Praise for *FIRE*

'This book is a revelation; an ambitious, poetic, sweeping account of the Black Summer fires ... a natural catastrophe on a ferocious scale beyond the realm of anything previously experienced, or for that matter, imagined ... a sterling primer for survival in the age of climate chaos which deserves very wide readership. This is a must-read book for the climate crisis era we are now living in.'

—Peter Garrett AM, *noted environmentalist, former Australian Federal Minister, and Midnight Oil frontman*

'*FIRE* is brilliant and powerful and deeply, deeply moving. It is not a book I will easily forget. And I suspect that as the years of climate collapse roll on, I will think of and turn to it many times.'

—Stephen Harrod, *Earth Grief: The Journey Into and Through Ecological Loss*

'Margi Prideaux's no newcomer to articulating the dire predicament we face due to the extraordinary complacency – and complicity – of our political leaders who dance around the edges of much needed change. Her wisdom gleaned from personal experience and her willingness to dive deep and untangle the wicked problems we now face provide us with more than hopium.'

—Petrea King, *Quest for Life Foundation*

'Margi Prideaux weaves graphic human stories through the reality of our changed environment. A powerful, must-read for today and the future. A truly incredible book, written with compassion and understanding from within the fire-scar of earth.'

—Becky Westbrook, *Evie and the Bushfire*

'An expression of despair, anger and bewilderment. The only way forward is not with more failed government policies, but through resolve and action at the grass-roots community level.'

—Alan Atkinson, *Three Weeks in Bali*

'Through *FIRE* Margi Prideaux shares her own deeply personal experience of the consequences of global heating. Margi's powerful story telling enables us to realise that the climate catastrophe is also deeply personal for us all. However, the desperation of the story does not leave us in despair; rather Margi leads us forward into action. There is hope for the future if we listen to the land, listen to ancient wisdom and act locally. Because climate change is personal.

—The Venerable Canon Rod Bower, *Director of Mission, Newcastle Anglican*

'I absolutely loved *FIRE*; the way in which Margi has weaved personal recounts through the book to support her research reiterates the dire need for action. Margi's work is truly a powerful 'call to arms' – one of utmost importance; a must read for all.'

—Melissa Jones, *CEO, BlazeAid*

Praise for Margi Prideaux's related writing

'Clearsighted, passionate and inspiring, Margi Prideaux has written a vital reimagining of the destiny of environmental activism. A clarion call for civil society to step forward and demand greater power. This important and wise essay will reshape the thinking of activists, environmentalists, NGOs and policy makers.'

—Micah White, *The End of Protest*

'Margi Prideaux has done more than anyone to raise awareness of the need for grassroots voices to be heard in debates over nature, climate change and the environment. She deserves to be widely read.'

—Michael Edwards, *Transformation*

'Writing with the deep knowledge of a scholar, the engaged fervor of a veteran activist, and the wisdom of a poetic visionary Margi Prideaux has produced an inspiring text for our time enlivened by its focus on the frightening ordeal we humans inevitably share with the animal wonders of nature also entrapped in this predatory capitalist world. Without exaggeration, a thrilling and indispensable guide to the future.'

—Professor Richard Falk, *Power Shift: On the New Global Order*; and *(Re)Imagining Humane Global Governance*

'[T]he exemplar of what happens when you combine two decades of cutting edge conservation at the practical level by a leading NGO, and critical thinking of what solutions, at the theoretical level, to some of the most pressing problems of our generation are required. This book is radical. ... an excellent piece of scholarship.'

—Professor Alexander Gillespie, *Conservation, Biodiversity and International Law.*

'Marrying a scholar's analysis with a poet's sensitivity, the book is essential reading for understanding both the constraints and opportunities for creating a more just and ecologically vibrant world.'

—Professor Paul Wapner, *End of Nature: The Future of American Environmentalism*

'[P]rofound insights into why so many well-meaning international conservation efforts are failing so many communities and so many species. Her spirited and brave call for truly collaborative governance with local communities deserves a full airing in the boardrooms of the big NGOs.'

—Professor Peter Dauvergne, *University of British Columbia*

'At once a window onto civil society and a critique of elite diplomacy, this book's powerful call for a new earth-centred democracy cannot be ignored.'

—Professor Anthony Burke, *Ethics And Global Security: A Cosmopolitan Approach*

FIRE

A Message from the Edge of Climate Catastrophe

Margi Prideaux, Ph.D.

Stormbird Press

First published 2022

NATIONAL LIBRARY OF AUSTRALIA

A catalogue record for this book is available from the National Library of Australia

National Library of Australia and State Library of South Australia Legal Deposit
Prideaux, M (1967) – Author
FIRE: A Message from the Edge of Climate Catastrophe
ISBN – 9781925856552 (hbk)
ISBN – 9781925856569 (pbk)
ISBN – 9781925856576 (ebk)

Cover by Stormbird Press.
Typeset by Stormbird Press with Felix Titling, Berlin Sans, and Kazimir.
Botanical illustration by Lisla, Shutterstock.

Stormbird Press is an imprint of Wild Migration Limited

Stormbird Press

Stormbird Press
PO Box 73
Parndana
South Australia, 5220
Australia
Phone (61 8) 8121 5841
Email production@stormbirdpress.com
Web www.stormbirdpress.com

The publishing industry pulps millions of books every year when new titles fail to meet inflated sales projections—ploys designed to saturate the market, crowding out other books.

This unacceptable practice creates tragic levels of waste. Paper degrading in landfill releases methane—a greenhouse gas emission 23 times more potent than carbon dioxide.

Stormbird Press prints our books 'on demand', and from sustainable forestry sources, to conserve Earth's precious, finite resources.

We believe every printed book should find a home.

FIRE
A Message from the Edge of Climate Catastrophe

Also by Margi Prideaux, Ph.D.

Global Environmental Governance, Civil Society and Wildlife

Birdsong After the Storm: Averting the Tragedy of Global Wildlife Loss

Tales from the River: An Anthology of River Literature

All Things Breathe Alike: A Wildlife Anthology

CONTENTS

For Jayne and Ashleigh, thank you for your beautiful rescue
in our time of greatest need.
And, Rodney, thank you for your respect for the old ways
and willingness to share this wisdom.
For Kangaroo Island—our fractious, fabulous community—
thank you for your embrace.
Geoff and Margi Prideaux

... and for Donna, because you are magnificent.
This journey in life would be harder without you,
my friend.
Margi Prideaux

We are not the first people to grieve the loss of land and ecosystems, the loss of a way of life, and the loss of how our culture functions; to have our liberties and autonomy limited.

I extend my respect to First Nations peoples across the world for their tenacity, determination, and sheer will to survive. It is from these peoples and cultures, who are intimately acquainted with the grief and trauma of loss of Country, culture, community, family, and identity, that we must learn.

I write from the island of Karta and acknowledge the songlines and spiritual relationship of the Kaurna, Ngarrindjeri, and Narungga Nations to this eternal place on which I stand.

Dear reader,

This is a work of nonfiction born of the depths of my community's suffering. I am not a reporter flying across a scorched landscape or a journalist camping in a disaster zone. I am not a politician with an agenda to grind. I am not an outsider looking in. I am an author and an ordinary person who, along with my husband, Geoff, never truly believed a disaster of this magnitude could happen to us.

This book shares our experience—the anger and the disillusionment—through the Black Summer wildfires and beyond ,and the months of recovery and discussion within our community.

While it has taken time to finish, the book remains just as relevant following the 2022 Australian federal election as it was in the weeks and months before. The colour of politics has swung towards the progressive hues of red, teal, and green, but nothing, materially, has changed. The failings experienced by too many Australian communities in the aftermath of Black Summer and the East Coast Floods, rests equally at the feet of both sides of politics. While the actors at the helm during and directly after these most recent of disasters have revealed their personal moral bankruptcy to the world, the system pre-dates them by years; the product of successive state and federal governments. Even the widely hailed progressive independents, freshly part of the Australian political landscape, have failed to understand that climate change is not only about the future. It is also about surviving, right now.

There is a familiar story told by western media of disasters and recovery. It is a story that quantifies the businesses directly impacted, the homes lost, the government support measures announced as an indication of benevolent intent, the scale of donated clothes and food, and after a short time, the gatherings of community as a demonstration of resilience. Once told, the media moves on. Yet, there is another longer, harder, silent, and often invisible story of the fabric of people's lives ripped and torn; of those lives being patched and rewoven through the fog of depression and fear that they have insufficient internal strength to get the job done. Overlaying this is a second story of a broken contract between government and the governed, especially in the face of climate chaos.

In the months after the wildfires, I sat down to write a version of that first familiar story. I recognised I had a ringside seat to a dramatic show and there was merit in the telling. Then, quietly my community spoke to me. It is the second of the two stories that are voiced in these pages. Often alongside Geoff, I formally interviewed nearly seventy people from across Kangaroo Island and had just as many informal discussions as the passage of time wore on. My community has known I've been writing and many times I found myself pulled aside on the street so people could share their story or implore me to write about something specific with brutal honesty.

Whenever I could, I asked them the same two questions. The first was to have them recall the moment that stays with them from the fire event; the moment on their mind as they fall asleep, hits them when they wake, or haunts them when their mind is idle during the day. The second question sought to take the pulse of how my community wanted to respond to the event. Acknowledging we will always have fire, I asked them what should we, as a community, do to protect ourselves from the savage scale of impact happening again?

In collating the first question's answers I have tried hard to capture the essence of my community's accounts. Yet, I know this book is an incomplete chronicle—an echo of limited vibrations—presenting a few precious memories among so many never told. We experienced a human and ecological catastrophe of epic proportions and I realised doing justice to every story would fill a shelf of books from here to the moon.

There is still deep trauma within my community and to protect people I care about, I have intentionally 'anonymised' everyone's input except where people have publicly spoken in some fashion. In some cases, I have deliberately combined stories to hide individuals in a crowd; my aim, always, has been to lessen pain. Readers with local knowledge may identify some people in a few of the accounts. Where this is likely, I have sought the teller's permission. Several stories—whispered across the community—are omitted entirely because they carry too much trauma and sit too deeply in the hearts of fragile souls to be rendered into words. The eyes of these souls will haunt Geoff and I forever.

While conducting these interviews, we have sat with people on burnt logs or beside wharves looking out over low-flying pelicans; we've stood in blackened sheds or among the burnt embers of a front porch still upright but badly damaged. Sometimes, we've had long conversations over the phone. Other times, I was sent accounts already entered in diaries, etched thoughts, or feelings, or recalled from screams in the night. My interpretation of these experiences has remained, always, in their hands, with my commitment to press delete if they have harboured any discomfort. Every one of us has been through enough.

My community's answers to the second question were insightful, often unexpected, and frequently wise. This book responds to all their ideas and views, as authentically as I can. This collective voice has taken me down paths I did not expect and pressed me to research things I've never considered before.

I've also been forced to reassess my own beliefs and assumptions. As a consequence, there are passages in this book that will challenge my conservation friends across the world. I have broken ranks and am speaking how I see it, because time has run out for diplomacy. I hope, from deep in my heart, these colleagues will make it the whole way through the book. If they do, they will see I haven't forsaken my roots. I am merely challenging conservation's intellectual inertia. However, I accept many bridges will burn.

It is impossible for me to express the depth of love Geoff and I feel for and have received from our community. In chronicling this journey, I hope to have honoured that love and to have done no harm. As sure as I still am that day follows night, we will only survive with each other.

Where I draw on published material, I reference this material in the usual academic way.

Margi Prideaux
May 30, 2022

Foreword

This book is a revelation; an ambitious, poetic, sweeping account of the Black Summer fires of 2019/2020, which raged across much of Eastern Australia, including as far as the remote Kangaroo Island located off the South Australian mainland.

We've long known that climate crises were coming our way, even if sections of national politics, in thrall to discredited conspiracy theories and beholden to the deep pockets of fossil fuel corporations, had failed to prepare the nation for the immensity of the challenge to come.

The Black Summer conflagration saw global warming arrive with a vengeance for Margi Prideaux and her Kangaroo Island neighbours. This is a gripping first person account of how a small community well experienced in fighting bush fires, faced a natural catastrophe on a ferocious scale beyond the realm of anything previously experienced, or for that matter, imagined.

'*FIRE ...*' is a genuinely deep dive work. By describing the actual events unfolding in real time, and drawing on first hand accounts from neighbours, Prideaux enjoins us to bear witness to the spectre of the climate careering out of control in your own backyard.

It is one thing to experience in the blink of an eye, homes and farms, forests and streams, native species and domestic animals, indeed anything that lay in the path of the monstrous inferno being obliterated. But how does this actually feel to those in the midst of the maelstrom? What actually happens on the ground in the days, weeks and months once the media has moved on and the public mind is diverted by more recent crises?

Here lies the importance of this book, for seldom are these questions asked, and rarely does anyone attempt to answer them in a way which brings some meaning to an event where everything humans take as normal has been rendered abnormal, and then some.

As a long time professional environmentalist and scientist the author brings a unique perspective to her portrayal of this calamity.

She writes movingly of the ensuing grief people experienced, lovingly of the living earth that was scorched in and around her, astutely of the machinations of the stuttering recovery that followed, and incisively about the role of environment organisations, local, state and federal governments, as they respond with mixed motivations and uneven results.

Along with recording and analysing this momentous scene change, by identifying the personal attributes and political strategies we—collectively—need to develop to prepare for a mega fire future, Margi has also sown the seeds of hope, hard as they sometimes are to discern in the midst of unparalleled chaos, and this too is a considerable achievement.

Margi has crafted a sterling primer for survival in the age of climate chaos which deserves very wide readership. This is a must-read book for the climate crisis era we are now living in. In short a magnificent effort.

The Hon Peter Garrett AM
July 2022

PANDEMONIUM

November 2, 2019–February 29, 2020

1

Stringybark

November 2, 2019

The warm sun is penetrating my work boots and the crumpled jeans lying flat across my shins, but the remainder of me rests in cool, calm shadow, my back pressed against an old soul who I love to visit. It is November and the sun smiles from its mid-morning pose. Beyond the shade, the landscape is bathed in flaxen light, shimmering off the dry stalks of grass. Not a cloud disrupts the piercing cobalt sky.

Hot, heavy air sits like a blanket on the landscape. Still, but alive with a buzzing so characteristic of the Australian summer. Insects hover and dance nearby. A cricket serenades across the paddock. Beyond these sounds the silence is so deep you can hear the thrum inside your body and Earth rotating in space. A roaring, alive silence known to people who live in places absent of modern human activity, where weather can be utter stillness.

Above, the branches of my old friend are wide and have twisted during centuries of wind and rain. Her torso, coated in rich hues of silver, cream, and brown, unwraps in places. Where the bark lifts from her trunk, it is fringed with threads–stringybark. Russet sap paints accents here and there, flowing through the cracks and gaps of the tree's weave. Young branches celebrate life with luminescent splashes of lime green leaves on deep red stems and the dark green adult leaves cluster together, casting the deep shade of a pergola awning.

Once, when she was younger, she looked upon a vast family spread across the valley below. Now her family stands in two groups, on the hill arc behind us, great limbs stretching to the sun that host eagles in their branches, and below next to the still gently-flowing water of the seasonal creek, their toes burrowed so deep they plunge into a bigger, constant running river, meters below the soil.

Sometimes when I visit, I wrap my arms around her base, barely stretching around half of her girth. It is a stereotype, to be a tree-hugger, but more country folk than you might expect feel strong connections to these giant old souls. Far from silent statues, their branches whisper of history and time, and of a cycle of life bigger than us. There is something calming about pressing your torso against their heft.

I often sit and imagine what she has seen. How many seasons she has watched roll across the landscape beneath her. Perhaps she wept when men chain-felled her family to clear the landscape for grazing. I hope she has come to a place of peace with the grass covered hill before her. Maybe, sometime further back, before white men arrived on her shore, there was a different landscape to what we now imagine. Certainly, the notions modern Australians hold about wilderness appear to be ill-informed. Fire, slowly crawling along the landscape, either lit by the land's ancient human culture, or by the less intentional lightning that hits the ground, would have created more space and light for grasses to grow. Perhaps the hills wouldn't have been as densely covered as the nearby modern National reserves. I don't really know. These are thoughts born of words I have read and heard, and I am not wise enough to seek answers from the tree, so I am left to hope the carnage wasn't as devastating as it has sounded.

Last year, I sat on the next hill and witnessed a beautiful scene. Eyes twitching, ears flicking, another soul was leaning against my friend, stretching her back and deeply yawning. It was a satisfying extension that reached her toes. Clothed in soft, deep chocolate-brown fur, with a silver ruff beneath her chin, she pushed herself up to stand. Her coat echoed the colours of the tree, with sunlight streaks of ochre, brown, and gold.

Then and now, the pungent smell of eucalyptus rolled down the hill as the sun drew oils from her leaves. I was struck by how this tree had been sheltering those who wore rich brown coats for hundreds of years. A thousand generations ago, the people who walked this island called her ancestors wanggami. It is a bewitching name. Now people across the world say kangaroo.

Today, I have claimed this precious spot, and the

wanggami are down in the shade of the creek. I am here to ground myself before I travel, once again, to the lands of my own ancestors in the northern half of this world. I am worried about so much. The summer is already here when the season should feel cooler, still.

It is hot and parts of the country are already on fire. Seven months ago, veteran firefighters, climate scientists and meteorologists sought a meeting with the federal government about the looming season. They were gravely worried—enough to push themselves into the brutal glare of political media. They sought to trigger the government to prepare for this fire season, but they were rebuffed and their concerns trivialised and ridiculed. Caught in the toxic climate wars of this country, the Prime Minister inferred the group sought to criticise the efforts of the current fire chiefs. A well-intended approach seeking to provide wise counsel was contorted into a political punching bag to serve the news cycle and the hubris of political egos.

The political feint didn't quite work. Everyone remembers a warning bell was tolled, and ignored. Everyone feels slightly on edge. We are worried about what's to come but can't quite grasp its texture and shape.

Two days after that first story of sitting beneath that tree, I step aboard a plane bound for an international conservation meeting in Germany. Once in the air, and over New South Wales, I am stunned by the smoke plume stretching out across the horizon. The news coverage has not prepared me for the scale of the disaster. Anger wells inside me that I am on a plane, again, contributing ever more emissions into this mess. Anger that so much is already lost, when the warnings were so clearly called. As my plane banks towards the north, I slump into my seat and hope Geoff won't be called into service while I am away.

Like many in my community, Geoff and I are both volunteer firefighters. We're newer into firefighting culture and network, and lack the well-worn wisdom of many younger and older people around us. Even though we might fall short in bravery and fitness levels, we understand that to live where we do means we have a responsibility to care for each other and do what we can.

I spend the flight doom-scrolling for breaking news. The disaster grows with every word and by the time I reach Germany I have changed the entire frame of what I intend to do and say while I am at this meeting. While I have a formal voice in the gathering, I am not a government official. None-the-less, I resolve to speak out, even if it means breaking my hard-won diplomatic standing. Over the next five days I strive to draw everyone's attention to the scale of the wildfires burning across Australia, and the link of those fires to a changing climate. I make urgent pleas for us to switch our conservation attention. I employ every word trick in the book, including stating the overused line that we are 'fiddling while Rome burns'. As the words leave my mouth, I watch the eyes of government officials flicker between boredom and disinterest. They only let me speak out of respect for my past accomplishment, and my adherence to diplomatic protocol, if not diplomatic content. It is clear they think I am wasting their time. They believe they have more important things to discuss.

We're investing hours of diplomatic time in forming an agreement about how important migratory species are to global biodiversity. I believe in this cause, yet I am struck by how much effort has to be invested to state the obvious, especially when, in my experience, it rarely transpires into action. Yet, here they are. Senior, skilled diplomatic officials, with a mandate to speak on behalf of their governments—a powerful potential to take a message of concern and urgency back to their home base—but there is no appetite for anything off the formal agenda. It is not 'their department'. It is not 'their diplomatic brief'. Inherently, they don't care. For the first time in my life, I feel what so many on the front-lines of conservation work in the developing world experience every day. The privileged, developed world simply doesn't understand. They are wrapped in cotton wool and disaster always happens to the less fortunate 'others'.

How I long to be gone from this charade and to be sitting beside my tree again.

2

Roar

January 3, 2020. 7.30pm

The sky is deep black, hours before nightfall. Not the familiar distant, ethereal black of night with cloud shadows and pinpoints of starlight, but a sombre, clawing, heaving noir that hangs like a blanket over the Earth.

I am overcome by a sudden urge to escape or run away from the people collected under the bright lights of the clubroom. The vibration of pain, shock, and anger is intensified under the flickering fluorescent lights and my own capacity to cope is paralysed by incessant alarm tones and screams from mobile phones.

Escaping to the moonless centre of the oval, I focus on what is directly under me, weighing the manicured grass beneath my feet; stumpy turf without weeds or beetles—a prideful symbol of humanity's control over nature. In this moment, this perfect expanse of green embodies everything I loathe about society; a swathe of homogenised surface at odds with a planet-level brutal wind. And the tempest is fierce; a righteously angry beast carrying ash and debris that shot-blasts my face and scratches my squinting eyes. As the wind storm whips and turns and thunders, my shock is amplified in a space of humanity versus Earth. The distant clubroom lights recede and ahead, pale white flashes glinted through the smoke. Aberrant forms careening and twisting through the treetops in the distance; a spectral dance performed for a displaced outcast.

Turning back towards the clubhouse, my eyes rest on Geoff, hunched over his phone to shield it from gusts of wind. I know he is delivering calm, careful words to people not here. We are alive. Yes, we are safe. For now. No, we don't know if anything is left.

Bewitched by the movement, I shift closer to the dance that caught my attention before. My grit-filled eyes painfully adjust to reveal a flock of corellas. A few more steps and their mournful shrieks break through the howling storm. Piercing cries that penetrate my soul. The universe's roar in mournful harmony with the flock's banshee cry. Jolted towards a reckoning, I sink to the ground mortified under the weight of brutal realisation. 'Humanity, what have we done?'

The first of Kangaroo Island's Black Summer fires, called Duncan and Menzies respectively, were started by dry lightning on December 20, 2019. Like most of our neighbours and friends, Geoff joined the fire crews on the Duncan fire ground that first day. Many more fires ignited in the days that followed. Duncan started in the bushland on a neighbouring farm, a short 8 kilometres from our home. It gathered momentum when it reached the commercial pine and blue gum plantations and onward into private and government-protected wilderness areas. Meanwhile, Menzies raged its own warpath further east. By day's end every fire truck on the island was in attendance at one or the other fire.

On the second day the fire station called for urgent backup from the mainland. From that day onwards, my voluntary role was to man the radios or support fire station logistics, occasionally taking a break to join Geoff in our private firefighting unit. As with so many others, around-the-clock shifts snatched away our normal lives, day and night without pause, as we fought alongside community leaders, farmers, townsfolk, and volunteers from across the country. The battle raged for another two weeks. Seasonal celebrations were cancelled as we wrestled the conflagration threatening our homes, our farms, and the wildlife we share this land with. Finally, on January 1, those fires were held behind containment lines. Duncan was stopped 50 metres from our farmhouse door.

Yet, we were collectively robbed of any relief. Another fire—by then named Ravine—had ignited and was already out of control. Lightning had struck on December 30 in the island's jewel—Flinders Chase National Park—to the southwest of our farm. This third major fire for the island's season rapidly built into an inferno that reached the island's north and south coasts at the same time. Firefighters and earth movers risked their lives to build fire breaks to halt the front but three days later, on January 3, the real ordeal broke through these containments, formed two pyro-cumulonimbus (pyro-cume) clouds that sent a fast-moving fire-storm north and eastward. This previously rare phenomenon incinerated farms, animals, and infrastructure, lighting decades-old plantations like candles, and overrunning vast ecosystems and their wildlife.

Ravine—so hot, so uncontrollable—literally devoured the landscape at lethal speed. Fire trucks shielded under halos of water witnessed lethal lightning inside Ravine's pyro-cume cloud. A weather station positioned centrally between the island's north and south coasts registered temperatures of 428°C with 140 kilometre winds before it stopped transmitting—at this point the fire was still some kilometres away. Aluminium that melts at 660°C pooled across shed floors. Firefighters took refuge where they could, or fled from its front where temperatures reached 900°C. Darkness eclipsed the daylight hours before the sun had set. Animals—sheep, cattle, kangaroos, wallabies, koalas—ran in panicked mobs and perished together in tortured heaps. Even the big, fast-flying birds succumbed to the fire, sometimes in mid-flight. Stunned and confused, wildlife had nowhere to hide.

Ravine destroyed our farm, our home, our dreams.

Ravine destroyed the farms, homes, and dreams of friends and neighbours, too.

Ravine stole lives: Two. A father and his son—brave firefighters—unaware of the threat bearing down upon them. Violent deaths that ignored the natural order of life, caught painfully short. A shocking loss that vibrated across the entire community.

By January 4 Ravine reverted to a devouring crawl, burning eastward for yet another two harrowing weeks, taking more homes, farms, and wildlife. When finally contained, but still active, it had burnt more than 2,115 kilometers^2 (211,500 hectares or 816 miles^2)of agricultural land, plantations, and woodlands of our small island—nearly three times the area of New York. Eighty-nine homes were reduced to ash and nearly 300 farm buildings destroyed, many with tools and equipment collected over farming generations. Nearly 60,000 farm animals and 830 bee hives were destroyed, and 150 kilometers^2 (15,000 hectares or 57 miles^2) of mature plantations were razed.[1] Farming, forestry, tourism, and the myriad of other business across the island were all hit, hard. A township was evacuated and elsewhere people fled to the safety of jetties and sports ovals at the easternmost point of the island. The whole island community was upended numerous times over the months the wildfire raged. So many old trees perished.

Across Australia the figures were similarly grim. The Black Summer fires decimated 190,000 kilometers^2 (19,000,000 hectares or 73,359 miles^2) destroyed over 3,000 houses, killed 33 people, more than 100,000 farm animals, and three billion native animals across Australia.[2] Black Summer burnt a globally unprecedented percentage of the continental forest biome, and took its place in history as one of the largest forest fires anywhere in the world. It raged across the continent for seven months. Smoke plumes and fire storms reached 30 kilometres in height, injecting aerosols into the stratosphere and circumnavigating the globe.[3]

Like so many others, our strong community shattered like exploding glass under thermal shock. With little more than an overnight bag, our phones, and laptops, Geoff and I stood with ash on our faces and smoke in our hair in an unknown world. Never has Kangaroo Island been so dry, and the relative humidity so low, so early in the season. This fire, and the devastation it caused, directly results from a changing climate.

While farmers bent their broken spirits to the task of shooting their burned animals, servicemen in fatigues cleared the roadsides and fields of carcasses that hung contorted in wire fencing or in crushes consumed by flames. When people met in the street, or over farm fences, they searched each other's faces for signs of an emotional burden weighing too heavily on each other's soul. Everyone was then, and remains now, desperate to not lose anyone else.

In time the dark, smoke-filled skies returned to blue. Our island collectively struggled to make sense of this event, as a community, and as individuals. For months, a profound silence cloaked our landscape. It was weeks before I heard the first bird call out across the ashen hills on our farm, or the sound of insects from the charred, blackened trees along our creek line. Children climbed aboard school buses that carried them through a charred and fragmented land.

Many of us lived in tents or shipping containers while we pieced life together again.

Eventually, the Royal Commission into National Natural Disaster Arrangements, otherwise known as the Bushfire Royal Commission, met, collected evidence, deliberated, and released its findings. Its mandate was to 'gather evidence about coordination, preparedness for, response to and recovery from [bushfire] disasters and improving resilience and adapting to changing climatic conditions'. To give the Australian government the means to sidestep accusation about its woeful response to the fires, the Commission was also to 'consider the legal framework for Commonwealth involvement in responding to national emergencies'. At its core, this Commission looked at the same evidence presented to dozens of previous commissions. As a broken community, even as the Commission began its deliberations, we were sceptical that anything would change.

Now, with the reports released, a brand-new federal agency formed, and more devastating disasters unfolding in the west and the east of the country, our community is punch-drunk and still struggling to rebuild. We are in new and uncharted territory. It is not terrible luck. It is not even wilful poor planning. The fire's ferocity took us by surprise because we did not accept how quickly and to what extent a warming Earth would disturb weather, people, and animals. We believed climate-related events would strike somewhere else, sometime else, someone else. We were content to manage life as we always had in the past and we allowed government to distract us from their wilful inaction. We trusted the system would protect us and what we loved. Our ignorance affected not only human lives, livelihoods, and homes but set in motion a backdrop of biological annihilation. So many old trees, gone.

Now we are all uncomfortably and consciously living in the changing climate curve without leadership or a plan.

But, I digress. First I must take you back to late December 2019.

3

Semantics

December 30, 2019

For ten days I have watched the 'operations team' in the fire station directing the onslaught to contain and conquer the first two fires, and now Ravine in its early stages. Over and over plans are constrained by decisions higher up the ladder of power. It is as if the government agencies are caught off-guard, despite the fire raging in the eastern states. No one in government seems to have planned anything. It is a shock to recognise they are not prepared.

Unlike the faceless bureaucrats working from city office blocks, this operations team is stationed at the coalface of the blitzkrieg, in a small building, in a small town, surrounded by farms and forests. They coordinate fire trucks to burn areas back where they can. Fighting fire with fire. They send dozers in to create bare-earth breaks where the terrain allows it and where decisions are approved, because often they are not. They pour over the weather forecasts from the meteorologists, day after day. From dawn to dusk and through the night, they weigh and war game, because the lives and livelihoods of people they know—a community they love—depend on it. At some level, this is the story that is known by everyone. It is the image Hollywood would portray if they retold the tale. But there is more to know. Beneath the formality of a firefighting structure, there are real human stories in play; experiences and decisions that draw on multiple lifetimes—of fathers and grandfathers—and I have nothing but admiration for the efforts of these warriors. I only wish they were ultimately in charge.

Ravine does not play by the same rule book from which our warriors have learnt—a fire lore written in the blood of burnt, weathered hands by three generations of farmers. A lore penned by sons and daughters standing on farms watching their fathers lighting their bushland to cool burn; a lore about wind direction and the landscape; about how plants react to flame; about understanding this country needs to burn, but gently, quietly. Fire is something you live with, you use, and you adapt to, because there is no one to help you except your wits and your neighbours.

Ravine has smashed this lore, and no one saw it coming until it tore over us, helter-skelter, hurtling fireballs.

The full story of Black Summer started many decades ago when scientists and meteorologists raised the first warning, but we were blind to its potential because politics was drowned in a semantic debate about our climate. The narrative of Ravine's story started in the lightning generated fires in the ten days before.

Five days before Christmas, Geoff had stood deep in the paddock looking at the sky. 'Maybe the weather forecasters got it wrong today', I remember him hopefully murmuring while walking down to turn the solar pump on to water the vineyard. The forecasts had projected thunderstorms. But, the sky was still big, bright blue, even though the wind was picking up. He hoped it would evolve to nothing and turned his attention to the vines.

Two hours later the first long low rumble rolled across the sky and a smoke plume climbed skywards on the near horizon. There were a number of fires, and one was on the neighbour's farm. I stood alongside Geoff as he prepped our 'farm fire unit'. These are typically farm utes (elsewhere known as pickup trucks) that carry between 500 and 1000 litres of water, a pump, and a hose. Often they are cobbled together from spare tanks and parts from the farm. Sometimes they are moulded, purpose-built units. They are always owned and manned by the farmer, without any formal support from the government-run firefighting force. They are nimble and able to go where fire trucks cannot, but they are also vulnerable. Today the fire was close to our home. We knew the drill. We exchanged a silent dialogue. It felt bad that day. There was foreboding in the air.

As Geoff set off down the road, I knew some 45 kilometres away, fire trucks hurtled out of the fire station and were also on their way, while our senior firefighters gathered in the station to coordinate the action. More neighbours in farm fire units like Geoff's were arriving on-site in a race to catch the monster before it raged out of control. This is what my community does. It is what we know. We are good at it.

But, that day the first house was lost, and shock rippled across the island. We don't lose homes here. We conquer fires. We have done so for generations.

Climate change has been the subject of many excellent books, millions of competent scientific papers, whole forests of reports, some I've even contributed to myself. There have been so many political interventions that I find it genuinely puzzling that doubt about the causes and impacts of our current climate chaos remain. That the debate rolls on is a product of politics and profit; and a concerted conservative media effort to discredit the scientific consensus in favour of political support from big oil and coal. That the science is still debated is unsettling. No science is ever fully certain. That is the nature of its inquiry. And despite that, right here and right now, the overwhelming weight of evidence tells us that Earth's climate is changing. What remains unknown is the fine-scale predictions of exactly when and how that change will play out.

None-the-less, I respect that people absorb information in different ways and trusting messengers is important. I am a new voice to some readers, and I recognise that people are cautious about the political agendas behind this vexed debate. Some people are more comfortable to accept that 'Yes, things are changing', but that change is an ancient natural background cycle. They fear the way climate change politics is reshaping the economic landscape of the world. They are worried that agendas are misusing the information. I get it, and I understand these perspectives. I just don't agree with them.

This is what makes writing about climate change so difficult. Because it isn't a defined phenomenon that any one person can pinpoint, I have to try and convince everyone that it is real, that it is urgent, and then come to the rescue with an immediate fix. Which is not how this book is going to go. Indeed, that fix is already long overdue; the world didn't marshal itself in time. For me, continuing to write about the failure to address climate change—about the unfathomable immoral behaviour of world leaders spanning decades—is a source of despair. My life's work has hinged around conservation, for better or worse, but, despite the earnest efforts of the collective movement, we are no nearer to reaching a balanced, stable, green future. The world was meant to get better. I now recognise it is too late to continue down that path.

Allow me a moment to summarise my current thinking. Earth's climate has changed throughout history. In the last 650,000 years there have been seven cycles of glacial advance and retreat. The end of the last ice age, about 11,700 years ago, marks the beginning of the modern climate era—and of human civilisation. In our deep, distant past these climatic changes were due to tiny variations in Earth's orbit changing the amount of solar energy our planet receives.[4] That's not what scientific evidence tells us is happening right now. The overwhelming scientific consensus states the current warming trend is the result of modern human activity and is proceeding at an unprecedented rate. The heat-trapping nature of carbon dioxide and other gases was already demonstrated in the mid-19th century. I have no question that increased levels of greenhouse gases are warming the Earth. Deep evidence of this is all around us—in ice cores from Greenland, Antarctica, and glaciers, in tree rings, in ocean sediments and coral reefs, and in layers of sedimentary rock.[4-8] I know that most leading scientific organisations worldwide have issued public statements that climate-warming is attributed to human activities.

However, my position is my own and I live in a community that holds a diversity of views. What is crucial to understand is that my narrative is not such a world away from the supposed opposite narrative that a warming world is part of a natural cycle. Both narratives agree—Earth's climate is changing. While I fervently support the campaign to arrest future emissions, that we fundamentally agree about the change happening is the most important message to understand, right here, right now. Wildfires and pandemics peak and then pass, but the effects of a changing climate are cumulative and will be forever accompanied by more wildfires, storms, floods, and more viruses. The world we are facing right now is hostile, and we need to adapt to survive. I don't mean the type of disingenuous 'resilience and adaptation' that my own government peddled after the fire—shifting the Australian economy to a gas-powered future and protecting the interests of coal barons. Most governments focus on all the big-picture stuff that keeps society ticking along without any change—hazard reduction burning, building new dams, developing new drought-resistant crops, and a drought resilience plan.[9] This isn't the depth of leadership we need. It is shallow lip-service to the severity of the situation we now face.

This is not a book about the politics of climate change. It is a book about what is happening to one community—my community—because of a *changing climate*. It is a book about the gross cascading failures of our political class to respond with genuine adaptation plans to the evidence of *climate chaos*.

We are country folk. Our days are filled with huge skies, birdsong, and clean, clear breezes fresh off the Southern Ocean. Or they were before Ravine. Here on Kangaroo Island, we have no traffic lights, no fast food chains, no shopping malls, or multinational department stores. We don't have a subway, or even a train. A traffic jam for us involves two cars simultaneously parking on the main street—or a car stopped in the middle of the road with someone standing beside the driver's door having a chat. No one minds. The delay is received with goodwill and apologised for with a full arm wave and a beaming smile. We know each other's faces, and we cross the road to greet each other with genuine interest and cheer.

Perhaps it is because our lives are pared down, simplified, that we readily notice change in our surroundings. Away from the cloister of city high-rises and sprawling suburbs, of endless advertising banners and roadside signs, of blinding street lights and the thrum of ceaseless traffic, we notice the weather shifting in our daily existence. On fine summer days the direct heat from the sun feels much hotter. It has a bite to it that burns the leaves of our plants, blisters the bare skin of our farm animals, and scorches the soil so that crops fail and water sources dry up. Some trees are dying and being replaced by more resilient species. Winter is shorter. The fire season comes earlier and lasts longer, and when it does rain, the downpours are more intense. These are the quiet, unverified reflections of a small community. But, the ancient evidence—the words that can be read from the pages of nature in trees, and glaciers, and rocks, and mud—is actually screaming a dire warning to us all. Our world is warming ten times faster than the average rate of ice-age-recovery warming.[5] We are on a collision course with a reality we don't really comprehend.

Both weather (the local conditions) and climate (the continental and oceanic-level system) impact everyone's lives across the world. Climate and weather determine how we stay warm or cool enough to survive, what resources are plentiful, and what foods we eat. No one is outside this massive system, no matter how rich or powerful they are. The perils of a warming world are many, and on this my community now agrees. Air-conditioning isn't going to save us. When the grid fails, the full brutal heat will be felt without question. A warmer world doesn't mean longer summers on balmy beaches. It doesn't mean more time to lay on the sand and read piles of books. A warming world is the gradual heating of Earth's surface—oceans and atmosphere. 'Warmth' is really a scientific shorthand for more energy being released into the global system. And a warming world—a more climatically energetic world—is unstable and hazardous to every living thing on Earth. This means that weather—the local stuff—everywhere, is dramatically, and in some places unpredictably, changing. In some regions the temperatures are beginning to dangerously climb, in others they are starting to plummet.

Droughts are getting longer, deeper, and may not lift for generations. As centuries-old heatwave records continue to be shattered across the country. Northern Australia—known for its rapidly melting ice cream cones and clinging t-shirts—has been warned their communities will soon be uninhabitable. Remote out-stations are running out of water as aquifers run low and water turns saline. Wildfires and storm events are already more frequent and powerful. Seas are rising. Now.[6-8, 10, 11]

Further out from our long shores, many low-lying islands are on the verge of being swallowed whole by rising seas. Coastal cities across the world are facing typhoons and relentless rain frequently associated with climate change-induced flooding. Almost daily we hear of another global city being impacted by rising seas. These cities will flood or move. In the coming two decades the impacts of a changing climate will creep into the daily lives of the concrete jungles that survive. Cities are already affected more than rural areas by increasing air temperatures because they're naturally hotter. Concrete, steel, and other infrastructure materials trap more heat than a green landscape does: the so-called urban heat island effect. Some cities will have almost no rainfall, but many others will have extreme downpours. All this has costly impacts on cities' basic services, infrastructure, housing, human livelihoods, and health.[6, 10, 11]

Even at the extremes of our world, ice and permafrost are melting into sloppy, carbon-releasing mud. Glaciers are disappearing. One hundred years from now the world will be very different, for everyone. So much will have changed. So much will be lost. It is a future best left to the imagination of fiction writers.[6, 10, 11]

Yet, hundred-year predictions, because of the long-time span, do something strange to the human mind. It makes the threat appear too distant; incomprehensible; out of reach. We subconsciously dismiss it. Unlike a global pandemic which represents a specific and immediate threat thereby forcing an acute response. I have included the longer span, because it gives me space to make an admission. Even though I have spent more than thirty years as a card-carrying member of the conservation movement; even though I have worked on the politics of climate change for the last dozen or more years; I now recognise that I had a veil of denial clouding my mind, too. I would authentically mouth the words of warning. I'd write them in moving essays. Yet, deep inside, in that space so far down that we rarely hear the voice, I too believed the impact was always going to happen somewhere else; to someone else.

I was wrong.

Really wrong.

Our community, here on Kangaroo Island, has experienced the muscle of a changing world that does not play nice.

Our challenge now is to use our experience and our knowledge to adapt to what is to come, to safeguard the things we hold dear—our history, our community, our food and textile supply, and the nature that surrounds us—and to overcome global and national political inertia and denial, pulling us in a different direction.

We are on a dramatic journey from climate denial to front-line witnesses of a global climate crisis. We are travelling into a world on fire.

But, back to late December 2019.

4

Mitigation, Interrupted

December 21 - December 31, 2019

He's fought fires his whole life but never thought he'd find himself here—on this swing seat at the front of his house, in a bubble of clear air, surrounded by thick clawing smoke that masks everything a metre from where he sits.

It has only been minutes, but these have felt epic and hard, as one shed after the next has succumbed to the blaze. Sides heaving with each breath, his lungs fight for the oxygen they need. The water is gone, and this is his third time seated in this quiet space. The third time inside an unfathomable twenty minutes. Each time he comes here he practically crawls along the ground, so thick is the smoke and intense the heat. Each time he sits for a surreal but precious moment of peace, knowing he must return the fight. He tries not to think of what is already lost to the flames. Tractors, trucks, the machinery that has made his life as a farmer possible ... and a lifetime of tools. It is too much to contemplate but 'I am not going down without a fight', he promises himself.

He knows how he'll escape if it comes to that. His ute stands ready out beyond the veil of smoke. He'll find it if he needs it, but he is not going yet. He is going to fight for that last shed with his last drop if he has to.

Then even that falls.

***

He is delivering grain to one of his neighbours when his phone starts. Facebook tags, messages and phone calls arriving all at once and each one yelling the same message, 'fire at the farm!' He spins the steering wheel and races back to get the ute, already set up with the farm fire unit. His next thought is where to get help? He reaches out to his network of farming friends with a short, sharp message and within 10 minutes a mate replies, 'I'm on my way!'

He arrives at the farm to see twenty or more farm fire units and a bunch of fire trucks already there, with the fire about to hit his farm's southern boundary. It is coming out of the National Park.

Eight gruelling hours later, they've pushed the fire front back into scrub in the 'Chase' in an area that was burnt two years earlier. The fire runs out of fuel and dies.

***

A reflective composure snaps into focus as she and her near-adult son stand atop a hill watching the fire approach. It is an epic scene, and she feels barely suppressed, numbing panic vibrating in her son, but calm rolls through her like a wave.

Beside them stands their neighbour. She checks herself noticing how his appearance somehow echoes the fire as it approaches; skin and bones, flaming red hair and a face full of freckles.

The wind hits her cheeks like a solid wall. This is not her first wildfire. Her life has been etched deeply by a devastating fire in her childhood. Her husband's family farm was also taken a few years ago. It sometimes feels like fire stalks her, yet here she stands, composed, emotionless, pragmatic to her bones in the weirdness of the smoky, dusty light and chaos of catastrophe. Only her love and concern for her son pierces her inner stillness. She knows they might lose it all this night, yet here they stand watching it come. Leaning into the fury of the wind, there is nothing left to do but bear witness.

***

All the mobs of sheep are pushed together—nearly 3,000 in total—and moved to his northern paddocks. The fires are to the south and west now, so he and his mates set about clearing bush to slow the next attack. It is a long day.

By 9pm the western sky of the farm is aglow with the same fire circling around the north west corner to the entrance of the river. There is only 200 meters from the break and the river as it snakes down to the coast. This doesn't bode well for tomorrow.

They drive two machines—a dozer and a rubber tyre dozer— to the area where they think the fire will run. They will start a break at first light. He needs to protect their western boundary.

He heads back to the house at 10pm and says to himself, 'Happy New Year!'

In the political world of climate change there are two main categories of human responses: mitigation and adaptation. Each are characterised by degrees of scientific complexity. Each struggle to achieve consensus, are beset by economic uncertainty, and challenged by deep value conflicts between the different interest groups. Vast disparities of power and influence inherent within international negotiations don't help. In this contested and fraught space, big oil has so far successfully blocked international consensus that their core product—fossil fuels—must be phased out.

In May 2021 the International Energy Agency (IEA) released its latest report, *Net Zero by 2050.* Their assessment was that climate pledges by governments to date—even if fully achieved—will fall short of what is required to bring global energy-related carbon dioxide emissions to net zero by 2050.[12] They describe an uncomfortably ambitious and narrow path that must be followed to reach the target of no emissions to give the world an even chance of limiting the global temperature rise to 1.5°C. Staying on that narrow path requires immediate and massive deployment of all available clean and efficient energy technologies—indeed, they call for an eye-watering 75 percent reduction in methane emissions from fossil fuel supply over the coming decade.

Six months later, during the next round of climate negotiations, focused firmly on the mitigation end of the discussion, the world's government only manage to agree to 'roll back fossil fuel subsidies' and 'phase down' unabated coal. They don't put even a toe on the narrow path described by IEA.[13]

An entire global convention—the United Nations Framework Convention on Climate Change (UNFCCC)—is dedicated to addressing climate change, while ironically expending a vast contribution of greenhouse gases every time it meets. This is the convention that negotiated what the world's press reported as 'the Paris Agreement'. This is the convention that was the 'Copenhagen meeting', and the 'Glasgow meeting'. It is the platform that governments use to sit in a room and develop agreements between each other about what the world should do—the risks we will take and the solutions we'll employ. It is the body that Donald Trump, former USA President, infamously withdrew the US from, and that Joe Biden, the incoming President, returned the energy-consuming superpower to. It is the body where Scott Morrison, Australia's former Prime Minister, ignobly proposed Australia use controversial 'carry-over credits' to meet its international climate commitments. It is the body that released a statement midway through the first wave of the pandemic warning the world we must do better:

> *'Climate change has not stopped for COVID-19. Greenhouse gas concentrations in the atmosphere are at record levels and continue to increase. Emissions are heading in the direction of pre-pandemic levels following a temporary decline caused by the lockdown and economic slowdown. The world is set to see its warmest five years on record – in a trend which is likely to continue - and is not on track to meet agreed targets to keep global temperature increase well below 2 °C or at 1.5 °C above pre-industrial levels.'*[14]

The UNFCCC is supported by an amazing scientific body, into which the governments of the world send their best and brightest climate scientists to deliberate what is happening now, and predict what might happen in the future. This scientific body is the Intergovernmental Panel on Climate Change (IPCC). There are, quite literally, thousands of scientific programmes spread across the world's universities that feed into this deep scientific process.

In September 2020, the World Meteorological Organization (WMO) and the IPCC, along with input from the Global Carbon Project, the Intergovernmental Oceanographic Commission of UNESCO, the UN Environment Programme and the UK Met Office released a new report, *United in Science 2020*. That report clearly declared:

> *'The average global temperature for 2016–2020 is expected to be the warmest on record, about 1.1 °C above 1850-1900, a reference period for temperature change since pre-industrial times and 0.24°C warmer than the global average temperature for 2011-2015. ... It is likely (~70% chance) that one or more months during the next five years will be at least 1.5 °C warmer than pre-industrial levels.'*[15]

Quoting these statements becomes numbing after a while. The information is shock on top of shock, until it ceases to have meaning. Yet, it is important to recognise it is the result of deep scientific consensus. The reality is that we know plenty about the role of human activity as a primary driver of climate change, and government officials certainly know more than enough to act. The climate dialogues are an impressive government-driven system for deliberation and negotiation on emissions and the multitude of economic dreams to trade, reduce, or mitigate climate change impacts. They have been the fodder for miles of media articles, years of shock-jock rants, and countless probing investigations. The misunderstanding that this system is outside of government feeds the fertile ground of disagreement between people who believe climate change is human-driven and the people who believe it is part of a long natural cycle. In truth, every line and every minute of the IPCC deliberation and report is government-led and government-sanctioned.

It would be possible to fill a number of books with a detailed account of what the IPCC science says. It is dense and a sobering read. The latest suite of documents, running out towards 10,000 pages, are infused with the precaution of a scientific community who has spent decades seeking to be heard within a typhoon of climate denial.[6-8] As a result they quantify absolutely every statement to be absolutely clear about how certain they are that their scientific findings are valid. A 'very high confidence' means that there is at least a 9 in 10 chance of a finding being correct. 'High confidence' means that there is at least an 8 in 10 chance. 'Virtually certain' might sound confused, or that the fundamental science isn't quite settled yet. It actually means the statement is 99 percent probable.

The present rate of changes in many areas of the climate system are proportionate to the rate of recent temperature change. But, some parts of the climate system are slow to respond, such as the deep ocean overturning circulation and the ice sheets. [6-8] What does this mean in the world we live in? With the primer about the IPCC qualifiers in hand, it is 'virtually certain' that irreversible, committed change is already underway for the slow-to-respond processes. We just haven't 'felt' it yet. Deep ocean warming, acidification and sea level rise will continue to change for millennia even after global surface temperatures stabilize. These changes are irreversible on human time scales. For this the IPCC has 'very high confidence'. At the regional scale, abrupt responses, tipping points and even reversals in the direction of change cannot be excluded. For this the IPCC has 'high confidence'. Some regional abrupt changes and tipping points could have severe local impacts, such as unprecedented weather, extreme temperatures and increased frequency of droughts and forest fires. Models that exhibit such tipping points are characterised by abrupt changes once a threshold is crossed, and even a return to pre-threshold surface temperatures or to atmospheric carbon dioxide concentrations does not guarantee that the tipped elements will return to their pre-threshold state.[6-8]

In short, it is all looking pretty dire. But, as I mentioned earlier, governments remain divided about what to do, and their deliberations sit in two distinct camps—those focused on 'mitigation' and those focused on 'adaptation'.

Mitigation Defined

Mitigation—basically how much we allow the world to warm because of greenhouse gas emissions—is where the lion's share of political attention on climate change has been focused. That may change now that Europe has experienced a summer on fire. Until now, and every year, politicians, scientists, industry, and conservation lobbyists spend literally millions of cumulative hours talking and writing about how to reduce the emission of greenhouse gases, especially carbon dioxide and methane, without tanking economies or hurting the hip-pocket of shareholders.

Mitigation remains, by far, the favourite child of the climate dialogues because people want to remain in hopeful denial that, somehow, everything will work out OK. Those in this camp want an economic solution found so that we don't have to change a thing, and governments are prepared to gamble on the future while they wait for inspiration to strike. The grand and celebrated plans to reduce emissions by 2030 and 2050 are, respectively, seven and twenty-seven years away. That's a fatal gamble.

In March 2021, Australia's leading scientists made a significant, global-scale, declaration about the fight to mitigate the climate crisis. They said limiting global heating to 1.5°C was now 'virtually impossible'.[16] That phrase is a plea, more so than the counterpoint to 'virtually certain', and while others in the science community came out to refute the claim as pessimistic, here we are another two years older, and still governments are stalling. Prof Michael Mann, the director of the Earth System Science Center at Pennsylvania State University, told *The Guardian* keeping global heating to 1.5°C would require global emissions to be cut in half over the next decade. It is 'entirely doable' and 'simply a matter of political willpower'. 'There's nothing about the physics that says it isn't [possible]', he said.[17]

And there's the rub. The wisdom rests with the science. Politics and power are what are failing us. The potential to address this crisis through mitigation has been scuppered. To paraphrase James Mangold, we have 'mitigation, interrupted'.

5

Adaptation

December 31, 2019 - January 2, 2020

She is the only local in the room. Vital island knowledge is missing from the meeting, and she feels sick at what this might mean. But her role is not to question. She has to play the part she's assigned and that is to follow orders.

Another fire on the mainland is drawing the state's response, she hears. 'There is nothing more coming than what we have now.' Her soul is sick with worry. The other fire is smaller but close to the city, so it has been prioritised by the government. For days these briefings have warned we're on the verge of losing control. She can't help but feel the decision makers don't fully comprehend what's at stake.

Her gut rolls with pain when she hears the words, 'We've got to prepare for the worst. Tomorrow will be a catastrophic day.' All around her there is an instant flurry of action. All these fire event management experts frenetically attack their tasks, seemingly speeding their potential to meet the need. They are serious but their faces show focused calm. Maps will be produced. Briefings written, crews assigned, food ordered, equipment fixed and redeployed. She knows they will work hard and without complaint, whatever happens today, or tomorrow. The fire is abstract in here. It is a challenge to be conquered. None of them seem aware of her standing paralysed in the maelstrom of activity. None know that this is her home.

***

Early morning they begin cutting off the burn scar from the unburned bush with the dozers. By eight in the morning they are nearly done, grateful the cold night has slowed the fire's advancement through the neighbouring bush.

They are low on diesel and not certain how far they have left to cut through the bush. The phones are out, and they don't know the neighbour's property well so they retreat. But they still have to cut off the fire's path.

Two hours later and they realise the past few hours have been pointless. A single bush they can't get to on the other side of our neighbour's bush throws a flame towards their western side. There is little time, but they work hard to widen the break at their boundary fence in preparation for the inevitable western hit. When the noise and the smoke from the wildfire gets too much, they retreat back to where the machinery and farm fire units wait. The wildfire rolls through an hour later. After twenty minutes of fighting in vain they surrender to losing 200 acres and retreat back to the next paddock. The fire is now in the river valley as well as racing across his pasture.

He contacts the neighbour to tell them he is lighting up a line to burn back towards the fire and the neighbour decides to do the same. The entire western boundary of his farm is now alight. Spot fires flare but are quickly extinguished by friends in farm fire units.

Eighteen hours into this long day they finally sit down. Somebody hands him a cold beer. He collects his thoughts and prepares for the next day.

***

The phones are going mad. The station is filled with people. Crews move in and out with the new rhythm of life. Mid-morning and the control centre briefing is called. People mill in, grabbing seats where they can and crowding against the wall where they can't. It is an austere room, purpose built to house the fire trucks, except in emergencies like now, when the space is filled with desks and screens, and phones, and whiteboards. Familiar faces now wear tabards denoting their role.

The phones are taken off the hook to silence the din for just a few moments. A hush falls. Every face is pinched with worry, and bone weariness is etched in their eyes.

The forecast for the next few days is in. Hotter, windier, a perfect storm for tragedy.

A senior official makes the pronouncement. 'It doesn't look good, people.'

***

He wakes at daybreak. He pads into the kitchen to make coffee. Mug in hand he looks out the window. 'FIRE!', he yells. An easterly wind is pushing a huge fire straight at the house. He charges around waking the others, expelling words no one in our community can sleep through. 'FIRE COMING, NOW!' There are flashing lights at the neighbours from another back burn that is coming straight at them. As adrenaline expels any vestiges of sleep, they race through what the next step should be. They are only three men with one farm fire unit so they decide to back burn towards the easterly wind from their side to create a buffer zone—to fight 1,000 acres of wildfire with a new fire shackled to their will.

As quickly and gently as possible, they light three kilometres of scrub, desperate to save their newly renovated boundary fence. So many hours and so much effort has been spent to rebuild that fence.

Then it is all gone.

***

There is a calm to the radio room, compared to the intensity of the room next door where attacking the fire front is being war-gamed, or to the bigger room further along where the organising happens to keep this large machine operating—food for firefighters, places for them to sleep, equipment repairs, maps, plans, and the constant jangle of the phone.

All day we listen to what's happening with the trucks, consciously tracking where they are and how they are faring. Occasionally someone from the control room asks for someone at the fire front to be contacted, and they reach out through this lifeline that connects all the fire crews together.

It is late. The other radio operator has been

redeployed to solve intractable equipment problems and I've been calling the trucks in for changeover so the day crew can get some rest, the trucks refuelled, and a night crew can return to face the fire. Each truck is supposed to radio in to say when they've arrived, but sometimes the radio signal fails or they don't hear the call to come home. Other times something urgent happens that delays their return while they try to control their situation. Sometimes, they're simply so exhausted they forget to radio through to say they are at base. I reach out to the final three every 15 minutes or so. Geoff, back from his night trying to deliver meals to all the fire crew on the fire ground, comes to sit beside me to wait. The door is closed and this room feels like a sanctuary. A place where there is order and calm, compared to the frenzy of the past thirteen days. The night radio operator pops his head in to say I can stand down, if I want to, but I shake my head and turn my face away to hide my eyes welling with tears. 'No, I want to see them safely home, if that's OK', I croak, hopeful he hasn't caught my emotion. I am not sure I understand where the tears have come from, but I am relieved that he nods and closes the door. Geoff leans against me, in solidarity.

There is only one truck unaccounted for and I am resolute I am not moving until they are safely back. I know I am being irrational. I could hand this administrative task to the next guy, but I can't.

I call again, 'KI Base to Parndana34' and I pause, 'Parndana34, it is time to return to base and stand down, and I am not moving until I hear from you', I say breaking all 'radio operation protocols'. Silence. Then the line crackles to life and a precious voice comes back through the line. 'This is Parndana34, KI Base', the familiar voice trails off to a chuckle. 'We hear you. It has been a long day. Say hi to your old man and thank him for the tucker, even though it was bloody cold!' Geoff slumps back in his chair and laughs. The tension of the moment lifts. 'We're on our way in', the voice finishes.

New tears flow. I love this community.

***

Twelve hours of slog.

They have called the fire crews three times now and finally a truck arrives around 10pm. They tell the farmers the plan is for the whole farm to be burnt as part of 'their' back burn. He can't believe it. He's been battling this blaze from all fronts for days, without their help, and now this.

He can sense the confusion about who is in charge of the fire. The crews from the mainland don't know the island terrain, so he pushes on with his own plans, regardless of what the fire truck crew leader says. Since the day's beginning, he's only had back-up from a few local farm fire units. And yet, he's managed to put out every spot fire. No land or fences lost. 'No bloody way' are they going to burn his farm.

Adaptation Defined

Adaptation—the other category of international climate change action—is a word we all know. Yet the current generation driving the world possess little experience with it, really. Generations before us were thrown into the turmoil of world wars, of a life shattering depression, of dramatic changes to work arrangements, and upheaval that resulted in shamefully overdue changes to the rights of certain groups. Humanity *adapted* and survived. Here on this island, those generations cleared farmland and built homes with rudimentary hand tools, basic equipment, no electricity, and the nearest doctor too many hours away. That generation cultivated a survival instinct that perhaps remains buried in us all, or perhaps has been lost. Nonetheless, the changing climate is forcing us to connect with that essence or build it anew. While elsewhere in the world the veil of denial still cloaks people's minds, here—on this small patch of land surrounded by sea—we now stand in the sharp new reality, learning to *adapt* to forces that are bigger than we can control. We have the opportunity to learn from our experience and accelerate building our resilience in the climate chaos world.

In the political cut and thrust of climate change politics, genuine adaptation is infrequently discussed. It is the poor cousin to mitigation. For decades it has been a footnote to the meeting agendas, or the last point of discussion at the end of days of negotiation. It is given far less attention than mitigation, even though adaptation prepares for and copes with a changing climate that can no longer be avoided. When international adaptation discussions do happen, they focus on how to shift large economies to renewable fuel sources. How to build big-scale infrastructure, and how to redeploy whole industries without anyone losing employment or stability. There are important discussions about providing money to developing countries to help them build big infrastructure or plan for large-scale relocation. But these discussions always focus on the big projects of governments.

There is even a global plan for Disaster Risk Reduction[18] but it is poorly funded, and often overlooked. Even with that plan, the focus is far too lofty to help communities facing the climate chaos front-lines—where the need for genuine, life-changing adaptation is the new reality.

Events early in 2020, through most of 2021, and into 2022, such as the unprecedented heat waves, wildfire seasons, floods, cyclones, and mass mortality of key oceans' ecosystems, should be screaming at us about how rapidly and fundamentally our global environment is changing with only 1.1°C of global warming.[16]

We have to adapt life, not for smooth economic transition, or to keep wealthy people earning massive sums. We have to adapt to survive and we don't have much time. We are approaching serious 'tipping points'—where large-scale components of Earth's climate system reach a critical threshold at which small changes lead to significantly larger changes—and while we don't know precisely which ones will tip first, or even when these events will begin the cascade, almost no one in the climate science field believes they won't happen.

I can't help but feel most governments are completely missing the point, right now. Looking at the Australian federal and state governments' discussions about adaptation in this one country, reveals a focus on strategies for use across the whole of Australia but none that meet the needs of communities where the impact is being felt. They propose high-level, large-scale strategies such as better air support or more fire trucks. They discuss allocating government budgets or streamlining the relationship between agencies in times of crisis. Granted, this is important and needed, but none of it is the fine-grained, local-scale planning that climate chaos vulnerable communities are desperate for.

Climate-threatened communities across the world need local, embedded plans that have been negotiated with them well ahead of time. They should cover how to keep fire from hurtling over a major road that is needed for evacuation, or the support needed for a specific industry that is critical to survival, like food production. These communities, and mine, need to know how to protect our children, emotionally and physically, if their school is impacted or a major fire rolls over. How will we restore power or phones if infrastructure is damaged or destroyed? What measures do we need our hospitals and medical services to have prepared? Will we need additional infrastructure, like pumps and tanks, and hoses? How can we smoothly communicate with each other about what's going on? We need to collectively agree on which patches of bush should be mosaic burnt through the winter, where permanent earth breaks should be established, and access roads created.

When the next landholder stands to fight a wall of flame careening across their crops or land, hours or days before any of the macro-scale government-led solutions even kick in, our embedded, community plan needs to support them with something more detailed than the knowledge that fire trucks *may* be deployed to help. That landholder should have the confidence and the peace of mind to know that their children will have a system of support automatically enfold them; that communications won't be lost during the height of the crisis because our community has a strategy to keep them going; that we have ALL turned our attention to help them; that their community has their back. Communities need to become internally resilient.

Other communities need this fine-scale confidence too but for different climate chaos threats. Not long ago, six million workers lost their income when major rice, corn, and sugar-producing areas in the Philippines were destroyed by Typhoon Haiyan. The Gulf of Mexico and East Coast of the US are experiencing some of the world's fastest rates of sea level rise and whole communities have already abandoned homes where generations once lived. Hundreds of thousands of people in Bangladesh now face an impossible choice between remaining on battered coastlines or moving inland to urban slums without means to feed themselves or care for their families. As I finish the final edits of this book, a third of Pakistan is under water, thousands are dead and hundreds of thousands are living in temporary camps. In 2018 in Japan, more than a thousand people died during an unprecedented heat wave, while India has been battling crippling heat waves and wet bulb events for a decade now, with the annual death of thousands of people across a growing number of India's northern and central states.[19-23] Mid-way through 2021 the Pacific Northwest of North America experienced an unprecedented heat dome which lasted five days. In British Columbia, Canada, temperatures in the small town of Lytton reached 48°C. A forest fire, likely caused by wilful denial and abetted by heat, forced more than a thousand people to evacuate and destroyed most of the town. Hundreds of people died across the Pacific Northwest.[24] In the early months of 2022, rain bombs burst over towns along Australia's east coast flooding regions well above any historical measures. The relentless deluge in Queensland and New South Wales is one of the most extreme disasters in Australian history, and the devastation is wide-ranging.[25] Scientists have recently modelled the droughts in Australia and discovered the major dry spells of the late 20th and early 21st centuries in southern Australia are without precedent over the past 400 years,[26] forcing farmers from their land, gutting communities and the viability of many rural towns.

This is all happening right now and requires people to adapt at life-changing levels, often with no government support. There is simply no choice. There is no cotton wool wrapping their lives. There is no rescue package coming. There is not even a wider societal recognition of the profound changes they face.

Given the human stories wrapped in these changes, It is perhaps a surprise that adaptation isn't what people think about when the changing climate crosses their minds. Probably it is because adaptation is not as sexy as mitigation. There is no exciting, noble fight in it. It is just a sad, tiresome slog of survival. It is complex and messy, difficult and often depressing. Sure, there are sparks of genius and amazing inventions that adaptation spurs into life, but in the main it is the pragmatic, hard-working, but not-so-alluring child that speaks with downcast eyes and hands clenched in anguish that people's lives must change, forever.

Adaptation presents big challenges for business and decision-makers, too, because it requires skills and knowledge to make long-term decisions. Far too often short-term priorities rule. Yet, we know that if decisions about major infrastructure investment, land use planning, and building design don't take the changing climate into account, there will be greater costs and risks in the future.

My community has seen this born out, writ large. 'Bushfire is integral to our ecology, culture, and identity; it is scripted into the deep biological and human history of the fire continent'.[27] Yet, as fires go, even in a fire-prone country, the Black Summer season was unprecedented. More than 190,000 kilometres^2 were burnt across the country.[28] There were 33 deaths directly from the fire, thousands from smoke inhalation in the months afterwards. Preliminary assessments indicate economic losses of several billion US dollars.[15] Compare this scale to the other mega blazes of 2021: the Californian wildfires burnt 10,396 kilometres^2, Brazil 13,235 kilometres^2, Greece 1250 kilometres^2. Australia's Black Summer fires have only been eclipsed by Russia's 2003 inferno, where the taiga forests in Siberia and the Far East region of Russia were hit by unprecedented wildfires, following record-breaking heat and drought, razing through 222,577 kilometres^2. In 2019, for the first time in recorded history, wildfire smoke reached the North Pole.[29-32]

Australia's Black Summer mega-fire was like nothing previously recorded anywhere on Earth. Since records began, no fire has burned anything like the 21 percent of a continent's forested land.[28] *The Conversation* editors emotively wrote 'Australia roared into 2020 as a land on fire'.[33]

Tom Griffiths, a noted fire writer, captured the season well:

> *'[Australians] always give their firestorms names, generally after the day of the week they struck. There are enough 'Black' days in modern Australian history to fill up a week several times over—Black Sundays, Mondays, Tuesdays, Thursdays, Fridays and Saturdays—and a Red Tuesday too, plus the grim irony of an Ash Wednesday. The blackness of the day evokes mourning, grief and the funereal silence of the forests after a fire-storm. [The 2019/20] summer will leave a black legacy, but there is no single, culminating event and no end to anxiety and fear, no defining day and no day-after yet. Individual Black Days have fused in a Savage Summer.'* [34]

If the fires revealed the strength and goodness of small, remote communities they amplified the gross failure of federal leadership.

And, as if neglect and omission were not enough, elected politicians encouraged misinformation and bot- and troll-like social media lies about the causes of the fires, declaring that they were started by arsonists or that 'greenies' had prevented hazard-reduction burns.[35] For absolute clarity, Australia's Black Summer fires were overwhelmingly started by dry lightning in remote terrain, with fuel loads that had been poorly managed by governments for decades, and a changing climate was the furnace that made them burn.

So here my community now stands, ill-prepared and under-experienced in the 'adaptation' world, regardless what our political class chooses to argue about. We are on virgin ground, trying to prepare for the unknown.

As I talked and interviewed people about the fires and what we do with our future, over and over I heard the same defeated, anxious words. Sometimes it was forcefully said, at other times almost a tentative whisper as if to speak the words out loud gave them more power, more control. 'We've run out of time' or 'It is too late now.' 'We can't stop what's happening'. Certainly, I resonated with their sentiments, but I couldn't leave them in this terrible, defeated space, and would engage them in discussion to try and draw them back from the brink of a deep, black pit of despair. Not everyone, but many, would become emboldened again and say, 'We love it here. We have to figure out how to adapt'.

6

Fire Weather

January 2, 2019

It is a place she feels connected to, her favourite place. A place more special than anywhere else. Snake Track, deep in the Gosselands. It is the type of forest only the most dedicated hikers go—or people who work for National Parks and have a reason to navigate its impenetrable depths. From the road, the place looks almost flat, but once you are inside it pitches into deep, steep gullies rolling down 100 metres inside a square kilometre; billy-goat country.

For a moment, she recalls the ridges and where the hills still see sun, where banksias are dense and dominant—vital habitat of the green carpenter bee, an iconic Australian species, the largest bee in southern Australia and a holy grail for insect twitchers. Kangaroo Island is now the species' last refuge, and almost all of that refuge is in the deep west of the island. These enigmatic bees need dead banksia trunks found in areas left unburned for at least 15 years, but preferably over 60 years. She counts the years back to the fire that burnt most of Flinders Chase in 2007. That fire not only removed substantial amounts of this banksia habitat, it also synchronised the flowering of many grass trees over this vast area. These grass tree flowers are the bees' other preferred nesting habitat.

While scientists had not found green carpenter bees in Gosselands in recent surveys, historically this was their habitat and there was hope they remained because the banksias were nearing maturity. She's always held concern about the Gosselands burning in one big fire event and losing these important plants.

There is more than just bees to revere. Deep in the Snake Track ravines, of twists and turns, is also endangered glossy black-cockatoo habitat. These are large black parrots sporting a bright red band under their tails. The females have fetching yellow patches on their heads and necks. This species prefers forested areas dominated by drooping sheoak, their primary food source, with stands of older sugar gum that have hollows to nest in. By 1996, the glossy black population had plummeted, because their nesting and feeding habitat was almost gone. Nests and feeding habitat are now protected and slowly the population has grown but their survival is still precarious. Sugar gums stand deep and low into these Gosseland gullies, towering up to twenty metres from the forest floor. Their old bark, smooth and grey, sheds in irregular patches to expose fresh yellowy-brown streaks. Creamy-white flowers adorn a fifteen-metre-wide crown through summer. These trees, tucked deep inside her connected place, showed no signs they had ever been burnt. Most eucalyptus trees can survive more than 250 years in the wild. These sugar gums were certainly old. The 2007 fires had not scarred this deep, wet place.

She gives herself a moment longer to reflect on the beauty of the almost untouched creek line, damp and wet, even in summer. No one can remember that creek burning, ever, she thinks with reverence. She recalls her last survey of the area walking in whole and coming out with her face ripped to bleeding pieces by the banksia. She chuckles sadly to herself. That the banksias 'fought back' wells in her chest with momentary happiness.

But now she faces south and the enormity of the building fires quells her soul's bliss. Now it is fatally dry on the ridge. Too dry, she knows. Standing fifteen kilometres north west of Snake Track, after one final, last heart-wrenching glance in its direction, she slams her mind shut to its fate. She is powerless to do anything else. Subconsciously she knows Snake Track will be gone soon and she doesn't want to look.

Drivers for Fire Weather

More than ten years ago, the Australian government commissioned the Commonwealth Scientific and Industrial Research Organisation (CSIRO), Australia's federal government agency responsible for scientific research, to assess the potential impacts of a changing climate on 'fire regimes' in Australia. Similar work was being conducted in the US. The intent was to increase understanding of the complex interactions between changing climate, fire regimes, and wildlife and wildland conservation 'to inform future fire management'. In this scientific world, 'fire regime' is the history of fire events at a given point in the landscape.

There was good reason to do this work. The deadliest bushfires for Australia in the past 200 years took place in 1851, then 1939, then 1983, and 2009. It appeared that 'fire weather' was becoming more frequent.[36]

The assessment, led by Dr Richard Williams and released in 2009, examined changes to fire regimes, projected the changing climate in order to predict the dangers, and considered what approaches were needed. Prophetically, the modelling of Williams and his team warned that, by 2020, extreme fire danger days in south-eastern Australia would be more than twice as frequent; that changing climate would influence fire regimes across the Australian landscape through changes to temperature, rainfall, humidity, and wind (and the amount of carbon dioxide in the atmosphere). Weather, they predicted, would become more severe, particularly in southern Australia and changing climate would become a dangerous driver for fire.[37] And, it is all coming true.

These scientists determined that changing climate will probably have the most significant impacts on both the fire regimes and the wildlife and wildlands of sclerophyll-dominated vegetation of south-eastern Australia and south-west Western Australia. Sclerophyll vegetation are plants with hard leaves, short distances between leaves along the stem, and a leaf orientation parallel to direct sunlight. We have a lot of this in southern Australia.

Their predictions do not stand alone. Dozens of scientific studies both in Australia and across the globe, published on either side of the CSIRO report, are reinforcing the warning. They also dive into the deep pool of why and how. Ten years later, in 2019, Sarah Harris and Chris Lucas provided another important layer of context with their investigation into the big climatic drivers for Australia—the El Niño Southern Oscillation (ENSO), the Southern Annular Mode (SAM) and the Indian Ocean Dipole (IOD)—as the cause of the recent upward trend in Australian fire weather.[38, 39]

Anyone who lives on the land or spends their days on the sea knows that climate (and weather) has a cycle, and it is long. As Earth breathes and sighs, different areas increase or decrease in temperature, humidity, and rainfall sometimes over a decade or more. Within a human lifetime it is possible to come to know some of these cycles and to expect and adapt to them accordingly. Traditional and indigenous communities have been doing this for aeons and modern farmers and fishers for generations. But human memories alter perception over time, and information passed from one person to another can morph and change in the telling. Where science is particularly helpful is looking, dispassionately, at data over sufficiently long time-scales to give us a picture that is bigger than our lived experience and is accurate across time. That is what Harris and Lucas did.

They looked at the data between 1973 and 2017 and found that the ENSO is the dominant driver of fire weather variability within a season across most of the Australian continent, although that influence is stronger in the central and eastern portions of the country. The IOD plays a significant role through the winter in southern and central Western Australia and in spring across south-eastern Australia. SAM's influence is more widespread. When its cycle is in a 'negative phase' the Fire Danger Index is higher, especially in south-eastern Australia. There are other complex interrelationships at play that all deserve full and thoughtful reading of Harris and Lucas' paper as well as the hundreds of other related studies. In essence though, these are the climatic influences that tune Australia's fire weather and therefore Australia's Fire Danger Index upward or downward within any given season.[38, 40, 41]

Understanding the climatic influences reinforces confidence in the meteorological weather predictions already feeding into fire management. But there is more to pick through. Clearly there is a long-term upward trend in the frequency of fire weather, especially in southern Australia. Understanding what is influencing that trend across seasons is important.

It might be easy to assume that ENSO, SAM, and IOD were the culprits, but it turns out that is not the entire picture. Before coming to their conclusion, Harris and Lucas looked carefully at another multi-decade climatic driver—the Interdecadal Pacific Oscillation (IPO)—to see if it explained the trend, but it had transitioned through only one cycle between 1980 and 2002 that vaguely lined up with the data. IPO didn't explain what they were seeing. Of course, there may well be another multi-decadal driver currently not known to science. But, Harris, Lucas, and most other climate scientists believe the far more likely driver is changing *global* climate, particularly in the southern portions of the Australian continent. Making matters worse, the changing global climate may also be impacting Australia's fire weather indirectly, by fundamentally modifying how the underlying climate drivers operate.[38, 40]

Studies such as these have done a good job of predicting large-scale shifts. But nothing is simple. Fire weather is expected to increase in most of southern Australia owing to hotter and drier conditions. Correspondingly, drought frequency is projected to increase. In 2014, the IPCC's regional assessment projected up to a thirty percent increase in days with very high and extreme fire danger by 2020—a reality that is upon us, now. It is high time we heed these warnings, because the next siren hails the doubling again of fire weather days in the next 30 years.[6-8, 42, 43] More plainly, the frequency of such events has already climbed from one event every two years during the late 20th century to around one event each year. In the coming decades fire weather will increase *across the world*, and will probably climb to two major events each year in parts of Australia.[6-8, 44] Many intense fires in south-eastern Australia are associated with strong winds channelled ahead of powerful cold-fronts, with the winds drawn from the hot continental interior. And, the not-so-great news is the frequency of these fronts is projected to increase by a factor of four.[45]

In our immediate future we can expect more frequent hot days and nights. Our fire season will be extended, reducing the opportunity to cool burn areas during the wetter weather. Higher levels of carbon dioxide in the atmosphere will also mean that fuel loads will increase in some regions because carbon dioxide speeds plant growth.[42] What we know from the past cannot be used as a reliable guide for what we can expect for the future.[45] In the prosaic language of science, fire management 'will become increasingly challenging', and the conflicted ground between protecting nature and protecting property will become more fraught.[42]

Forest Fire Danger Index

By mid-way through 2020, the data had been crunched and a retrospective scientific picture was forming about the weather conditions that generated Australia's Black Summer wildfires.

Those tasked with assessing fire weather have a crucial role in all our lives, yet they are unseen specialists we rarely acknowledge. I have come to think of them as invisible saints. Imagine having the role of faithfully, objectively compiling a Forest Fire Danger Index (FFDI) every year to measure the degree of fire danger in Australian forests. Imagine what you would imagine.

Their work combines a record of dryness, based on rainfall and evaporation, with meteorological variables for wind speed, temperature, and humidity. People who understand this data—fire behaviour experts and fire weather forecasters—use the FFDI values to build a picture over time, looking back and forward, too.

The accumulated FFDI values for spring 2019 were the highest ever seen over large areas of Australia—significantly higher than any other season on record. Basically, high temperatures and low rainfall, inside the grip of a prolonged drought meant there was more fuel to burn and weather that made that fire hot and furious.

As we know now, their predictions were spot on and the results were catastrophic, in the truest sense of the word.[2, 46]

History had foretold this day would come. Despite the FFDI predications, three massive fires in Victoria over the period 2002–2009 burnt some 30,000 kilometers^2, or 40 percent of the state's public land. In the worst of these bushfires, 173 people lost their lives in Australia's worst civilian tragedy. Each of these three fires was followed by intensive government investigations, the most serious of which was the Victorian Bushfires 'Black Saturday' Royal Commission. It found that 30 years of continuous changes in the organisation of public land management had disrupted forest and fire management, increasing the fuel loads in most forest types. Science tells us that burning to reduce fuels is important for nature and the protection of life and property. The greatest number of submissions to the 'Black Saturday' Commission concerned fuel-reduction burning. Despite specific recommendations coming from the Commission (as well as from an earlier government inquiry) for a three-fold increase in the fuel-reduction target, Victoria remained divided on the effectiveness, propriety, and implementation of fuel-reduction burning—divided among ecologists, divided among the community, divided among and within the key land-management agencies.[47, 48] It is clear to me, when I talk to people in South Australian parks and other agencies, our state harbours that divide too. Despite the FFDI data, division drives the budgets and staffing of agencies, gutting them of their effectiveness; dis-empowering their ability to move forward as they know we must.

Rapid Rise of Mega-fires

It is not just the changes in weather we need to consider. It is the scale of what is being unleashed.

In 2014, scientists were already warning that the increased fire incidence will increase the risk of mega-fires in southern Australia to people, property, and infrastructure.[42] Mega-fires are wildfires that now burn at high intensities in each season, despite massive investments in fire suppression. They continue despite intensive and expensive enquiries.[47, 48] Were those scientists in 2014 writing their projections now, they would have certainly added the overwhelming impact to agriculture and horticulture and the mental health of farm families.

Mega-fires were the subject of an international conference held in Tallahassee, Florida, in 2011, spawned by increasing awareness that fire suppression was 'running out of road'. Jerry Williams, the former National Director of Fire & Aviation Management, United States Forest Service, was the keynote speaker and wrote:

> *'[P]rotecting people and sustaining natural resources can no longer rely on suppression capabilities, alone; protection will become more dependent on how we manage the forests where high-impact mega-fires incubate.'*[49]

William's point was that drought and fire exclusion policies have been implicated in the mega-fire problem. High-impact mega-fires can be traced to land management decisions that result in dense forest conditions with high biomass and fuel build-up over extensive areas. As droughts have intensified, more of these accumulated fuels have become available to burn at intensities that exceed suppression capabilities.[50]

The conference gave rise to discussions about 'tipping points', and greatly increased risks to ecosystems not previously threatened by fire—critical ecosystem functions created by the confluence of changing climates and accumulating fuels.[50] Indeed, Adams wrote in 2013 that global evidence posits that we are on the cusp of fire-driven 'tipping points' in some of the world's most important woody biomes including savannah woodlands, temperate forests, and boreal forests, with consequences of major changes in species dominance and vegetation type. The evidence also suggests that the vast carbon emissions from mega-fires are now contributing to the changing climate, and will be responsible for large swings in water yield and quality from temperate forests at the regional scale.[50]

More recently, an international group of authors has written that an ever-increasing focus by governments on fire suppression was a trap, as it allowed fuels to accumulate to levels that would eventually burn at intensities well beyond the capabilities of any firefighting service, anywhere,[50, 51] and beyond ecosystem tolerances. Our pattern of conservation management seems to be marching us towards a doomed future.

Nothing is simple, least of all understanding how much and what types of vegetation and leaf litter becomes dangerous under extreme fire conditions, and it is no surprise that the effects of changing climate on fuel loads is complex. While accepting that conditions vary at landscape scales and in different regions of Australia, simplistically, vegetation production (and hence fuel load) tends to be linked with annual rainfall. Changes in rainfall patterns from a changing climate influence the amount of fuel load that is present and the rate at which that fuel dries. In areas projected to receive more rainfall, the fuel load may increase. In other regions, where rainfall is projected to be lower, it is anticipated that fuel loads may decrease. But, that's a simplistic view. The fertilisation effect of elevated atmospheric carbon dioxide is also increasing vegetation production. Unhelpfully, this seems to favour woody plants and shrubs over grasses, altering the amount and distribution of fuel for fire because woody plants, shrubs and their leaf litter typically contribute to a higher fuel load in landscapes. And, the relative carbon and nitrogen content of leaf litter may also change, resulting in slower leaf litter decomposition or reduced palatability to grazing animals, further increasing fuel loads.[37]

For landscape-scale wildfires to occur, four conditions are needed: the presence of spatially continuous fuel (i.e. vegetation and leaf litter); fuel that is dry enough to burn; an ignition source (e.g. lightning or human causes); and weather conditions favourable to fire spread. In vegetation-dense ecosystems, such as temperate Australian forests, a continuous block of fuel is generally present, except for in the few years directly following fire or other disturbance. Thus, the second precondition, fuel dryness, becomes the constraining influence for large wildfires in this region. Typically, we think of drought as something that impacts farmers and crops, but drought equally impacts natural ecosystems. Drier periods cause low fuel moisture content, particularly in living vegetation (i.e. foliage and twigs). And, the level of dryness is relative. Drought triggers leaf deterioration and shedding in eucalyptus forests, blanketing the forest floor with fine fuels which increase the rate of fire spread. For fine dead fuels (leaf and twig litter), moisture content is largely driven by atmospheric conditions and by soil water content for fuels in close contact with the soil. As they dry, previously damp gullies and rainforest patches become unlikely to act in their usual role of blocking the spread of fire across the landscape.[52] The landscape, simply, becomes easier to burn.

With large-scale and high intensity fires—mega-fires—the world will witness biome-scale changes in forests, including some of the world's most iconic forests, in time-scales as short as the next 50 years. Scientists are warning of rapidly approaching tipping points—where the vegetation changes begin to influence climate itself, as well as the wide range of other functions and services these ecosystems provide us all. Outside of removing all homes and infrastructure and human activities near or in forests, including in many cases the surrounding agricultural or pastoral activities that we all depend upon for food and textiles, the challenge governments face is to accept the reality of increased ignitions and fuel loads, and implement appropriate preparedness measures. 'Managing mega-fires, or at least incorporating mega-fires into land management, policy and planning, has to become a priority'.[50] These changes are bigger than the loss of homes and infrastructure. They threaten the very foundation of the biodiversity that surrounds us and upon which we depend.

Many researchers now fundamentally believe that the extraordinary losses of wildlife from Australia's Black Summer fire will be matched by wholesale changes to plant diversity and abundance across much of the forest estate of New South Wales, Victoria, and parts of Queensland and South Australia. The loss of soil carbon is still being measured, and while there will be an initial increase, water yield will likely take decades to recover to pre-fire condition in key catchments.[53, 54] Already, these are previously unfathomable changes, and mega-fires are just warming up.

7

Helter-skelter

January 3, 2020

His crew of farm fire units is bigger now. To their own rig they can add the friends from last night and another this morning. The predicted heat and a strong northerly wind are the opposite of what they've been hoping for. These are their most dangerous wind conditions and by dawn wind-lines are already showing signs of what is in store.

They drive all three farm fire units to an already

flaring area and sit to wait for the embers to ignite more spots in the unburned bush.

It doesn't take long before they are chasing another big fire across the paddock. This news travels fast and they are again joined by a few more farm fire units. One brings radios for communication. What a huge relief.

***

Early in the morning, Geoff takes two mainland-based radio technicians to the northern side of the fireground so they can set up a radio tower to enable better communication between fire trucks in a region with notoriously bad radio coverage. The men, newly arrived on the island, are noticeably jumpy about being driven into an active fireground. Their convoy skirts the northern fringe of the fire area before stopping at the staging area and parking amongst on-call operators and heavy machinery. The day is already hot, and clear enough to track the large plumes of smoke billowing up in the southwest.

As the technicians step away from their vehicle, onto the recently burned ground where the new radio tower will sit, the compression of their footsteps ignites in flame.

Footsteps on fire. An omen of the coming apocalypse.

***

Her husband has been monitoring and fighting the Ravine fire for days. She has hung in at home with the kids, trying to keep life normal.

Waiting.

Fires have raged through Flinders Chase for over three generations of her family's farming lives. Their farm sits on the laterite plateau of the island; a giant lightning rod that has shaped the region's fire season for thousands of years. Hers is a family tuned to fire. A family that has stood at the front lines as fire fighters and managed their land and their risks as farmers. Her own roots spring from half a world away where fire takes a different shape and texture. She knows how much she doesn't know but trusts her family's direction.

They have begun the day with breakfast on their front porch. She asks them if it is the day for her to go. Despite the air being full of smoke and ash, they assure her there isn't much risk, yet.

But, as the day progresses, she notices subtle changes in her husband's stance. He spends longer watching the fire and seems more drawn inside his head.

***

Tall and sure he stands with his crew in a shed awaiting instruction and the meals that will sustain them for their shift. The fire truck is tasked to press south to defend what they can of the buildings in the Chase. Plans have been hashed over for days it seems. He is not from this island, but senses a strange calm in the township, as if everyone is waiting for the unknowable.

He stretches and moves to the door, staring towards the western horizon where the smoke haze is thick. Glancing back at his crew he is glad they are calm, but the waiting after hours of travel is getting tough.

Finally, the food and water supplies arrive. He steps back into the cool of the shed. 'Up! Everyone on the truck', he shouts, and confidently strides out into the glare of the sun.

***

The dreaded words are spoken. 'Take the children and dogs and go to town', he tells her. Her subconscious has known the news was coming for hours, but now she feels ill-prepared. In a flurry of nervous worry, she flings belongings into bags, including snatches of mementos she will later wonder about. In time, she will discover this was a common occurrence across the island. Strangely packed bags, and so much left behind.

Within minutes, her children are secured in the car. She meets him at the end of their road. He has been looking for the safest direction for them to travel.

Together they stand, husband and wife, friends with a shared heart, shielding their children from their exchange. Around them everything still stands. The house, the trees, the spots the children play. Deep wordless meaning passes between them. Then, after a decade of chastising her for her driving speed, he leans in and whispers, 'Drive like Schumacher and don't look back'. The enormity of what he is saying—of the imminent danger ahead—sinks deep into her soul. She knows, in that moment, she might not see him again.

***

He loses the battle with the grass fire and another 100 plus acres. The fire runs into two creek lines where the bush is dense. A grader has joined him and together they fight to cut off the fire where they can.

He lights up along the grader break to widen the area where the fire can't burn. It holds. By mid-afternoon everyone is watching and waiting, again.

Then seven or eight farm fire units get calls that their own properties are in danger. They have to leave. His friend, who brought the radios, says he can stay for another 30 minutes before he must go too.

***

She plunges down the road, her children in the back, tears streaming down her face. There is deep smoke and fire on one side and blue sky on the other. Pressing her foot hard to the floor, she tears herself from her love to protect their loves, driving as fast as she can (maybe even beyond what is safe) into the blue.

From the opposite direction, fire trucks belt past. Her young son, old enough to be aware but not mature enough to understand, says 'Mummy, look at all these people going to help daddy', and her heart breaks further because she knows the truck's destination is the park, not the farm.

The men of her family will face the fire-breathing dragon alone that day.

It will be the longest day of her life.

***

They stand in their 'Safe Zone', a well grazed, green, kikuyu paddock to the west of the house. A small group of people staring wide-eyed and virtually speechless at a massive wall of smoke. It is impossibly, improbably tall. Then flames emerge from the smoke, far taller than any tree and deafening noise bear down from the west.

The air is on fire.

This is not a fire to know.

***

This fire won't let up. He spends the next few hours soaking hot spots. Everyone is getting jumpy, knowing one spark could mean it is all over. If they lose it, the rest of the farm and his sheep will be lost.

Two of them return to the house to fix their fire pump and find a fire in the pines along the road on their southern boundary. They begin to wet the area with a now broken pump and call for help from the others. The dozer comes. They realise then that somebody had already seen this fire. They had cut branches and wet the area down, most probably saving his paddocks. He would love to thank whoever this mystery person was.

The afternoon is cooling off. The wind has changed to a strong southerly. Two friends are out of water, so they decide to head home for the night. They plan to return in the morning with food, water, and petrol for the fire pumps.

***

She's been watching the fire app for days. This fire is deadly serious and has been a constant concern, but she's not felt directly threatened and is confident to stay at home with her children. If she needs to, she knows she can evacuate to the beach. She's lived here her whole life, and this doesn't feel close enough to be an immediate threat.

She wanders out on her porch, tea in hand, and looks to the western horizon. While she stands there a huge plume explodes in the sky, like a nuclear bomb has gone off and her mind speeds to process the unexpected information. With an odd detachment she notices it looks just like the pictures she saw in school when they learned about the nuclear test sites.

Then, adrenaline kicks in with a fierce rush. She feels it course through her body, propelling her into action. That plume is too big to not be a threat, and she recognises that it is smoke she needs to flee from. She and her kids won't survive on the beach. They won't be able to breathe. She's got to go, and now.

She has never moved so fast. Moments later she is hurtling down the road with her bewildered precious cargo in the back seat of the car.

***

The rule books sent him out into the field to see what was happening, gather first-hand information and to return to the station to chart out the next plan of attack. But by the time he had reached the south west corner of the island, an emergency call confirms the world had tipped on its axis. Three men are trapped in a burning house, their escape route engulfed in fire. He knows them. We all do.

***

She belts down the road, pushing her car as fast as it will go. The smoke is dark above, but there is still a sliver of bright light at the ground.

A glance at her son in the back seat breaks her heart so deep she knows it will never mend. He watches mournfully out the window as his beloved dog streaks across the paddock trying to catch the car.

She knows she can't stop.

***

They try to attend the call for help, directing four trucks north. A helicopter attempts to guide the convoy through a safe passage, but his knowledge of the area tells him it is too constrained, and he can't risk the men's lives in the trucks. He's fought fire his entire life, but today his world is turning bad, and quickly. Smoke is masking any semblance of visibility. Day has turned to night. Knowing there is little time before they are caught in a lethal embrace, he directs the convoy onto burnt ground and prays they survive.

***

He has been fighting the Duncan fire on his own for weeks and is exhausted in his bones. For the past hour he has trudged over the burnt paddocks, looking at the damaged fences. His eyes have been focused towards the ground.

He hears an engine and, bewildered, looks up to see his neighbour's ute tear across his paddock, the driver manically shouting words he can't quite hear as they hurtle past.

As if watching himself from afar, he turns towards where they have come from and sees a black, fire-filled cloud rolling towards him.

Adrenaline charges his legs and he races to shelter under the water tank beside his house, as hot ash and smoke on fire descends around him.

***

Fire barrels towards them, even as the blanket of blackness cloaks the convoy. The car rocks on its wheels as the fire storm races around them, but he focuses on the radio, talking to the trucks, reminding them how to stay safe—water halos on, firefighters all crouched in the foot wells, oxygen masks on everyone's faces. There are sixteen souls in those trucks and he needs to keep them calm; to keep them alive. What roars past and over this group is deadly in the extreme. It is like nothing his decades of experience have prepared him for.

In this moment he knows his crew are huddled in the same desperate embrace that is taking place at multiple sites across the island. This fire is too big. In this moment he know that everywhere, men and women will seek what shelter they can, dig deep within themselves for survival knowledge, and pray. He fears many won't make it.

***

In a paddock a quarter of the island away, I stand in the late afternoon watching the sky turn angry, roiling red.

Then the wind hits and I have to lean hard forward to not be thrown off my feet. It carries twigs and stones, and then hot embers. My mind throws up questions. Why embers? The fire is too far away. Why stones? Wind can't carry stones. Then rational thought snaps into hard focus.

As I race for Geoff, across the island mobile phones screech. Friends yell to friends to take shelter, hunker and hide where we can. A monster had been unleashed and its wrath is bigger than anything ever experienced.

Geoff and I get in our cars and flee from the beast. In a space of half a kilometre day turns to deep, black night.

***

Halfway between the south and north coast, the visibility is already down to meters. Tall flame is everywhere. Then the wind suddenly swings and belts them hard. Fire rages 25 metres away. A hose on full fog is set up to protect them, but the heat is so intense it is as if the water isn't there. They try, in vain, to save the buildings. The heat is more extreme than all his years of experience have taught him how to fight.

Above the truck, lightning cracks inside the pyro-cume cloud.

The radio carries screams from other trucks being burnt over.

This is a hellstorm.

***

The biggest fire-storm he has ever experienced has just rolled over him and he's sure more is coming. He has to get his crews to safety. After checking each of the trucks, he leads them back to the road across open fields. Practically blind in smoke too thick, he focuses on keeping his voice calm and steady, because the trucks that follow can see nothing but his car's tail lights and embers flashing past. Through kilometres of fire tunnels, and billions of embers, they pass trees alight from their roots to their tips. Flames lick the roads and up the sides of their trucks, super heating every surface. All the while he searches for familiar landmarks within a cauldron of lava.

In time, the crews all reach safety. Back at the station, he sends them home. They've been through enough.

Across the island, communications are down. The crisis is smashing every plan and process that existed until this night.

He gets back into a car and plunges back into the smoke and flames like so many true warriors on this fateful night.

***

He has been sent to rescue more people trapped in the fire, and a knot twists in his gut every time the loader he is following has to clear another downed tree. Frustratingly slow progress is exacerbated by the concern of what he will find. With relief, the group is found alive and once safely on board, he turns the convoy towards the highway where other trucks and cars emerge from burnt ground. People, shocked and amped, cling together, bonded as one group. He piles survivors into any vacant spaces the vehicles can offer and slowly leads a convoy of vehicles north to a sports club oval. At least that is open ground.

Radio instructions tell him to stop on that oval overnight. But, there are more than thirty souls now in his care, and too many fire trucks that are needed elsewhere. Intuitively, he knows the advice is flawed, so he takes a small vehicle east to see if he can get through. The journey is surreal. The homes of friends are on fire on both sides of the road. Destruction and death are everywhere. But he finds safe passage and returns to the small group on the oval, with instructions for how they can move forward.

With everyone departed, he is left alone in the dark, on the oval. A fireman for his whole life, now he stands—another warrior—without water or a truck and watches the historic hall burn.

***

Nearly every farmer that had given up their time to help him has either lost their farms or is about to. The fire is about to hit him from the south with no chance of stopping it.

He grabs what he needs to from the house and heads to the evacuation point on one of their burnt-out paddocks to meet the fire truck. He gets to the road before he remembers the mob of nearly three-thousand sheep boxed in a paddock and races to open gates with the hope that they'll survive.

***

She stands in the middle of a blackened paddock holding what is left of their sheep on burnt ground. The fire storm thunders overhead. They've been fighting fire from three directions for weeks. In the distance, their home is ablaze. They are exhausted beyond measure, but on this night she and her husband stand together, come what may.

***

Through the impenetrable black, fire balls roll up the hill towards his house. The pump keeps choking, he thinks it is because of the heat, but then it springs to life just in time.

He puts the hose on fog before he is hurtled off his feet and against the stone wall by the force of the fire front. He hears the deep internal crack as his head hits stone, and he blacks out.

***

He's been alone for days and hasn't slept, but every fibre of his body is tense and ready. He sits in his ute in a burnt paddock watching the fire take out the blue gums next to their neighbour's property only a couple of kilometres up the road. As if he's in a movie—where the improbable happens—it begins to rain. The glow of the fire slowly recedes to nothing. He can't believe it.

He goes to check on his neighbour who decided to stay and defend his house and then returns to his own home for a one-eye-open rest.

8

Fire-breathing Dragons

January 4 - January 5, 2019

She watches as the coroner lays sheets over two bodies—violent deaths that have ignored the natural order of life and caught so painfully short that an entire community is impacted. Cold hands of pain and suffering press into her heart at these brave men's inconceivably selfless sacrifice.

They could not have imagined the fires would be virtually unstoppable.

They drive past the checkpoints and the fire still burning to the east; after weeks of fire they are numbed now to what had seemed a terrible risk before. This time is different. She struggles to process how much the landscape has changed. For kilometres, hundreds upon hundreds of animals lie tortured and dead across the road or twisted into fences in tragic piles. There is violent ferocity to this now-still scene. So many lives petrified in place.

Shocked at the reality, she demands they stop the car and that they each get out and bear witness to what has happened.

This is not a moment to deflect or to glance away; to avoid the pain.

This is a moment to be present.

To embrace the sorrow.

***

Stunned they look out across thousands upon thousands of animals—cows, horses, sheep, wallabies, kangaroos, possums, and eagles—that have perished together in choke points as they fled the fire and the heat of the storm front's lethal wave. Animals mummified in flight, now lifeless charcoal statues portraying final moments besieged by deadly thick smoke and gripped by fear.

In the days to come, the community learns the names of the firefighters. Shocked whispers and gasps, a precursor to a collective slide into deep sorrow that will echo around burnt buttresses.

***

Already the air ricochets with the gunfire of farmers ending the lives of animals. Those beings who had survived but are so damaged they face tortured, short weeks of life—a staccato rhythm of bullets under a sombre landscape-level oratorio of agony. Sheep with udders burnt away. Cows no longer seeing the world; their hides melted from their bodies leaving angry, violent red as their life-force screams with pain. Possums, wallabies, and koalas, eyes glazed, fur burnt from their bodies, the bones of their spines exposed in perfect white lines. And feet, so many feet gone, leaving only bony stubs.

Her eyes are raw from the toxic mix of crying and ash.

***

The trees seem like charred skeletons with snow at their feet. From one horizon to the other, there is nothing but black and white, and all he can do is stand and weep.

***

He feels his mind switch off somehow; anything it takes to get the job done. Standing at the drafting gate, he faces the grim decision to destroy or not as each sheep runs or limps through. So many animals. So much suffering. His heart contracts in his chest. He has to get the job done as soon as possible.

He becomes aware of a stabbing pain in his jaw and realises it is from his tightly clenched teeth.

In the distance gunshots ring as other farmers bend to the task so he doesn't need to shoot his animals himself.

He feels sick.

He'll be doing the same on his mate's farm tomorrow.

***

She stands in the paddock over the remains of their faithful work dog.

Tears.

***

It wasn't the fire that shook my core; that rewrote my sense of self. Not the thirty-metre flames, or massive fire storms that ripped the canopy of calm above our island two days ago. Not the showering hell-fire still raining embers across our land. It is a big, terrible event—one that continues to the east of our farm even now. That event has shape and form.

My soul becomes wounded—untethered—while standing in a familiar space rendered desolate, monotone, and utterly, profoundly silent. Not a bird, not a hum. Not a single living sound, save the Earth's sad sigh. The giant trees along our creek-line stand as tall, blackened skeletons from their toes to their tips. Where once hills were dense with greens and ochres, now they are covered by tree bones with drifts of white at their feet. It is a landscape rendered entirely mute. Not even the wind blows. From horizon to horizon is a coil of thick, ghostly demise.

At my feet lies the remains of an eagle's charred skeleton. I can see parts of its spine and the bones of one shoulder. I knew this soul. With their mate they had circled above our heads as we'd stood within our vines. We had watched as they taught their young, from the top of a giant swinging tree. They probably died mid-flight. I imagine their wings trailing gracefully above their heads as their beautiful bodies plummeted to the ground. This reflection opens my awareness to hundreds of smaller birds similarly scattered across the paddock. In fences are the twisted, tormented remains of too many animals for my heart to contemplate, so I avert my gaze. Bewildered—this is almost too much to absorb—I am unprepared and unaware my moment of reckoning still races towards me.

I turn to watch Geoff walk up the vineyard hill, bending slowly every few steps to caress his blackened vines. His movement is tentative, achingly gentle, as if fearful of heaping greater harm upon the already dreadful injury. This vineyard had been one of hard labour, and of love. As I watch, he stops and stands. Face toward a distant horizon, his expression suddenly caves violently inward.

I feel his silent howl ...
... and my soul shatters.

The Black Summer fires were genuinely an unprecedented catastrophic event across southern Australia. There are not sufficient adjectives in the dictionary to reinforce the scale of the cataclysm to human and nature. The extensive area of forest burnt, the sheer heat of the fires, and the extraordinary number of fires that developed into extreme pyro-convective events were unmatched in the historical record.[55] That they happened should serve as a warning that we must be prepared for more in the future, because the systems igniting them are unfathomably powerful, and well beyond human scale.

It was an ignition from the sky.

Contrary to the dog-whistle myths that many politicians like to spread,[56] lightning that occurs with relatively little accompanying rainfall, known as dry lightning, is one of the main ignition sources for wildfires throughout many parts of the world. It is not arson. It is nature. This is not necessarily the case in all regions. In Brazil or Indonesia, fire has become part of an annual, corrupt resource grab. The tragedy of those fires deserves another full book dedicated to their cause and effect alone, but that is not my task today.

Not surprisingly, developing a model that can predict dry lightning occurrence is a holy grail for meteorological researchers.[57, 58] Large-scale driving factors for lightning storms include the big atmospheric and ocean drivers previously discussed, as well as a changing climate. It is amazing to recognise that the average chance of fire per lightning strike varies a lot and depends greats on the season.[58, 59] For example, researchers in Canada have calculated that the average probability of fire from a single lightning strike for adjacent provinces in Canada is 0.07 percent for Alberta but two percent for British Columbia.[59] Here is where the other factors come into play. Southern Australia has a temperate climate with the summer period experiencing the most severe fire weather conditions, as well as being the time of year when lightning is most likely to occur. I can personally attest to repeated experiences of dry lightning thunderstorms on Kangaroo Island where you become acutely aware that there are many, many lightning strikes, and the probability of a fire feels, at least, very high.

Lightning starts fires by striking directly into dry, flammable material. As lighting often hits the ground deep in impenetrable regions of large wilderness areas, there is a serious risk of fires smouldering for days before taking hold. They can also become root fires that burn within the root system of a tree, smouldering for weeks underground, long after the surface part of the fire has been extinguished.

Capricious Foe

Bushfires are often described by firefighters as being chaotic and capricious. Mostly this is because of the turbulent winds that drive fires on bad days. But is also involves the highly complex nature of fuel and combustion. Leaves, twigs, and branches are mostly made of cellulose. When heated, cellulose reacts in two ways. One way produces volatile gases and flame. The other produces char and glowing combustion. There are thermal and chemical feedbacks between these two reactions, which means that a fire burning in vegetation looks chaotic. One moment it appears fixated on consuming something and in the next moment sparks explode with furious energy. To the human eye it looks like fire does not follow any rules.[60]

Inside turbulent fire, the temperature of the reaction zone can reach 1600°C, with the base of tall flames reaching 1100°C and the tips of flames a relatively cool 600°C. A kilogram of dry vegetation contains enough energy to power a 100Watt light globe for 50 hours. In a fire that energy is released in a few seconds.[60]

Wildfire is a volatile and dangerous zone to be a human. Fire unleashed is truly capricious.

Clouds + Fire = Hellstorms

Some fires amplify themselves in horrific ways. It was a previously rare event that changed our lives, here on Kangaroo Island—a pyro-cumulonimbus (pyroCb); the fire-breathing dragon of clouds.

> *'A cumulonimbus without the 'pyro' part is imposing enough—a massive, anvil-shaped tower of power reaching [8 kilometres] high, hurling thunderbolts, wind and rain. ... Add smoke and fire to the mix and you have pyro-cumulonimbus, an explosive storm cloud actually created by the smoke and heat from fire, and which can ravage tens of thousands of acres.'* [61]

Pyro-cumulonimbus, or pyro-cumes for short, occur infrequently, but their impact can be fierce. Their fire spread is highly unpredictable and they're generally not suppressible.[62]

These dangerous cloud events form above sources of extreme heat, like erupting volcanoes or very large wildfires. The heat source needs to be relatively large and intense, and the wind not too strong, as smaller, weaker fires in higher winds develop turbulent, puffy plumes that don't form the same way. Within the right wind, heat and moisture conditions, super-heated thermals of air and moisture are drawn upwards towards the inversion layer of cooler air.[63-65] Anecdotal evidence suggests that near-surface wind surges associated with nearby thunderstorm outflows, the arrival of cold fronts, or sea breezes, can trigger the transition from a wind-driven fire to a more upright plume and pyro-cume.

It is not a surprise the events surrounding pyro-cumes sound a bit sketchy. These are mega-heated events. But, when these factors align, a fire-breathing dragon rises into the sky and looks around it with the intent to destroy. Physically what happens is the heat column, carrying burning embers and super heated smoke rises rapidly. It hits the cold inversion layer, and is forced sideways before it roll powerfully back towards the ground, slamming and spreading with force and speed, taking fire and heat with it. Once formed, pyro-cumes often generate their own, extreme low-level winds, and sometimes light rain or hail, and even tornadoes.[63, 66, 67] They are also known to generate their own lightning inside the fire plume that can ignite additional fires far ahead of the main fire front.[67] The combined effects of these phenomena dramatically increase the fire-spread and danger to those on the ground. These are not dragons to be trifled with.[66]

The aerosol of smoke from pyro-cume clouds can persist in the atmosphere for weeks, and in some circumstances reduce ground level sunlight much like the 'nuclear winter' effect.[66]

Because they are rare, and understandably difficult to study, the current methods of fire-spread prediction, including the use of traditional modelling approaches, falls short when attempting to predict pyro-cumes and the behaviours of the wildfires they spawn.[62]

There is significant concern within the scientific community that the changing climate is increasing the occurrence of pyro-cumes globally. This concern is driving more focused research into these meteorological phenomena.[63, 64, 68, 69]

In July 2019, a group of Australian researchers led by Giovanni Di Virgilio released an assessment on future changes in the risk of pyro-cume occurrence for south eastern Australia. Their view is that atmospheric instability and dryness is a better indicator of pyro-cume development than surface fire weather conditions. They noted that over 90 percent of pyro-cumes occurred on rugged landscapes.[70] Previous research has found that interactions between winds and rugged terrain also generate the expansive flaming zones associated with pyro-cume development and increased wildfire severity.[71]

Di Virgilio and his colleagues contend the atmospheric conditions, including tropospheric instability and dryness, and surface fire weather conditions such as temperature, humidity, wind speed, and precipitation, associated with pyro-cumes development are projected to increase in frequency predominantly in the southern Australian spring. This effectively extends the dangerous part of the fire season into spring, when historically these threats have typically been a summer phenomenon.[70] These fires will be more difficult to control and will cause considerable damage.[70, 72] This shift in seasonality has huge implications for resource allocations by fire agencies, for the periods when controlled burns can safely take place, and for how people living on the land manage risk.

Sadly, we are looking towards a future with more hellstorms.

Cold Truths

With all this information, it is easy to become despondent. Uncontrollable fire ignition from the sky, fire-breathing dragons, and looming tipping points can leave us with a sense that the world is out of control. In some ways it is. Certainly, where I live. But we are a tough community. And we need to accept what is going to happen right here, in our little patch of the world—our island floating in an ocean of possibilities. We need to know what we can't control, so we can decide what to do about the things we can.

The great fire writer, Stephen J. Pyne, has confidence

communities can rise from this. Fire-prone places are becoming more fire-driven, more fire-susceptible. Unlike many regions, he argues Australia is better positioned to respond. We have fire institutions and fire scientists who lead the world with fundamental advances in fire behaviour, fire ecology, and fire anthropology.

> *'First to experience, first to lead—Australia can turn what promises to be a problem Pyrocene into an opportunity; only the US has a comparable technological and cultural capacity. Europe outside the Mediterranean, for example, has almost none of Australia's experience and fire culture to tap into. Other continents have fire and folklore but lack institutional heft. In a planet increasingly informed by fire in all its manifestations, a world that is segueing into the fire equivalent of an ice age, its experience counts. Australia is a firepower. How it uses that power matters to the rest of us.'* [73]

There is a responsibility in that call from Pyne, but there are immediate matters we need to overcome. Chief among them is an acceptance that fire has always been here but its nature will be more damaging and fiercer in the future; that what is coming is not the natural fire our landscape is adapted to. This requires everyone to move to a space where we accept that we must adapt to survive.

You would think that would be simple. We acknowledge the face of disaster and take steps to adapt and protect ourselves. Sadly, not so. In an age of clicktivism and social media information flow, there is another challenge to overcome. People really want to ignore this. In February 2020, Henriette Jager and Charles Coutant wrote with dismay to the prestigious scientific journal *Nature*, confused that a global crisis that will forever reshape the ecology of the Australian continent, as well as the structure and direction of many rural communities, was not stimulating a collective worldwide commitment to address the changing climate. But that instead, the world—including the cities in Australia—was responding with a massive effort to knit, crochet and sew booties, koala mittens, joey pouches and even nests for rescued wildlife.[74] Even the wildlife carers so crucial to our collective recovery efforts and loved by our community agreed, this overflow of well-meaning but off-target sympathy captured how misunderstood the real situation is to the rest of the world beyond the burn scar.

There was also a phenomenal outpouring of financial support to conservation organisations professing to save koalas and other wildlife that grossly eclipsed the scale of the human aid. I saw first-hand when the chips are down, many in the conservation industry prioritised fundraising—foolishly forgetting that people are part of nature—collecting millions of dollars to support wildlife rescue and feeding stations, while farmers on Kangaroo Island bent their backs to destroying their suffering farm animals without a whiff of support. These were the men and women who had faced weeks of unrelenting firefighting to protect those very ecosystems and wildlife.

Never have I felt so disconnected from my peers. Never has it been so clear how disconnected the conservation industry can be to people. The blunt truth is that wildlife won't survive the next fire without those same humans that fought and lost everything in the Black Summer fires.

In the weeks after the fires, I watched a debate raging on Facebook about the sharing of images of animals suffering. People, here in Australia and half a world away, were aggressively attacking the distribution of truthful images of the fires and the harrowing nature of the damage it caused, concerned about the impact of the imagery on their personal emotional welfare. Their claim was that showing such stark, sad pictures would 'turn people away from caring'. That speaking openly about the changing climate would 'frighten people into inaction'. Attempts to raise the issue on the political stage were met with the sharp rebuke that 'now was not the time to talk about climate change'. The media lapped up the debate celebrating the then Deputy Prime Minister McCormack and Prime Minister Morrison's denial of the link between wildfires and climate change.[75]

Too soon, in my opinion, the conservation movement and others capitulated, softening their tone, and sharing images of the 'hopeful' fresh green shoots instead of the stark black landscape. A blanket of comfortable denial was wrapped around the world again and the conservation 'till continued to ring'.

I learned the cold truth of many natural disaster survivors. Our experience was quickly and aggressively tuned to serve PR machines that wanted to promote 'hopium' and the myth that nothing was really changing in the world. What was deeply unsettling is no one beyond the communities destroyed in the fires seemed to notice.

9

Warriors

January 6 - February 29, 2020

The fire has travelled east and is about 6 kilometres from his farm, and it is huge, gathering momentum as the temperature and wind increase. He knows this island is in for strong northerly winds followed by a strong southerly in the late afternoon. The same as the week before when their other farm was smashed so hard. They've always believed sou-westerlies were their friend. No more. The fire breaks containment lines and makes its way towards his friend's place and he pushes his ute hard to get there in time. When he arrives, he's relieved to find others there to help. This fire has gone on so long, it is amazing anyone still has the energy.

***

They stand on the top of the hill, as farm fire utes belt down their bush tracks. They are amazing and tenacious and her heart thanks them for saving this precious patch of wildness.

***

She answers his call to hear him say 'you have 15 minutes until it hits'. Robotically she moves through the motions of the 'fire plan' she knows so well. Fill buckets with water. Sinks and troughs all full as well. Wet towels ready. All the flammable materials outside had been moved weeks ago, or were burnt away when the first fire hit their farm, sheds and house. But for this fire event she is not alone. There are others with her, and one of the children has a fever climbing. That reality changes everything.

With the confidence of a mountain, she knows her husband will stay between her and the fire, but this time she is second guessing herself. Should they still be there? Is somewhere else safer? Where once her resolve would have been as solid as stone—to stand and fight because you are safest at home—on this day she is no longer sure. So much has already been lost across the island. So much has already been lost on their farm. Nothing in this fire has been predictable. Her family knows fire, deeply. It has been part of their DNA, forever, but this fire had proved 'unknowable'.

She steps outside for a moment, looking at the intense red glow on the horizon, knowing both her husband and son are inside the crimson haze—inside this ever-present wildfire that won't die. Ash and smoke have swirled around her for nearly three weeks, and here the threat of flames is back again.

Once back inside the house, with the door firmly closed on the looming chaos, something shifts in her mind. The fire might come or might change direction. There is no way to tell. She knows how to survive if it bears down on her home. Now, it is a sick child she will focus on. There is a fever to quell and nothing will break her resolve.

***

It doesn't take long for the fire to reach the outskirts of the township, just missing his friend's property but rolling across the farm on the other side of the road. A couple of people stay with him, while others help the fire trucks on the other side. It rages for an hour before making its way south, destroying more as it goes.

***

Startled from shallow sleep by the ringing phone, he looks at the clock. It is 5am. 'I just put a fire out at the corner of your house, but there is more coming. If you get here now, you'll save it', a friend yells. Without conscious thought, within minutes he is back in his farm fire unit barrelling down the road towards his home. Flames are everywhere and trees are crashing to the ground as he drives. He knew the threat was coming. He's been worried and raising the alarm about the fire escaping from the pines for days. Now, there is no time to think.

An hour later the house is safe and he wearily moves

his sheep onto burnt ground, to protect them as well. He stands on the ridge to watch fireballs hurtling over the top of the neighbouring plantation. Big red orbs, igniting and exploding gas ahead of their path, before snaking down into the neighbour's vineyard.

This is devastation.

***

He drives upwind to find the fire coming straight at him. It is dark and he and his dad work frantically to shift things of value out of the sheds. They'd sent friends who've been helping home to be with their families. The fire is flying across their top paddocks. And everyone has long since given up believing this fire will be predictable.

The fire gets around them travelling up the roadside and hurtles across other paddocks.

He stands for a moment, defeated.

Resigned now, leaning over, he pats his old man on the back and they leave the farm for the main township of Kingscote.

They know they'll lose it all tonight, but they've done what they can.

These searing accounts of surviving the fire are laced with grim warnings, and too many untold stories of heartbreaking loss and humble acts of care and bravery that helped to save lives and livelihoods. The eyewitness testimonies I have captured matter: not just as a record of loss and destruction, but as a dire warning. It is communities who stand at the coalface, not governments or bureaucrats who make the decisions. Individuals who know each other and risk it all to protect what and who they love.

As we stand on the cusp of escalating changing climate

tragedies throughout the world, beyond the edges where people have congregated in cities and sprawling suburbs, our first line of defence from disaster are the people in our communities. These are the people we see daily on the street in the local town. They are the souls we sit beside at the pub in the afternoon, play sport with on the weekends, or chat to while we are waiting to collect our children at the bus stop. In Australia, we have well-developed systems of volunteer firefighters, emergency rescuers, and ambulance services. These willing folk represent a huge mix of people including lawyers, doctors, butchers, and chefs. They expend years of personal energy and commitment in maintaining organisational structures that meet governmental standards and mesh neatly with bureaucracies.

They are trained to an high standard. They are proficient in all areas of emergency work, and in terms of bushfires, are sometimes more highly trained and experienced than their paid career counterparts, because their skills are generational, developed and handed down over multiple lifetimes. Some volunteer firefighters have fifty or more years of experience fighting fires and in the incident management roles that coordinate the fight of those fires. Volunteer firefighters are what I know but I have no reason to think the other volunteer emergency services are any different. They all have the advantage of intimate local knowledge including hazards, access tracks, and resources. This volunteerism stretches beyond fires and floods. Voluntary emergency work undoubtedly attracts a few thrill-seekers, but nobody does this work because they love it. They do it to keep their communities safe. They do it because there is no paid rescue force beyond the city limits. Across almost all rural communities in Australia, the first-response person racing to your aid in the event of a heart attack, stroke, accident, flood, or fire is most likely a neighbour.

In administering this unfathomably large public service, Australian governments expend an embarrassingly paltry budget to outfit these crews with trucks and equipment to face down flames or floods, to scale cliffs to rescue the injured, or to attend car accidents. Don't be fooled by the figures governments trot out. It pales compared to what it would cost if they had to pay the current volunteer workforce that underpins it. That these volunteers turn up disaster after disaster is a government expectation—one that too easily slips into a dismissive presumption.

During the Black Summer fires, Australia's then Prime Minister, Scott Morrison, infamously stated that volunteer firefighters did not need compensation because they 'want to be there' facing flames and destruction, crippling heat, and life-threatening situations, day after punishing day. He then left the country for a family holiday in Hawaii supposedly unaware that the most dangerous fire event in living memory was sweeping across the country.

Australians have never been shy about speaking out about our leaders and the response from the firefighting community was swift and brutal. It left little doubt as to how egregious that political *faux pas* was. In a social media clip that would go viral, Paul Parker, a firefighter from Nelligen on the New South Wales south coast, leaned out of his truck window and shouted a message to the waiting media.

> *'Are you from the media? Tell the Prime Minister to go and get fucked',* he yelled, before ramming his fire truck into gear to drive away. *'We really enjoy doing this shit, dickhead!'* He finished as his truck sped off.[76]

Up until 2019, Australian politicians from both sides of politics had been reticent to link wildfires with changing climate, but Black Summer was different. After years of worsening drought and increasingly curt warnings from the Bureau of Meteorology and fire chiefs, the connection could no longer be denied and the public was deeply wounded by the cavalier dismissal from the political ranks.

When an apparently chastened Scott Morrison flew home from his Hawaiian holiday and started touring firegrounds, firefighters from Cobargo, in the New South Wales south coast hinterland, refused to shake his hand. Morrison tried to make up lost ground in a series of belated announcements promising more air tankers, more money, and more time-off for firefighters who had already been toiling for months as if these people were somehow now on his payroll. It was far too little, and egregiously too late. People wrote open letters to the press brimming with hurt and anger. Firefighters across the country voiced their disgust with the government, but they still faced hellish wildfire day after day. Few walked away.

While visiting the fire zone on Kangaroo Island, with the then South Australian Premier Steven Marshall on January 8, Morrison grasped, pitifully, at empathy before making a further gaff. 'Thankfully we've had no loss of life', he was filmed saying. 'Two. We've lost two', he was quietly corrected, referring to outback pilot Dick Lang and his son, Adelaide surgeon Clayton Lang, who tragically died on January 3 after their car was trapped by flames. 'Two. Yes two, that's quite right', he briskly replied. 'I was thinking about firefighters, firstly', he said, trying desperately to recover ground, yet making the blunder even worse.[77]

Both statements rippled across our community. We were aghast at the ignorance they implied. Morrison's brief may have been focused on the formal firefighting force. His attention may have been elsewhere, but the gaff spoke to something more—the unconscious discounting of at least half of the volunteer effort that is crucial to our survival beyond the halls of power.

This dismissal has existed from both sides of politics for decades. Dick and Clayton had not been on a fire truck, that is true, but like so many landholders on the island, they had their own firefighting equipment. On that fateful day they were returning home to sleep after days of fighting flames—as farm firefighters.

Here is the dirty secret in Australia. Stephen Pyne might laud our firefighting community—the envy of the firefighting world—but the truth is it is not big enough, and can't reach far enough, so we have grown an unofficial, unrecognised firefighting force beyond the grip of government control. Self-funded, self-directed, these are farmers and landholders who take their own equipment—utes, tanks, pumps and hoses—out to face the flames. Often, they are the same men and women who man the government-managed firefighting trucks, only to go out again to stand side by side with friends and neighbours on the days they are rostered off, because when fire threatens your community there is no time for rest. Fire waits for no one. Men and women alike, they are the warriors in our communities.

And there are other warriors. As soon as disaster strikes, emergency service stations are immediately crewed with volunteers who organise logistics, prepare meals and drinks, and man phones and radios. Twenty-four hours a day, until danger abates, these roles are filled by people taking time away from their families and their paid labour, without any compensation. Outside of moments of disaster, other volunteers man the ambulance stations on standby across 24 hour rosters; again without pay or compensation.

In the cities, Australian metropolitan firefighters are paid annual salaries between A$68,000 and A$86,000, and upwards of A$140,000 at management level. Meanwhile, the ferocity and scale of the fires beyond the city have strained the rural service's capacity and stirred public debate about whether unpaid firefighters deserve more. And with government agencies and political parties so out of touch, an assumptive reliance by the government on volunteers, and a corresponding lack of resource and funding, it is no surprise that the sheer quantity and ferocity of today's wildfires have put a strain on volunteer goodwill.[3, 78]

Australia is not alone in relying on volunteers: Austria, Germany, France, the United States, Japan and China do it too, but none of these countries have the sheer scale, climate or ecology so primed to burn. Roughly 195,000 Australians volunteer with the nation's six state and two territory bushfire services, which, over Black Summer, corresponded to approximately 150 hours of labour per person/per year. The basic maths of that equation equals 29,250,000 hours of unpaid labour every year, by people who take responsibility for highly skilled, life-threatening, life-saving work. But such a diverse mix of people who volunteer with the fire service makes the monetary value of the volunteers difficult to measure. According to Queensland Urban Utilities spokesperson Michelle Cull, writing for *The Conversation*, their contribution to society can be conservatively estimated at A$1.3 billion each year.[79]

After his poorly chosen words, and bowing to decades of lobbying in the background and a new public uproar from firefighting brigade members across the country, Scott Morrison belatedly outlined a federal plan to pay volunteer firefighters who work for small- and mid-sized employers up to $6,000 to cover lost income, if required for duty for more than 10 days. At the time this seemed a modest step forward, even though it pales against another announcement that volunteer firefighters with federal government jobs would receive four weeks of paid leave.

But these decisions address a short-term public demand for recognition, without actually resolving the question of whether the government should continue to depend so heavily on a volunteer force in the face of unprecedented changing climate that imposes heavier physical, psychological and financial burdens on firefighters than ever before.

There is even more disappointment in the system. Despite the heroic efforts of so many unsupported landholders, the South Australian government review of the Black Summer wildfires (the Keelty Report), went so far to suggest there is a need for 'greater governance of [farm fire unit] activities, with a proposal to *regulate* volunteer participation on the fire ground through the 'Australasian Inter Service Incident Management System' structure. The suggestion is likely made with good intent, but it risks a layer of management and control that threatens the very agility that makes farm fire units an asset.

Farm fire units fight fires, not because they want to, but because there is an unshakable bond between them to protect the homes, farms, and livelihoods of friends and neighbours. They don't want to submit to rules and regulations that force them to adhere to set routines or to be summoned to fight fires if that could jeopardise the running of their own farms.

One farmer shared a sad story, in the early days after the fire, of a back burn that nearly engulfed his farmhouse. The story is anecdotal, and I can't defend my assertion, but it appears the specific back burn was managed by the governmental firefighting crews, without prior notification that it was happening and little awareness that there were men on the farm. It is a catch twenty-two, because everyone is technically supposed to evacuate the region. Inside the declared fire area, the only people who are supposed to be there are the formal emergency services people. But across rural Australia it is well known that landholders stay, because they must, especially now that wildfire is burning longer and bigger than before. There are not enough trucks or crews to manage the mega-fires we are now seeing in Australia. Farm fire units are a vital part of the firefighting efforts. Without them so much more would be lost. Communities simply could not recover from the scale.

In this case, even when the farmer made contact, something not easily achieved in a region with patchy mobile phone coverage—and without something as simple as a shared radio network—there was tension about who should be in charge. This is not a surprise because there are two separate firefighting forces, with separate chains of command—one directly contained within a network of family and friends, and the other spread over government departments—and little crossover of information. In dangerous situations, tempers flare like the wildfires they face, but near misses like a back burn being channelled towards a farmhouse, with no warning to the inhabitants, and then a demand to take over the protection of the very place that was threatened does little to engender trust.

No one is wrong. Everyone is doing the best they can in the moment, all the way up to the top levels of government. But there are grave problems that need to be overcome. The way the government administers the firefighting force assumes there is no 'civilian' activity within the fire zone. Yet, in many farm communities, and especially within ours, landholders don't leave their farms or their land. They stay and defend their homes, sheds, equipment, sheep, cattle, and fences, their heritage bush, and the properties of their neighbours because they must. There is not enough government resources for them to walk away and they know there will be no compensation to help them rebuild after the event.

It is ironic that tracking farm fire units' whereabouts is one of the problematic issues experienced by trucks that come into regions to support the local firefighting force, but not so much the local firefighters themselves. For the local force, farm fire units are an asset to be cherished. They are nimble and they go where they need to, but communication with them is adhoc, because they don't have the same radios as the trucks.

The Keelty report noted that:

> *'Many portable radios now have GPS capability and this is used by other emergency personnel in other states .... This type of GPS tracking included in portable radios may help to identify [farm fire unit] personnel and their location as they are often first to the scene of a bushfire.'* [80]

The Report suggested:

> *'... a significant investment should be made in portable VHFs (rather than retrofitting UHFs) to support private operators ([Forest Industry Brigades], [Farm Fire Units] and private contractors) in fireground operations.'* [80]

It seems like such a small thing. Give people radios so they can better coordinate with each other. This is one of at least a dozen simple things that could make a real difference: to put proper radios in the hands of those agile volunteers. But by the time the Keelty report had made it through the editing process of government departments, the simple suggestion of outfitting farm fire units with appropriate radios didn't make the list of recommendations. All that was recommended is a desire to 'regulate' their activities better, and for a 'policy' to be developed around standards of equipment and fire protection clothing carried by these self-funded units.[80] So we have to buy our own radios, it seems. We are being urged towards UHFs, not VHFs, because the authorities don't want farm fire units cluttering up bandwidth. It has left many of us scratching our heads about what it will take for the government to actually recognise the enormity of what we are facing, now.

In truth, giving more support and recognition to farm fire units undermines the very support and recognition formal firefighting brigades are fighting to maintain. They are also unrecognised and unsupported by the centralised power structure. They are caught in the same self-perpetuating construct as the rest of us—chasing after baubles and beads.

There is resilience inherent in Australian farmers and rural landholders, and a wisdom born of a land that has fire. Yet even that metal was tested during the Black Summer wildfires. The stories I have had the privilege of hearing; the feats of bravery and determination during this one fateful fire season could fill a shelf full of books.

On Kangaroo Island the fire was too big, too strong, too hot, and eclipsed the accrued experience of generations. Friends and neighbours stood shoulder to shoulder, for weeks on end, without the barest recognition from their government for their efforts. Too many mothers were forced to flee with their children, leaving their partners behind to do what they could. So many people were evacuated by neighbours because the fire came up too fast and too hard that they were caught off-guard. Whole townships were threatened. These tales surround us, every day. The knowledge of this event ripples in the air we breathe now.

We know and value the two firefighting forces within Australia each have a different focus and a different master. The farmers and landholders of the valiant farm fire units are nimble, first-responders who fight fire because they want to protect their property and the places they live. They serve no one but their own conscience and the community they cherish. Across the country, the government-controlled firefighting service also serve the community, but they operate under the structure of government rules in return for firefighting equipment and trucks. Both are needed, but sometimes they operate in conflict, especially when the firefighting crews are volunteers from beyond the region and don't know the local terrain.

We need them both.

We need to protect them all.

They are our front-line warriors in a war we will be engaged in for many decades to come.

BEDLAM

April 1 - December 31, 2020

10

Undone

Fog sits deep in the valley. The sun is up but makes only the gentlest impression across the treetops. Our paddock is verdant green, cloaked with a layer of deep, white mist; the skeletons of branches thrusting above. It is beautiful, but not 'picture postcard pretty'. It is beautiful because it is my home, the seasons continue to roll on, and I am still here to appreciate it. I realise now that simple reality was never a given.

The tree trunks just outside the door of our temporary home in a shipping container remain deep, charred black. They will be forever black, I guess. A flush of vibrant growth hangs close to their branches in a desperate bid to survive. It frustrates me that the media and conservation movement want to celebrate this as evidence of 'recovery'. These are not happy trees. They are fighting to survive and repair deep burns; to build themselves anew, just like all victims of trauma.

It is not the first time, or the last, that I stand with one hand on the closest arboreal friend and whisper 'I am sorry'. A tree can only be as strong as the landscape which surrounds it. Without them, large gaps in the canopy will allow even more of the summer heat to reach the earth and dry it. A wave of sadness floods from my head to my core. My counsellor tells me this is a physiological reaction; my brain triggering a hormonal release. Some vestige of ancient DNA when internal reactions were necessary for our daily survival. Now, in this prolonged grief in which we are cloaked, this hormonal wash is, frankly, unwelcome.

My phone pings with well-meaning Facebook messages; strangers celebrating the rebirth of our landscape. Past visitors remember their trip and share pictures of scenes that no longer exist. Hope and love and reminders to rejoice in 'the beauty of nature's capacity for regrowth' arrive via text messages with a peppering of positive, happy emoticons: love hearts and smiling faces. They chirp merrily about visiting again 'post pandemic', and then segue into discussions about how tough their current travel-less life is, stuck inside their homes. I don't reply, or share, or 'like'. Their messages rasp. I am exasperated, because they force me to don a veneer of polite happiness, and I am too tired.

***

The sun is high in the sky and her eyes are intense. Speaking this story has been held in check for two long. She's been through the big fire a decade ago, and before that survived Hurricane Katrina. She thought she knew disaster. Now she tells me, with frank honesty, this howling hell-scream of a storm, was worse than anything before.

***

The edge of his voice cracks as he explains his utter sense of helplessness. It escalated so fast, and he was caught on the outside. There was no way to access anyone. He is furious, now. 'There was no information. What the hell! People were dying'. Every cell of his being wanted to help, but in the communication vacuum all he could do was stand and watch the sky from afar.

***

Down the phone the conversation suddenly stops. I hear faint sobs. 'All I had was time to grab my bag and run' she quietly says. 'I could see the lights in the station and my heart wanted to go there, but I knew I had to obey the siren'.

Slowly, as I listen to her I belatedly understand that people across our island thought they were leaving others to perish that fateful night, but they've not wanted to say this out loud, fearful of adding to the immense grief that reaches every corner of our community. My already broken heart breaks again for their silent pain.

***

Back bent with the weight of nine decades on this Earth and face etched with wisdom and knowing, he lifts his eyes to meet mine, for the first moment in this difficult conversation.

'Never before' his voice of time whispers. 'We've fought off demon spawn, but never before have we faced their master'.

And then his expression collapses into the deep sorrow only seen on the faces of those who have seen too much life.

In the weeks after the fire Blaze Aid and the Army arrived with welcome muscles and enthusiasm for the physical work we all faced.

The army rolled up and picked up burnt fencing wire. They carted away the wreckage of sheds and fire-twisted farm machinery, and after struggling against a paralysed government-run decision-making tree, found creative ways to turn their attention to the unexpected problems landholders faced. They were on the ground, face to face with landholders. They saw the scale of devastation and the ghostly expressions in our eyes. As a life-long pacifist, the Army's green and khaki uniforms are now etched in my heart for their compassion. For us, they removed the remains of a shed, rolled fencing wire, and dug a long trench to bury a new pipe between two dams on our property. They also sat and talked with us, about anything and nothing and everything in between. There was unexpected solace in sitting with people trained to face the perils and trauma of battle. They were young, but they 'got it'. It was a heady time having so many willing souls and understanding faces around to help.

Similarly, the Blaze Aid volunteers quickly arrived on the island to help with rebuilding the thousands of kilometres of fencing that had to be replaced. They brought skills and equipment and their own army of volunteers from across Australia and the world. They were here for the long haul, setting up a camp in the centre of the island, and visiting farm after farm to sink posts and hang wire, as materials became available. As the pandemic hit, they isolated themselves in their camp, operated as a 'Covid bubble', and kept their unrelenting work-pace on farms.

The Minderoo Foundation also arrived and, before long, temporary housing was being rolled onto properties for those landowners who had lost their homes; rapid deployment of shipping containers fitted out with beds, a kitchenette, washing machine, shower, and toilet. These shelters were practical and smart coming with water tanks and generators as part of the kit, recognising many of us had no water and power. These 'pods', as they came to be known, were a lifeline. With accommodation already scarce, the pods avoided a large-scale homelessness crisis.

In life-defining moments you discover there are few places to lean upon. Despite your profession, class, or monetary worth, despair about your loss of security creeps in. With each choice you contemplate, strong emotions propel you to either drastic new heights or onto a cliff's edge from which there is no return. Minderoo compassionately provided dignity, shelter, and safety. They gave us the priceless gift of time: allowing our feet to stay planted on our land with space to breathe, re-evaluate, and plan. Without the drastic sense of urgency that would normally take over someone who'd become suddenly homeless, having a temporary home allowed us to take advantage of opportunities as they unfolded. 'Minderoo' became a noun in my mind for hope, time, and gratitude.

Without doubt, the first six months following the blaze were almost euphoric for a few with willing souls around to help. But this was not the experience for others. This period also represented a dark crisis for those who fell through the cracks and, for one bureaucratic reason or another, didn't qualify for the generosity from the Army, Blaze Aid, or Minderoo.

Allow me to describe a few examples, to paint a picture about life directly after a disaster.

Because of a shortage of fencing posts, a government official ordered that available posts could only be purchased for 'external fences' or for properties with 'living stock'. On paper, in a high-rise city office, this probably made sense. I can fully understand that the decision sought to ensure equity, but the unintended consequences hit hard for many people. First, it assumed that everyone affected farmed livestock. For us, our vineyard sits in the middle of our farm and needed an 'internal' fence rapidly reinstated to protect the surviving vines from the wildlife who, without habitat, were stripping the vines of their bark, and threatening the vineyard's long-term survival. Without access to posts, our vineyard only stands today because of the profound generosity of two farming families. From the first, we were loaned temporary electric netting that stretched out along a fallen fence-line, and given irrigation pipe that allowed water to be quickly reinstated to vines. The second family turned up with wisdom and tools in hand to help us lift the burnt fencing and reinstate it as a short-term measure. For large blocks of vines with substantial fire damage, replacement of wires and retraining of so many vines is an extremely laborious and costly exercise. Understanding the extent of loss and the impact such loss would have on our future, our friends drove from the opposite end of the island, weekend after weekend, for the months it took to re-fence our entire farm.

The fencing travesty hit others too. Nearby, close friends lost not only their fences (and home, and sheds, and all their machinery) but also their entire flock of sheep. They had lost their entire farm income but didn't qualify for access to fencing materials because they had no living livestock, and so lost a whole year of income while they waited for fencing supplies so they could restock their farm.

Other friends have a heritage conservation property and despite their lifelong commitment to the heritage estate the government so often crows about, found themselves wholly beyond any formal help, with decision rules putting them firmly outside of consideration.

Early on, the South Australian government determined it would take responsibility for clearing the wreckage of all the destroyed houses, because they almost all contained asbestos. At the time, this felt like a gift. Removing asbestos can be costly especially when you live on an island. Each house was swiftly assessed and a schedule of house removal created. This decisive commitment went through us all as a wave of hope, until the days stretched into weeks and then into months, while government departments hand-balled the responsibility backwards and forwards. We learned that hope was hollow. There seemed no end to the meetings called to decide where the asbestos could be safely buried. Meanwhile, the asbestos dust we were now not permitted to touch was blowing in the wind across our landscape, in the air we breathed and the water we drank. And every day of this tortured wait, many of us opened the doors of our pods to the vista of our wrecked lives. Depression was heaped on recurring trauma—a potentially lethal mix. Then, when they finally made a decision, the process for clean-up got funky. Each week there was a specified schedule of the house wrecks to be cleared from specific zones, but the timetable would change, without notice or explanation. Houses that had been abandoned for decades and already sat rotting in the middle of eucalyptus plantations were being cleared ahead of houses that had been lived in the day of the fire. The unpredictable scheduling affected those who had no intention of remaining on-property on the day their homes and memories were carted away, suddenly finding themselves present while the truck rolled in and a digger picked up the wreckage of their lives. Mobile text messages bounced around the community, laced with tears.

The management of surviving trees created another unexpected drama. The government agency responsible for the power supply infrastructure had legal authority to enter all properties and fell trees deemed dangerous to power lines. More than a few of us arrived back to our charred house sites after a day away building new fences or repairing other fire damage somewhere else on the farm to find bright crosses painted on the trunks of ancient surviving eucalyptus trees. No one called. No one consulted us. No one asked if these trees could come down. No one inquired whether we still even wanted the power lines. As with so much else that happened in this period, we had slipped from being legal landholders in control of our destiny to victims of tenuous, undefined welfare under the care of a bumbling bureaucracy. It was galling and depressing.

I am not alone in taking a stance against this power-grab. As a lifetime activist, I am probably proudest of my resistance in the form of a bucket, soap, and brush. Through a haze of tears, I remember one day scouring away the disparaging crosses and smearing the cleansed trunks with fresh charcoal to hide my crime. Two giant trees still stand on our farm because of this, and their canopies fed the surviving parrots through that first season.

Then came the struggles to have power reconnected to farms. By now the infrastructure had been long fixed, and we were waiting to open accounts with power supply companies. It took weeks of phone calls to convince well-meaning but clueless help-desk operators that our mystical National Meter Identifier (NMI) burned along with the power box. It isn't impossible to have power reconnected without the NMI so why we were forsaken to an administrative maze with no way out remains a mystery, even today. Eventually, the government agency enabled electricians to just set up new boxes. It took more than six months, but the power companies caught up and sorted themselves out.

The once simple task of proving our identities to different agencies became another painful ordeal. Without having access to basic documents including birth certificates, driver's licences, passports, and bank statements, we discovered, the only way to reinstate identification is to have identification. In the early days, directly after the fire and while its impacts were covered in the media, help desk personnel were sympathetic and showed some residual understanding, but as soon as the pandemic hit, this sympathy evaporated and responses became clipped and curt. Once again, we were forsaken to a hamster wheel, and round and round we ran. More frustrating hours were wasted trying to sort these issues out than I care to recount, and having to recite our traumatic story over and over again wore many people down.

By mid-year we were in the clutches of three traumas—a wildfire, a pandemic, and an Escher-like bureaucratic landscape that expressed little compassion or understanding. We had become homeless people constantly fighting an uphill battle, and often felt stigmatised by those tasked to help us.

Rebuilding homes and refurnishing lives has been, perhaps, the toughest journey of all. It is not a subject I ever imagined I would write about, even as I began the process of research for this book. I naively imagined there would be government support to guide us through the process. Keep in mind that none of us woke the morning after the fires with our heads full of dreams for new homes. All of us were worsted and beaten. Yet, we had to make swift decisions about contracts and budgets and building designs that we were, frankly, ill-equipped to navigate. How I envy those new home builders who have had years to dream and plan, carefully exploring options, and focusing on the design they desire. Not only were we emotionally and physically empty vessels, we didn't have a safe and secure base from which to plan.

After experiencing the significant emotional distress of shock, anger, depression, and hopelessness of losing literally everything we just wanted a pad where we could feel secure, comfortable, and safe.

Within weeks of the fire, Facebook was awash with building companies promising to build houses fast and cheap. Anyone who looked under the hood of these offers discovered they were filled with variation clauses that could escalate quotes. Moreover, they failed to consider the fire reality of the region they were competing to rebuild in. These were bear traps that a few unlucky ones fell into, and regretted. Others sought local builders who we could trust, but soon discovered builders need plans, and plans have to be developed by outside people. Builders themselves were now faced with navigating building designs, development applications, and all myriads of other legal and technical issues through all-consuming, stress-filled months of effort.

Meanwhile, an entire new 'recovery' industry was being created within our community when a workforce from the mainland swept in to pick up the pieces. These staff were ostensibly employed by the government to support us through our recovery and rebuilding process but, as most of us, had never been through a disaster of this magnitude before, we had no idea where recovery stopped and rebuilding started. Clueless about what to do, we turned to these well-meaning souls for guidance and support, only to find it was beyond their remit. They helped where they could, and intervened where possible, but even they were drowning in a ridiculous and complicated sea of rules, regulations, paperwork, and applications. Most alarming was the discovery that, despite Australia's past wildfires, this workforce had no play book. It seemed like everyone was in the dark.

It turns out the internet, even then, was awash with 'Disaster Resilience Handbooks' and 'Community Recovery Guidelines', some important ones published as part of the Australian Disaster Resilience Handbook Collection.[81] Clearly the information was available. As a 'client' of the process it feels like no one thought to look at it.

One government document, published in 2018, states that:

> *'Recovery is a long-term, multilayered social and developmental process that is more than simply the replacement of what has been destroyed and the rehabilitation of those affected. At its centre, recovery is the complex process of individuals and communities who have been impacted by a disaster event working to resolve the impacts that the event has had on the trajectory of their lives.*[82]

But then the report goes on to say:

> *Recovery provides an opportunity to improve aspects beyond previous conditions by enhancing social infrastructure, natural and built environments, and economies.'*[82]

That alone would have been nice to know. I saw very little evidence of our community doing any such thing. Committees were appointed with community members on them, but there was no outreach to the wider community. They seemed to operate on the basis that whichever perspective was present was comprehensive enough. There were also lots of agency staff involved. As a result, almost everything they determined had to do with government agency territory—infrastructure, roads, buildings etc. I don't want to disparage the goodwill of the individuals involved, but we were not in the driving seat of our destiny. At no stage has there been an opportunity for the '*individuals and communities who have been impacted by a disaster*' to develop a post-disaster plan about where we are going and how we adapt, let alone '*resolve the impacts that the event has had on the trajectory of [our] lives.*'

Post-fire, it seems some lessons may have been learned. The more recent publication of the Handbook, Community Engagement for Disaster Resilience, reminds responders and agencies that:

> '*Effective community engagement is responsive, flexible and recognises the community as the central reference point for planning, implementing and measuring success in any engagement process. Inclusive, respectful and ethical relationships between engagement partners and the community must guide every stage of the engagement process.*' [83]

Better late that never, I guess.

Early on, the local government, responsible for building approvals, made a well-intended commitment to turn around all bushfire development applications within two working weeks. In the end, most of us had to wait more than six shameful months, either because of inertia within the team responsible, insufficient staffing levels, or concern about making mistakes. It really isn't clear. Whatever the reasons, the time was painfully protracted for people living in shipping containers and sheds.

Once these development approvals were finally granted, we then faced a building material shortage caused by the federal government's home-builder incentive scheme—designed to keep the building industry afloat during the pandemic—that saw timber, and steel, and glass consumed by building upscale house extensions in untouched cities, rather than building modest homes to shelter bushfire-affected families across the country.

So, we waited, and waited, and waited, from our makeshift homes in sheds or pods. It was a hard, hard first year.

What I came to understand in that first year is that Australian governments, at all levels and of all colours, were wholly and profoundly unprepared for this disaster. They lacked any comprehension of what was faced by individuals on the ground. Inside government departments people seemed to maintain their normal work cycle of rostered days off and holiday leave without anyone recognising the need to bring in extra workers or relief cover for when key decision makers were away or just overwhelmed with the volume of work.

No reflective post-fire guidance was provided to the building industry about rebuilding expectations. Perhaps, most flagrantly, they appear to have failed to review the designated bushfire prone areas and the building rating ascribed to these areas in response to the country's major, climate-driven disaster, and in South Australia for the first pyro-cume event to have devastated more than half a million acres on Kangaroo Island.

The opportunity was there. Obviously, something got reviewed because in July 2020 the South Australian government released a new *Ministerial Building Standard MBS 008*.[84] The *Minister's Code for Undertaking Development in Bushfire Protection Areas*, in essence, requires the road and driveways to be safe to use for access, have a turning circle near the house of 12.5 metres, and for the house to be set away from hazardous terrain and dense vegetation. We must have 5,000 litres of dedicated water for fire suppression, powered by a pump that can run independent of main electricity, with pipes that don't limit water flow, and any non-metal pipes buried underground.[85] Fire hoses should, sensibly, reach all parts of the building.[86] Pretty much that was the extent of the reaction to the scale of the event. Grossly undercooked, but at least what was determined was modestly sensible.

Based on this evolving standard, our building application was approved in March 2021 with the build site for our new house rated at Bushfire Attack Level (BAL) 12.5. The BAL rating is the Australian government standard for measuring the risk of a home's exposure to ember attack, radiant heat, and direct flame contact.[87] The BAL rating determines the construction and building requirements necessary to protect homes in bushfire prone areas, and builders have little interest in voluntarily building at higher levels than they need to. It makes them uneconomic compared to the cut price builders that swoop in. The playing field is not level.

For a very basic summary, BAL 12.5 requires non-combustible roofs and gutters, and sub-floor and outer-walls to be built with bushfire-resistant timber, at least, and any gaps at material joins to be less than 3mm to prevent embers penetrating. If windows are less than 40cm from the ground they should be of 4mm safety glass and protected by metal screens or bushfire shutters. Any vents should have ember guards and roof penetrations should be non-combustible.[88]

Yet, wildfires are so hot they can melt metal, vaporise vegetation instantly, and scorch the earth, consuming all organic matter in the soil. Inside the fire zone temperatures can reach 1600°C. Often it is not the flames that cause lethal damage to buildings and humans. It is the radiant heat coming off the fire. Where the fires burned on Kangaroo Island the radiant heat flux from the raging inferno would have easily been in excess of 100 kW/m^2, and would have frequently reached 160 kW/m^2. Putting this into perspective, the average radiant heat flux from the sun at midday on an Australian summer's day is about 1 kW/m^2. At 2 kW/m^2 bare skin burns in about 40 seconds. Standard glass windows will shatter at 10 kW/m^2 and wood can ignite after exposure to 25 kW/m^2.

BAL 12.5 assumes the house will need to withstand ember attack with heat flux up to 12.5kW/m^2. Most of the sites where houses burned during the Black Summer fires will have far exceeded this. Such is the nature of living in a rural area, where there is a lot of naturally occurring, burnable material. Yet, these same properties have been designated—by the government—at this BAL again and I fear that many people will have rebuilt homes that may not withstand the next wildfire, not because they are stupid, or unthinking, or wilfully disregarding chance. Everyone rebuilding after Black Summer is bone weary, exhausted, and desperate for a home again. They don't necessarily have the developed skills to research independently and have relied on the government for sound guidance. Most have no energy to fight with builders about building to higher BAL ratings when the government's own development approval process states the lower levels are acceptable.

There is some government and industry focus on planning and regulations—the early stages of building design to reduce flammability, fuel management, early warning systems, and fire detection, and suppression.[42, 48, 89] But nothing approaching the scale of adaptation we must engage.

Geoff and I didn't want to take that risk. We were lucky we faced the situation equipped with decades of research skills. Against the trend, we built a small house, with no bells and whistles, at a higher BAL than government standards—BAL 40. We invested in a serious, independent firefighting system built into the structure of our house and sheds, as well as wet-break around the built structures on the property. We built with a non-combustible roof, walls, enclosed sub-floor, 6mm toughened glass, all with ember guard screens with mesh apertures of less than 2mm, and all gaps in joins less than 3mm. All vents have ember guards and roof penetrations are non-combustible.[90] Our deck is also totally non-combustible steel with flame-proof decking. BAL 40 assumes increasing levels of ember attack and burning debris ignited by wind borne embers, together with increasing heat flux up to 40kW/m^2 and with the increased likelihood of exposure to flame. That's a big jump from the heat flux of 12.5kW/m^2.

The only reason we were able to see our way clear and complete a build to this standard is because we had done the research the year before Black Summer when we were considering how to alter our existing old house to better withstand a future bushfire. We never got the chance to implement that plan, but with the new build we made it a condition from the get-go. That decision added twenty percent to our build budget, which we compensated for by reducing the size of our house. Many people in our community could never even contemplate that stretch, given most of us, although believing we were fully insured, discovered we were chronically under-insured.

Before the Black Summer fires, the home insurance company AAMI estimated the additional cost for up-scaling from BAL 12.5 to a BAL 40 build. They suggested an increase of building costs between A$19,000 to A$73,000. Houses in BAL Flame Zone—the highest risk category—could cost an additional A$65,000 to A$277,000, to meet requirements.[91]

While it probably seems self-evident, research has empirically demonstrated that a building's—and therefore its inhabitants'—survival is far more likely if a 30-40 metre defensible space is maintained, in addition to the obvious need for sufficient firefighting water and equipment. This includes, sadly, the removal of all overhanging trees or trees touching buildings, and the maintenance of very low gardens and surrounding lawns to reduce the impact of radiant heat on flammable structures. The effect of radiant heat in damaging window glass and allowing entry of embers into buildings, may be the single biggest risk to a home.[92]

Andrew Sullivan, a researcher with the CSIRO, helpfully puts this into perspective with a fictional scenario. Imagine a garden bed outside a window of your house, covered with helpful, water-saving organic mulch. That mulch and the other dried material under your plants contain enough energy when it is burnt, in the form of radiant and convective heat, to break the window and ignite the curtains inside your home in a few seconds.[60, 93] It is sobering, especially when you walk around your house and recognise the surroundings for what they are—fuel. Don't think that water poured onto that mulch will save things either. I poured thousands upon thousands of litres of water into and onto the garden beds around our house. Everything went, even my so-called flame-proof or fire-retardant plants. I now recognise that wildfire is so intense that water would have evaporated in a few minutes. Even the succulents were smouldering ash when we returned.

Rebuilding safer in a bushfire zone was never supported through the recovery process. The wildfire victims were cut loose and had to navigate this complicated world of building on their own. By the time 2020 was drawing to a close, most of us were completely undone.

11

Splinters of Glass

In that intangible moment between awake and asleep, cold sweat and terror claws through. The temperature seems to drop and damp creeps in. This is when her barriers are down. The sharp, grey smell of wet ash assails her conscious senses. Images of the landscape come to the fore, like an old glass plate negative with the world turned monochrome. She lies there, alone, and knows she now lives in the same geography, but it is not the same place. Her home remains but everywhere around is burned to the horizon. Nothing has changed. Everything has changed.

***

Across the desk his smile is broad, reaching up into his eyes; this giant in our community. We talk lightly about business and what has changed following the fire. He is working hard to keep the store stocked with what his community needs to rebuild. I tell him how grateful we all are, and he tries to deflect the gratitude, as he always does.

When I ask how it was during the fire, a cloud passes across his face, and tears well though he fiercely fights them back. He tells of so many young men arriving, day after day, one after the other, with burned out pumps and broken equipment, amped on adrenaline that he knew couldn't last. Every one of them was desperate to get things repaired so they could throw themselves at the fury of the fire-storm once more.

So many young souls, unprepared for what they faced.

He shakes his head to force away the pools welling in his eyes again, and forges on with his story.

He tells me how he made a quiet space at the back of the store and would sit these young men there with a coke in their hands, while his team worked beyond their sight-line fixing what they could. He was desperate to give them space to calm and regroup, knowing pumps and care was all he could offer them in that moment.

He worries about them, all these months later—all the things they experiences, all the things they saw. He worries about everyone. We have all been damaged.

I walk outside the store and crouch down, my back against the wall and cry.

My community.

***

I stand at the base of my beautiful tree. I've been watching the other, younger stringybarks around her push out new growth in their desperate grab for survival. A few are succeeding. Many are not; their new growth withering away. There is a lump in my throat as I feel her silence. Pressing my cheek to her mighty girth, I whisper, slowly, hoping to invoke tree-time. 'Please come back. I am sorry'.

She is deeply still and offers no reply.

By mid-year, the days for Geoff and I have fallen into a new routine. We work in the vineyard or write from our one remaining shed that stands precariously because solid beams mysteriously combusted without the entire structure disintegrating. We navigate living in our pod by reinstating long-ago living habits from our time aboard a sailing boat. We know all about cold damp. We know about condensation dripping onto your face as you wake. We relive a routine of topping up our water supply every few days, and resorting to using a single power line to avoid having to drudge into a rainy night to reset a circuit breaker. This preconditioning means we don't do it as tough as some others. Fellow journeyers in this recovery space joke and laugh about the limitations of their temporary shipping container homes, thankful always for Minderoo, but their eyes betray a deep-held fear that they will be living this way longer than they can bear.

For the past six months we have all shifted through shared phases. First it was the aftermath; working out what was left, what had to be protected, and ending the misery for those souls too badly damaged to survive. For a few weeks, the air sounded of gunfire as thousands and thousands of animals were released from this life, with luck for another, kinder place. Then farms and fences had to be rebuilt. Parks needed to clear trails and fell those trees that were losing their fight for survival. Sheds were needed fast. Only when this immediate work is completed will houses even start. Meanwhile, families are fragmented. Children do not see their fathers for days. Businesses, having first adopted fire recovery mode, now have to pirouette in the pandemic; dance steps many can't master. Immediate feels like such an inadequate word. The immediate is still happening eight months after the fire.

The community momentarily falls back into its tribes. We stop listening to each other beyond the clique of our familiar groups—farmers, tourism, townies, sports club, environmentalists—and circulate with who we know best, developing opinions about the other tribes that are not always savoury. Partly this is driven by funding opportunities. Various grants become available to rebuild social infrastructure, and tribes have to compete with each other to secure what they need to rebuild.

It becomes clear we have entered a long-haul survival game where only the fittest will pull through unscathed. By mid-year, I ponder whether we were collectively fit enough.

Often, when I am lost in thought, my ringing mobile phone acts as an intrusive shrieking alarm that leaves me feeling interrupted and disgruntled. But when I see her name on my screen, my heart always smiles. Hearing her say 'Hello, my friend', is one of the most soothing sounds to reach my ears. 'This is another welfare check', she always continues, the genuine warmth in her voice wrapping me in a passionate hug. My friend lives on the other end of the island and reaches out to me from the solid, understanding base of a family who has lived for five generations in this place. She knows fire. She knows loss. She knows recovery. She knows what I need. Almost weekly these precious calls offer a life raft. I never know when they'll arrive but my mood genuinely lifts when they do. Each time I take the call, I feel sure I have my emotions together, at last; certain I am moving past the anger, grief, and pain of past events and always eager to say so. But instead, for the next half hour, I offload inane details about pain-filled moments or speak of descending further into my dark internal world where no trace of light penetrates the walls of a blackened tunnel. At times I cry. Sometimes I am outrageously furious about one thing or another. Sometimes I am choked by a gripping silence that strangles my throat. Often my thoughts are hog-tied making even the slightest decision a trial.

Week after week, for months, this same friend, her husband, and often their son, made the three-hour round-trip to help rebuild our fences when we were too fatigued to make sense of what to do. They brought tools, fencing wire, and posts and rolled up and disposed of what needed to be destroyed. They helped us bury our large replacement irrigation pipe, knowing and pressing us, because if we didn't do it then it would be left above ground to be burnt in the next fire. They taught us new skills, they listened to us talk about what we know—we grow grapes and make wine, but they have infinitely more land knowledge built on generations of farming crops and sheep. They told us stories and made us laugh. They shared mid-day meals with us, even though a full stomach made it hard for them to work though the afternoon. They knew a meal is all we could offer, and their generosity was profound in the receiving. They had their own pains and pressures, but still they came. Those pains and pressures continue, and still my friend calls.

Maybe this depth of compassion is a small community thing, or even an island thing, where there is an unspoken understanding about resilience through community bonds. These conversations have a distinctly different shape and texture to the ones we have with friends beyond the island. No one outside of the catastrophe means harm, but their questions focus on the wrong things. They can't know so only ask what they think is right. 'When will your house be built?', 'Do you have enough clothes?', 'What did you think of that stupid statement the Prime Minister made?', or 'I am so sorry this has happened to you'. Then, they lapse into a retelling of the event from their own perspective. Sometimes we can do that. At other times it is too hard, not because of the event, but because it is a retelling of what we've said so many times already. For us, it is not the fire itself but the aftermath that is causing the pain, but saying that out loud sounds like we are ungrateful for the help we've received. With my island friend, if we veer off into the uncharted ground, she lets me ramble, while other off-island friends try to change the subject because the nerve is too raw, or because they don't want to hear it. 'Don't dwell on that', they say. 'Look for the silver lining'. They create a black tunnel where people engage in avoidance and emotional numbing.

One point of beauty amongst this tragedy has been the unexpected donations made. Many of the homes and properties lost or damaged in my community are rural properties, either for farming or land owned by citizens who chose to live a lifestyle outside of the mainstream. Even though we are many tribes, we collectively pride ourselves on our self-sufficiency, and for good reason. For many of us the shops are 75 kilometres or more away. That's not a trip you make on a whim because you've forgotten to buy milk.

While charities and government agencies focused on shelter and infrastructure for rural people, and community members organised centralised pick-up points for donated food and clothing, Sophie Thomson (media presenter, author, and gardening expert) and Anne Morrison (President of the Kangaroo Island Garden Club) recognised how deep and serious the loss of vegetable and ornamental gardens was, as well as fruit and nut orchards. This was damage that went unnoticed by most, but very early on Sophie identified how this overwhelming deprivation would impact the mental health of more than a hundred landholders. Firstly, she began arranging the donation of plants, equipment, and materials, while Anne reached out to the island's gardening community to help bushfire-affected gardens to be rebuilt.

Each time Sophie comes to the island with a load of plants, she runs workshops on the intricacies of rebuilding a garden after a bushfire. It is not straightforward. The soil structure has been damaged and needs specific attention to rebuild. Fruit trees may have sustained internal damage, and while they might re-shoot, could still die within the next season. She also begins the tentative conversation about how to rebuild so you don't lose your garden the next time. Her compassion, infectious enthusiasm, and workshops are a lifeline for many of us, drawing us together to quietly discuss the deep loss we are feeling but finding difficult to discuss more widely for fear it will be trivialised by others. Our gardens are a primary food source, a source of stability, and a daily focus for many of us. They nourish our souls as well as bodies. The loss of these places is deep, and we feel vulnerable without them.

Sophie's other profound gift is to battle against a bureaucratic machine that belittles the role growing food plays in people's lives. She organises the materials, space, and building force for a new community garden in the middle of the burn scar. It is magical to see it rise from the ground, and for the community to come together to plant it out. By now the pandemic is in full swing and supermarkets are rationing basic food purchases. Where before we would have taken this in our stride, now 50 or 100 kilometres away from these shops, and beyond the daily rationed purchase allocations, we have nothing to fall back upon. To be able to harvest what we need, whenever we want, is a mental and physical lifeline.

Lovingly and tirelessly tended by local volunteers, the community garden becomes a vital weekly grounding point that, along with the welfare check from my friend, keeps me alive through deep moments of despair in the first year. I always visit the garden when there is no one around and, for a few precious moments, feel at peace. Being able to pick food and press my fingers into the soil is soothing to my soul.

In these moments of solitude, I can forget I am trapped in a nightmare and can almost believe life is restored. After months of having lethal adrenaline coursing through my system, these moments bring my blood pressure down and calm my system.[94-97] The effect lasts for a few hours, or until the next recovery drama raises its head.

This tangible feeling is not without scientific basis, and it is important to better recognise this. Sophie should not have had to wade through dismissive inertia. There is extensive scientific literature, examining the benefits of gardening and community food growing for both physical and mental health, especially after a major disaster. The evidence is as clear as night and day. It is striking that it even needs to be said.[98-105] Nancy Brown's important work into disaster resilience and community gardens holds important recommendations for emergency managers. She recommends they look at the underlying causes of recent catastrophes and genuinely explore what loss means in relation to the communities they serve. It is a mistake to assume that rebuilding infrastructure is the only need, or that in Kangaroo Island's case, farming was the only important loss. There are far too many well-meaning but ill-informed assumptions being made. A community is a complex thing, and there are many forms of loss that are shared. Community gardening clearly addresses a number of underlying problems post-disaster and offers a clear avenue for disaster resilience building that should be tapped. It should never be so lightly dismissed.[98]

There are other elements of community and gardens that should be factored in. In the months since the fires, Anne maintains contact with more than 100 impacted gardeners and welcomes these gardeners around 450 times—equating to around 25 visits each month—to a makeshift garden centre she and her husband have created in their carport. Visiting Anne to pick up donated plants, or hay, or all manner of gardening materials, is an opportunity for a chat with someone who understands that recovery is a long slog, not a convenient package of a couple of months. She knows gardens are important in creating home and security. She knows the value of gardens are not insurable—that they often represent decades of toil and considerable financial investment to establish. Their loss is felt deeply. Her commitment to our recovery, like so many other unsung volunteers across Australia, has been an effort entirely outside the recovery system engineered by government—unsupported and unrecognised, but deeply vital.

Life from within the changing climate curve is tough when all around you bear the scars of each other: children evacuated from burning farms by mothers driving like maniacs through fire and thick roiling smoke past their child's treasured dog, or sheep, or horse. Young people, restrained in the back of a car knowing they were leaving their pets to perish while hearing the choked sobs of their mother, don't recover from that easily. Meanwhile, fathers and farmers remain on their land fighting to save burning sheds that held the tools of their grandfathers, their faces streaked with tears as friends literally dragged them from the fire's path. The shock of losing cherished family heirlooms casts a totally different shadow on the situation and takes a long time to recover from, emotionally and physically.

Young firefighters who crouched covered in wool blankets in the foot-wells of fire trucks breathing oxygen with a water-halo overhead huddled in a desperate bid to survive a fireball exploding above them. Their biggest fear was not for their own survival but for that of a friend exposed in the foot-well of a ute parked alongside because the fire truck has no more space. Everyone survived but the possibility of loss marked these young men deeply.

Physical wounds are made worse, and likely permanent, because injured people who should have been hospitalised kept fighting the fires or accepted only rudimentary treatment. Others abandoned medical care altogether so they could fight uncompromising blazes that continued to threaten their homes and livelihoods.

The ferocity of the fires tested and broke time-honoured practices. In the past, all generations of family stood shoulder to shoulder to fight impending threats. But when older members had to be evacuated for their own safety, despite believing they possessed the strength to stand and fight as they had for their lifetime, they lost their dignity. These brave guardians hadn't lost their nerve or been shuffled off. They just faced an adversary that was too fierce, too big, and too consuming for them to survive it. Ravine is the fire that robbed them of a part of themselves.

Dozens of people had the harrowing task of entering the remains of badly burnt neighbouring homes to sift through hot ash and rubble for bodies. That almost everyone survived is a miracle worth rejoicing, but the emotional legacy of having to search has left deep scars. In the retelling of these events, the harmed adopt a manic tone in an attempt to plaster over deep hurt with humour.

What isn't written within these pages are the whispered stories of those encounters too painful to voice; the events that trail off before the teller has finished their story, as if their brain has said, 'Enough, you cannot survive this image so I will distract you with blue skies'. We all know these stories, but never voice them.

All these experiences are connected across the community. An entire community teetering on the edge, their lives threatening, at any time, to splinter into a thousand shards of glass.

We all now face an increase in long-term health risks from prolonged exposure to the smoke and ash. Many of us spent too long in dense pollution. Bushfire smoke contains a complex mixture of particles and gases that are chemically transformed in the atmosphere and transported by the wind over long distances. Managing the health impacts of fire smoke should be integral to landscape fire planning and bushfire emergency response, yet it is not.[106-109]

There has also been an unwelcome offshoot of the government-funded mental health support. At the behest of agencies, who need stats on paper more than real-world results, there is now a push to survey those who have lost property and homes. Trapped like lab rats in a cage, fire victims are prodded by authorities in a quest to discover what is already self-evident in mental health literature.

Having never been through this level of disaster before, many people don't recognise their mental health is being impacted and suffer further, needless trauma through the interrogations. Despite being the daughter of a mental health professional myself, I consent to these intrusions more than once, belatedly recognising what the full agenda is only after the survey has started. While a fury burns in my chest, I try to mask it with a veneer of peaceful calm to avoid offending the well-intentioned workforce tasked to examine my experience and perspectives. It is not that the questions are the wrong things to ask, nor that they mean harm. It is the timing and the skill of the questioner that leaves an etch of violation behind. Traumatised people should be given the path to seek professional help themselves, to talk with their neighbours over fences, to meet with people they trust, on their own terms. They should not be subjected to a stranger's advances into the depth of their feelings, and certainly not to have their reactions peppered with suggestions for how they might 'feel better'. They should certainly not be subjected to data gathering exercises without explicitly and willingly understanding this is what they are contributing to.

Then there is the other trauma in our community. The unexpected grief as people suffer survivor's guilt or feelings they are profiteering from misfortune even though the service they provide is necessary and done with integrity and deep humanity. An event the size of Ravine ripples through the community outside of the physical burn scar. Nobody is left unscathed. Local tourism businesses are desperate to restart their income again, after months of closure, but remain fearful of causing community offence when they tell tourists it is OK to visit. There is the exhaustion of shop owners who find themselves unofficial counsellors to a parade of customers who walk through the door; or the exasperation caused by a legion of tourists wanting to relive the tragedy for vicarious pleasure, yet contribute nothing tangible, and leave nothing but a community member sapped at the end of their day.

Some of our most vulnerable—the innocents in our community—

are still struggling to come to terms with what has happened. Too young to understand why their father stays alone on the farm even though there is no house, or why their mother spends evenings quietly sobbing in anguish. In the news and media, they are exposed to coverage about great walls of flame consuming what they are connected to; trees, swings, sheds, and more. They watch trucks surrounded by dense black and red and hear recognisable voices yelling about the burning heat. They see balls of fire, rolling down roads towards anonymous cameras; a disaster played out in an age of technology.

Watching replays of the disaster doesn't happen when children are in the safe embrace of their parents. It happens when groups of children are watching on their friend's phones, in a school documentary project, or when the media celebrates an anniversary of the fire, which pumps ratings and sensationalises our experience. When these images intrude, families are robbed of sleep for weeks. Mothers relive the terror, not of the fire, but of the loss of their friend and lover—the father of their hearts—through the nightmares of their children. Fathers cradle their sons and daughters through long nights of darkness, assuring them of safety, even though they have been robbed of that assurance themselves. These traumas are private moments that are masked during the day by the most cheerful and optimistic among us.

I fear for them; for us all. The emotional after-effects are deep and long. If we are not mindful; if we are not conscious; the damage will manifest across time leaving a generation of us inextricably lost to the fire.

Very soon after the fire, I enrolled for counselling and even spoke out in media interviews about a looming mental health crisis and the importance of mental health interventions. With a father who dedicated a lifetime as a psychologist and stress management counsellor, I wanted to be an ally in challenging public prejudices and projecting positive outcomes about people suffering with mental illness. Yet, despite being open to the process and committed to overall recovery after months of counselling I wasn't getting better. After a while, I began having regular and open conversations with Geoff about wanting to end it all. Deep, internal anger was triggered multiple times every day. Finding some way to ease the pain, through no longer living, was becoming seductive.

After surviving Ravine, anxiety built up in my body long before I comprehended the full impact on my mind. Standing in the ashes afterwards, smelling smoke, and witnessing the surrounding devastation triggered every part of my body to believe my home was unsafe. And the future only promised more devastating climate chaos. That reality was simply too big for me to bear at the beginning. With excessive cortisol surging through my veins, my body entered a fight-flight-freeze response and stayed there. Every day, or hour, or even minute, I ricocheted between wanting to face the threat head on, run far away, or stand frozen in the headlights. As a survival mechanism, the body has a memory of trauma. For me, that memory was triggered by the smell of smoke, a conversation or media coverage, or the wind. When these things occurred, I would turn to Geoff, desperate to say, 'I think we're in danger and we need to leave'. But I could see he was battling his own scars; he would not be able to reassure me that we were going to be alright. So together, we walked through our trauma.

As winter rolled into spring, I shut myself off from all but those closest to me. I shunned conversation. When I was forced to communicate, I would fume for days afterwards about perceived slights. I began carrying a hostile level of internal rage that was at odds with the degree of set-backs and bureaucratic bungling. I concealed the fury deep, working hard to hide it from everyone but my skilled and trusted counsellor, and my friend who kept calling. My mental landscape was becoming vicious and completely out of character. I was tipping dangerously towards self annihilation. Something wasn't right. My counsellor saw it and referred me to a psychologist with specialist trauma skills.

I recall sitting the test to measure Post Traumatic Stress

Disorder (PTSD), casually answering questions about suicide, anxiety, and rage with absolute, chilling detachment. Thinking back to that day now sends a shiver up my spine. My psyche was locked in a dangerous battle, and the side that wanted to live was not winning. My resulting score was 53 of a total score of 80. Any score above 33 is suggestive that PTSD treatment should immediately start. Despite the detachment, the result was still a shock, albeit a detached one. I thought PTSD was limited to people suffering from physical trauma or who had witnessed horrific events—like war. I couldn't wrap my head around how it related to me. But there it was, in black and white.[110, 111] Under my new psychologist's gentle and incredible care, I got ready to start Eye Movement Desensitisation and Reprocessing (EMDR) therapy.

Now I know that PTSD is a mental health condition that's triggered by either experiencing or witnessing a traumatic event. Symptoms can include flashbacks, nightmares, and severe anxiety, avoidance, negative changes in thinking and mood, and changes in physical and emotional reactions, as well as uncontrollable thoughts about the event. It infects every aspect of your life—home, work, school, and relationships.

EMDR is based on the idea that symptoms occur when trauma and other negative or challenging experiences overwhelm the brain's natural ability to heal, and that the healing process can be facilitated and completed through bilateral stimulation while the client is re-experiencing the trauma in a safe environment. I didn't go into it blindly. I am a researcher. Writing and researching is how I make sense of my world. So in the cold damp of the pod, I read, a lot. I wanted to understand what was happening and how EMDR worked before I was willing to open myself further.[112-115] It was hard—at times harrowing, actually—to go deep inside my mind, following the pathways my subconscious wanted to track. There were suppressed thoughts that surfaced and deep, gripping guilts that roared to the fore. Through an ocean of tears, and across many months, the process helped my mind to unpick the layers of blockage that were causing me to revisit the trauma event as if it was happening in the present—in every moment of every day. Now, the trauma is still there. I can see it clearly, but blessedly it has moved into the past, as if time is a physical distance. I have stepped back from the abyss and can imagine a future.

Given my trauma stemmed from a dangerously changing climate, I wanted to find out if I was alone. I had heard of eco-anxiety and eco-trauma. But I wanted to know if these were merely catchy slogans of the self-help industry or clinically recognised conditions. I soon became aware that physiologists the world over are witnessing a growing epidemic around climate change related mental health conditions, including people suffering with intense feelings of grief from climate-related losses of species, ecosystems, and landscapes.[116] And, these impacts are not isolated to people striving to protect nature. They are also keenly felt by people living on and working from the land—by farmers.

An important study conducted in the US was released in early 2021, demonstrating that climate-related extreme events, such as wildfires and floods, have severe mental illness sequelae. Moreover, unchecked climate chaos threatens to severely impact the mental well-being of huge portions of populations.[111]

The published medical and physiological literature about post-wildfire trauma also reveals a serious up-tick in rates of PTSD, depression, and generalised anxiety post-wildfire in both adults and children. Several new terms have arisen in the scientific literature reflecting an increased awareness and understanding of the impact of natural disasters on mental health—ecological grief, solastalgia (a form of emotional or existential distress caused by environmental change), and eco-anxiety.[117, 118]

Loss arises when people are dispossessed of things they value—natural and human-made alike. Beyond the actual loss itself, things like safety, memories, health, and agency are also bundled into this space. In 2019, Petra Tschakert and colleagues published an important review of 106 cases of loss and damage spread over 47 countries, with harm resulting from one or several of the eight types of climate stressors and climate impacts assessed: floods (47 percent), droughts (43 percent), increased temperature and heat waves (42 percent), storms (29 percent), sea level rise (22 percent), glacial melting (10 percent), reduced sea ice (10 percent), and bush, forest, and wildfires (8 percent).[119] Keeping in mind, this assessment was conducted before the cataclysms of 2019, 2020, 2021, and 2022 that have rolled across the world. None-the-less, what they found was important.

Tschakert and her colleagues provide the first detailed, quantitative account, that I am aware, of the different dimensions of harm across many case studies. Intangible harm—including loss of identity, self-determination and influence, order in the world, dignity, and continued existence of a natural landscape—is now reported as much as tangible harm—including physical health, indirect economic benefits and opportunities, productive land, and human life—in both developed and developing countries. Together, these documented experiences amount to slightly more than one thousand ways to experience climate change harm here and now. Not in some distant future, but in the present. Some of these are well-known in published literature and climate impact discussions (such as the loss of crops and harvest and resultant food insecurity) while others have been less visible, for instance the break-down of social cohesion or looming existential threats.[119]

What my lived experience has uncovered, for me, is that adaptation to a changing climate needs to move beyond infrastructure, institutions and individual values, which are mediated by power and politics. The mourning of the loss of ecosystems, landscapes, species, and ways of life—ecological grief—is likely to become a more frequent experience around the world.[120] Yet, vulnerability is too often treated as an adjective and assumed to attach to individuals or groups of people ('vulnerable women' or 'vulnerable children') without recognising that vulnerability is a dynamic process over time and context.[121] Too often, the media and politics dismiss the trauma of an actual event, or the grief about a future, or slow-moving event, rebuffing the harm to people's mental health and social engagement.[122, 123] When, in truth, the research refutes this attempt to silence pain. Rather, we need to engage each other on this upsetting topic to promote coping and to ensure our communities take the right course, not cling to denial and remain headed in an ill-prepared, dangerous direction. The psychological impact of hearing grim predictions about increased vulnerability depends on how we help each other to process the implications of that foresight. There is a new skill we all need to foster about how to break bad news and help each other integrate that bad news.[122]

We also need to learn to think and plan ahead about the unknown. In 2017, Marc Girons Lopez and colleagues investigated how best to prepare communities for the potential of a natural disaster and how to support each other and operate during the projected event. Lopez and his team found that efforts to promote and preserve social preparedness before the threat of disaster tangibly helped to reduce disaster-induced losses by almost one half. They also found that people's engagement with emotional experiences around the disaster became fundamental to processing and making meaning of them. It seems clear the benefit of co-responsibility extends beyond individuals to communities and the supportive services within these.[122, 124] It is ironic that scientists and social scientists need to quantify what seems blindingly obvious when it is spelt out. But the benefit of Lopez's paper is that, when stated, the blindingly obvious becomes harder for government agencies to ignore.

What has been heartening to discover is that research into communities who have experienced collective trauma has found that communal emotional responses lead to greater solidarity within the community. During these events, perceived 'belongingness' is protective against the development of PTSD and was the largest predictor of good mental health.[122, 123, 125, 126] This single piece of information gives optimism for the future, because together as communities—not isolated in tribes—we are stronger and we can adapt to survive.

In the immediate aftermath of disasters, survivors tend to seek out their own networks of support, if they are available. Many people have a natural stoicism and minimise their focus on the psychosocial impact of their distress. This resilience has psychosocial advantages that buffer the ill effects of disasters on people's mental health.[127] But, there is a risk in assuming stoicism is enough. There may be an interval, sometimes an extended interval of months or years, before some people develop disorders.[127, 128] We won't be out of the woods and a fully healed community for more than a decade.

As if the mental health impacts are not enough, there is disturbing physical health impacts we will have to face too. During Black Summer, over 10 million people across Australia were covered by a blanket of thick smoke for months. In the past, the smoke from bushfires and controlled burns has generally been in the form of sporadic, short-term spikes in air pollutant concentrations. The duration and scale of population exposure to bushfire pollution during Black Summer is unprecedented, reaching levels up to 10 times those deemed hazardous.[129] Prolonged exposure to wildfire smoke over December 2019 and January 2020 alone is estimated to have resulted in over 400 deaths and over 3,000 additional hospitalisations across Australia, and not only among people with respiratory conditions but also among healthy people.[130] Both heat and air pollution exert effects, and when combined the total effect, may be larger than the sum of individual effects. Wildfire smoke contains high concentrations of fine particulate matter that penetrate deeply into the alveoli, can move into the bloodstream, and can cause systemic inflammations. Firefighters especially, but really everyone who spent nearly two months in the toxic soup that was our breathable air, were recurrently exposed to carbon monoxide, hydrogen cyanide, sulphur dioxide, hydrogen chloride, phosgene, isocyanates, oxides of nitrogen, acrolein, acetaldehyde, asbestos, polycyclic aromatic hydrocarbons, acrylonitrile, vinyl chloride, formaldehyde, and polychlorinated biphenyls (PCBs), and benzene. Some of these are known carcinogens. As if that is not enough, fire atmosphere can produce acute changes in pulmonary function that can lead to chronic lung dysfunction. The physical health impacts include respiratory distress, chronic obstructive pulmonary disease, asthma, and cardiac arrests. International evidence reveals low birth weights and inflammatory effects as well.[129, 131, 132] A recent Australian study examining fire fighters' exposures found the cumulative impacts of mercury exposure should be investigated further.[129] There are also concerns about long-term brain health after extreme smoke exposure.[133] And the bad news continues.

We are a long way from finding a path out of these dark woods.

12

Wither Wilderness

Eleven weeks after the terrible event, I lay awake, face turned towards the window, staring into the dark anxious for sound. As so often happens in this post-fire world, hours ticked by in this empty space. Then, as I fought despair and tried to push my mind towards sleep, a precious call breaks the stillness.

'Mopoke, mopoke, mopoke', a voice echoes with a familiar rising and falling chant.

Resting for minutes in between, the owl continues its call, softly and beautifully, while tears roll down my cheeks and I drift into grateful unconsciousness.

Winter is coming. It is stepping towards us to provide solace, peace, and rebirth. The days grow shorter; the light has a soft grey hue, and the drizzle in the air reduces summer to an etching. This precious island landscape—our home—has begun to heal. Where once the paddocks were black with ash and burn, now shoots of grass thrust forwards and cloak the hillsides in shimmering emerald green—a celestial promise of new life that will be born to the spring.

Soon the deep rains will come, and summer will curl into sleep; the memories of firestorms will fade into dreams or nightmares. Winter will guard the sleeping form, bathing it in water and cooler weather. There will be no threat of fire for a brief while. The summer landscape can rest and recover.

Lambs will be born, and not long after, the surviving birds will begin to collect twigs and leaves and wool for nests. I envy the birds for their optimism and faith that spring will arrive to wake summer from its slumber. But I curse my own species' lack of devotion to the next dawn.

Journalists immediately reported from active Black Summer firegrounds and described something neither an 'event' nor 'just Australian', but a planetary phenomenon. Fire is no longer a local or national story. Australia is the canary in the coal-mine, a belated warning of planetary peril. The world is watching us. We are the burning frontier of a warming world, the perilous cliff-edge of the Sixth Extinction. Black Summer may be the first fire season that

Australians have tried to calculate the mortality of wildlife and wild places, and the cost has been immense.[34]

The human mind struggles to grasp very large or very small things. On average, most humans can see less than five kilometres into the distance. So, perceiving the true extent of the destruction of wildfires requires imagination. We use imagination to contemplate many things beyond our human scale—nanoseconds, the Universe, and the geological time. But, because our imaginative thinking is based on our prior experiences, we are often fall prey to bias and inexact estimations. Our colonial past also skews our understanding, because we've been taught to think of landscapes as empty (of humans), rather than full (of biodiversity). When we hear the Black Summer fires razed 190,000 kilometres^2 and that three billion animals died, we can't quite grasp the enormity.[134]

It is easier to catalogue the experience, especially for those outside of the burn scar or disaster zone, as 'generically bad', and to move on. Yet understanding the scale of destruction wrought by wildfires, hurricanes, floods, and droughts is vital if governments and societies are to adapt in the future. We also have to critically address our colonial blinkers about empty landscapes at one end of the spectrum, and our deep green philosophies that wildness only exists without humans at the other.

In evidence given to the Australian federal Senate Inquiry into Australia's Faunal Extinction Crisis, Daniel Rogers, Principal Ecology Advisor to the South Australian Department for Environment and Water testified:

> *'... from a threatened fauna perspective, the animals that relied on the habitats that burned on Kangaroo Island have essentially gone through an extremely significant and rapid habitat-loss event. In a very short period of time, we've finished with little habitat left, and what's left is highly fragmented and isolated. ... It's also important to recognise that a lot of the native wildlife of Kangaroo Island were, as I say, thought to be reasonably secure on Kangaroo*

> *Island, such as the southern emu-wren, whipbirds and the Bassian thrush, which are now seen internationally to be threatened in direct response to the fires. Species such as the Kangaroo Island southern emu-wren has lost over 70 percent of its habitat, simply through these fires, and is now being considered nationally for listing as endangered under the act. That is simply in response to the fires.'* [135]

That's just Kangaroo Island, long heralded as a biodiversity ark. Beyond Kangaroo Island the Black Summer fires were devastating. Michelle Ward, a University of Queensland conservation biologist, has pointed out that many of the species affected across Australia in the Black Summer fires were already threatened because of drought, disease, habitat destruction, and the impact of invasive species.

> *'... mega-fires may have made the situation much worse by reducing population sizes, reducing food sources and rendering habitat unsuitable for many years.'* [136]

Tim Flannery, a prodigious academic and writer on all aspects of changing climate, (and climate change), who releases books that appear, like magic, with perfect timing, highlights with brutal clarity how fire will be the signature of the Anthropocene. Australia burned like nothing previously recorded, anywhere on Earth. The area burned included 21 percent of Australia's broad-leaf temperate forest area. As I read this account, I was further shocked to learn that typically, in dry years, fires in Australia burn only around two percent. 'Since records began globally, no fire has burned anything like 21 percent of a continent's forested land'. The Black Summer fires were a staggering ten-fold increase. On other continents, over a similar period, the high-end figure is 4-5 percent.[28]

In the months since the fire, I've had far-ranging discussions with a dear friend about the directions the world is travelling, the scale of loss we've just experienced, and what this all means for the precious landscape we live within. Her conservation property—only 3.5 kilometres from my farm as the eagle flies—is a place of unparalleled beauty where more than a decade has been invested in protecting every inch. She 'walks the talk' too, running a sustainable, organic produce business. Western Kangaroo Island is considered one of South Australia's major biodiversity hotspots and the De Mole River Catchment area is a jewel within this system. The river begins at an elevation of about 300m just north of the Ravine Des Casoars Wilderness Protection Area, close to where Ravine ignited, and flows west-north-westerly until it reaches Investigator Strait near Cape Forbin. This is a rare and unique area, even by Kangaroo Island standards. It forms part of a 103 kilometre^2 catchment area where 41 percent of the land is under some form of government or private nature conservation agreement. Nineteen percent is plantation forestry, 16 percent is grazing landscape, and the small remaining percentage is cropping, roads, and dams. Here it feels like conservation strives to sit in harmony with primary production. Conservationists flock to walk through its dense bushland and enjoy the relative abundance of so many species all but lost to the rest of Australia. It is, in simple terms, conservation heaven.

Outside her one remaining building stands a De Mole River Correa—a lone bush she planted years ago during a revegetation effort to repopulate many of the threatened species of the area. Growing into a dense round shrub up to three metres high, its stem is covered in rusty egg-shaped lobes, the underside of its long leaves are a blanket of rusty hairs, and it boasts one solitary flower head that erupts into a display of tubular, green, darkening to mauve, lobe-shaped flowers.

During one of our long wandering conversations, she bitterly laughs as she recounts her surprise this morning when stepping outside and realising the Correa had survived. So much has been lost, it has only been recently that she has been able to see what remains. But the forward journey is a hard one. Feral cats have invaded. People have been walking without permission across her land, potentially spreading the phytophthora she had worked so hard to control. 'During the fire, it felt like we were under constant attack', she told me. 'It went on and on, and gave me insight into what it might feel like living in a war zone. In fact, I was empathising with the animals and what they might be experiencing as well; how threatened they felt; not knowing which way to turn or what the best option was'. Looking at her today, in the bright sunshine of autumn, I can see one battle is behind her, but the after effect of war has taken its toll. But she is strong, still. Beneath her natural inclination to walk through life with a gentle footprint, remaining calm and generous under pressure, is now a warrior dedicated to leveraging change.

Season after season, she has worked with scientists to venture into survey vegetation and eradicate weeds on her land. She has invested hundreds of thousands of dollars in labour, time, and expertise in protecting this vitally important section of forest and wetland. She had already commissioned a Significant Environmental Benefit (SEB) Management Plan that outlined the need for prescribed burns but struggled with the bureaucracy to follow through. 'I had a list of threatened species on the property that was three pages long', she says. 'But there was no support. We see huge flows of money going into the pockets of big cashed-up conservation organisations and into the government agency charged with this care, but the community is working for free'. Even though she had placed a Heritage Agreement over her land, and the government considered her property part of the 'heritage estate', the implied perspective was that she was a private landholder and on her own. We share deep dismay about the government's response to her property during and after the fire. But, with a generosity of spirit so typical of her, she chooses to see light where she can find it. 'There was a defining moment of unity during the fire when neighbours stood on the road and talked. The fence between us all was down. It was beautiful when people from all those walks of life connected. I want to hold onto it', she says with brightness, although there is a poorly disguised crack in her gentle voice. The recovery battle has been hard on us all and the community is fracturing, I know. From a heightened viewpoint on her now blackened landscape, the view is one of acres of weeds, but no one seems to care.

She and I share a world-view: this landscape we both love will only survive if the community works together to save it. I forget my own challenges for a moment and my heart breaks for her and her struggles against the government's abdication of what she believed was a shared heritage bond.

There are unspoken truths to confront in this changing climate space. Conservation must adapt. The Black Summer fires destroyed decades of conservation in a single season. Chris Dickman and Lily Van Eeden coordinated a study for WWF that found almost 3 billion wild animals—143 million mammals, 2.46 billion reptiles, 180 million birds, 51 million frogs—were killed or displaced in the wildfire.[137] The full impacts on Australia's biodiversity will not be fully understood for years to come, as extinction debts are slowly, painfully realised. Sure, trees will regrow. 'Nature will rebound', people are fond of saying, but we know these fires burned hotter, deeper, and were far more extreme than this landscape is adapted to.

Some coarse surrogates are being developed now. Brendan Wintle, Sarah Legge, and John Woinarski have projected that, across Australia, 327 (272 plants, and 55 animals, including five invertebrates) of the ~1800 listed threatened species in Australia had a significant portion (>10 percent) of their known distribution within the Black Summer fire footprint. Thirty-one of these were already critically endangered. Among the significantly impacted species, 114 have lost at least half of their habitat and 49 have lost over 80 percent.[138]

Parks didn't protect them. Arguably, the aggressive dismissal of all historical knowledge—indigenous and white alike—and the misuse of environmental laws sealed their doom. And, who was it that stood in the face of the firestorms? Farmers and other private landholders fought harder than anyone to save nature along with their farms. Many of these people are the descendants of others who have walked these lands. These are the same individuals that have been hampered for decades by a scientific bureaucracy. Land clearing laws that 'count' rather than 'feel', 'prescribe' rather than 'support', and have been woven into an impenetrable mess that is, arguably, designed to exclude landholders from managing the risk of fire to biodiversity on their own land. This includes those with generations of knowledge of wind and rain, when flowers bloom, or birds begin nesting. Our balled-up, metric-driven interpretation of laws, suppressed cool, controlled fires that might have saved a significant portion of those species and habitats. Landholders were dis-empowered while bureaucracies were invested with even more power because we don't trust.

Everyone forgot that science, wonderful as it is, exists to inform and serve. Its nature is always incomplete as it quests for deeper and wider insight. Science is not a manager. It is a tool. And it has no capacity to capture history that it was not a part of shaping.

Wither wilderness.

13

Hopium

Until that single moment, as I stood at the base of our vineyard the day after the fire, my life had been one devoted to conservation; more than thirty years as a professional and activist on the environmental front lines fighting the boardrooms of power and greed. It was my sole, driven focus. I was climate-aware, conservation-tuned, well-read, with a CV that arrogantly proclaimed a sophisticated level of knowledge about the environmental issues that beset our planet.

Once I had dismantled the protective brick wall in my mind, a painful truth was exposed. It is already too late to save the world as we know it. The tools we have developed are designed for a time already past. The fire revealed that no level of physical protection can defend an ecosystem from extreme climate events. Campaigning to protect the boundaries of parks is a useless distraction. Fighting to save species while travelling on carbon-gushing planes is morally bankrupt. Praising the pitiful, incremental, emission reduction steps of powerful countries is negligent. I no longer believe in the conservation movement, in its present form. I no longer believe that politics, with the current pressure, will rise to the challenge. Our global community—our entire lives—is so deeply entrenched in a soulless economic growth frame we cannot unpack in time. Even while fires and floods rage across Europe, Asia, and the Americas, even with a heat dome inexplicably appearing and killing in North America's Pacific Northwest, oil and gas companies still have the support of governments to explore for more black gold. The forked tongue of reality is galling when laid bare.

What is needed is radical adaptation. Now. But to speak those words out loud is to commit myself to the marginalised and dismissed fringe. For months, I am reticent and angry. If all the data and analysis turn out to be misleading, and the coming decades are calm and safe, then I have harmed my standing in a movement I have committed a lifetime to serving. If the predicted collapse comes within the next decade, then anything I say now is moot. There is no safety in this space. So, I stare at these reflections, and discover the pain I am feeling is because

> it hurts to let go. I am letting go of everything I thought I was, everything I thought I knew. Messages of love, hope, and support keep coming to me, but I am powerless to respond because I am somewhere else.
>
> Seasons pass while I stare vacantly into despair, contemplating self-destruction.
>
> My whole life's effort rendered useless.
>
> Until it was not.

The online website, Urban Dictionary, defines 'hopium' as the metaphorical substance that causes people to believe in a false hope. As the opposite to 'copium', which represents the rationalisation of the current situation, hopium represents the belief that the situation will someday improve.[139]

Well, it won't. At least not in our lifetime.

Hope, according to Stephen Jenkinson, is '...very often a refusal to know what is so. ... Hopeless[ness] is the collapse of that refusal, and it looks a lot like depression'.[140] Like Jenkinson, more and more social scientists are speaking out. Humanity is locked in a cycle of putting faith in things they cannot control, in abrogating responsibility to someone who is very likely to disappoint—be that governments, corporate actors, or the section of humanity driven to pursue hedonistic, self-serving pleasure without any concern for the shared costs. By focusing on hope, people keep themselves locked in an emotional unsafe space where they put all their energy into their hopeful wishes as the solution, rather than in following the initially tougher path of self-reflection, that when done with honesty and clarity, unshackles them to see solutions that they can control, steps they can take, points of empowerment that they can own.[141] Jenkinson advocates we consciously become hope-free, leaving hope and hopelessness behind.[140]

Thoughtful, hope-free expressions are coming forward,

especially from the climate science community. One of the best has been penned by Joëlle Gergis, an award-winning climate scientist and writer based at the Australian National University.

> *'During Australia's Black Summer, more than 3 billion animals were incinerated or displaced, our beloved bushland burnt to the ground. ... After everything this year, what we hear when we listen to birdsong has changed. ... Recovering the diversity and complexity of Australia's unique ecosystems now lies beyond the scale of human lifetimes. What we witnessed was inter-generational damage: a fundamental transformation of our country. ... As we live through this growing instability, it's becoming harder to maintain a sense of professional detachment from the work I do. Given that humanity is facing an existential threat of planetary proportions, surely it is rational to react with despair, anger, grief and frustration. To fail to emotionally respond to a level of destruction that will be felt throughout the ages feels like sociopathic disregard for all life on Earth. ... We are being forced to come to terms with the fact that we are the generation that is likely to witness the destruction of our Earth. We have arrived at a point in human history that I think of as the "great unravelling". I never thought I'd live to see the horror of planetary collapse unfolding.'* [142]

Gergis penned this piece early in 2020 following the fires and then the mass bleaching event of the Great Barrier Reef. She is no lightweight flake writing pretty words from the margins of a debate that should be closed. She is a lead author of the United Nations Intergovernmental Panel on Climate Change (IPCC) Sixth Assessment report, and an expert adviser to the Australian Climate Council.[142]

Since her essay was released, the phrase 'the great unravelling' has flowed like water through a group of writers who have shifted their consciousness from one of hope that we can still save the world to an acceptance that we can't, in its entirety, and that we either need to spend the years we have left making peace with the loss or working to protect what is left. After a lifetime of work in the camp of hope, I've kicked my hopium habit and now grieve the greater loss that I see happening across the world. I have contracted to focus on what is immediately and tangibly close to me—the creek line at the bottom of our farm, the bushland over the hill, the wildlife kin I share this place with, and the community around me.

Although conservation has literally been my life, I've been forced to throw out all that I believed, and all that I thought I knew. I am now looking towards new relationships and partnerships with neighbours and community to collectively survive what is to come. We cannot afford the old demarcations of conservation and parks; of laws and division.

The pain and loss of this year tested my personal resilience and reshaped my beliefs, but it has also stripped away a veil. Recently, I gave evidence to the Australian federal Senate Inquiry into Australia's Faunal Extinction Crisis (provided in the Annex of this book). Knowing my words would be recorded as an official written entry in Hansard (the official record of debate in Commonwealth parliaments), I was prepared to announce in public it is too late. Too late to continue as we are. Too late to continue with our old plans. I came out as hope-free.

Drunk on Hopium

Hope can also feed dangerous divisions. Steve Biko, the brave anti-apartheid activist, once said, 'A community is easily divided when their perception of the same thing is different'. I appreciate the wisdom of this statement now. Division surrounds us. The uber-rich elite separate us into camps, fuelling our divisions in their quest for resource and power. And the conservation sector feeds that division by casting us in tribes—those for and those against nature.

Drunk on hopium, even after the massive losses from the Black

Summer fires, the conservation industry persists with the myth that we must lock away tracts of land for nature, because only that will save nature from a changing climate. Big conservation argues the people closest to the land are too ignorant of the facts. Their powerful voice fuels a distrust of anyone using the land and sea to grow or harvest food or fibre—dismissing the connections many in modern agriculture, horticulture, viticulture, and fisheries have to a healthy landscape—while blithely continuing in their roles as consumers who demand cheap food and fibre from the very production systems they vilify. They demonise those who depend on wild resources for their food, while speaking from the privileged access to city supermarkets with ladened shelves of packaged goods. The conservation sector's mantra of 'parks and distrust' tolls like a drumbeat at a wake.

I recently found myself standing in a room of conservation landholders discussing the development of a plan for endangered species management in the few islands of land that have remained unburned. These are 'my people'. I know their language. I understand what drives them to conserve what they can, but after the experience of Black Summer I found myself standing apart from them, feeling philosophically drawn to the farmers in the room. They held no hope. They were practical people looking for practical solutions.

I ventured to speak up and ask if we should be designing a bigger plan—one that included the remnants of bushland, along with the farm and forestry land that stands beside it. I mentioned that we shared creek lines that were corridors between the islands of vegetation, and that we needed a fire plan that encompassed it all. A day earlier, I had a conversation with another conservation landholder, who spoke with venom about how a farmer had approached them in the depths of the fire to suggest a back burn along their shared boundary, to prevent the bigger approaching fire from overwhelming them. The conservation landholder was affronted that the suggestion had even been made, and I recalled standing there bewildered as to why? To me, it seemed like a practical and generous offer. It is not easy to manage a back burn. It takes skill, knowledge, and equipment. We'll never know if it would have made a difference on the day, but it might have. How was it that the two perspectives were so divided? All this was rolling through my mind as I spoke up in the conservation meeting and made my suggestion to the room. I have history with the conservation movement, so I am rarely yelled down, but not one of the conservationists there on that day met my eye or even subtly nodded in agreement. Their silence was palpable. I was giving voice to a heresy.

In contrast, the farmers, lined up against the back of the room, all turned their heads in my direction with keen interest. It wasn't the time and I wasn't well enough prepared to push the discussion further into the open, but I saw the dangerous division clear enough. I resolved to pursue this in the months and years to come.

Division seems to stem from an unresolved debate about what the landscape really looked like prior to European settlement, and about how and how much fire was used by the First Nations of these lands. 'Some believe that fire is essential to maintain Australia's ecological diversity. Others believe that fire is just another way that humans disrupt ecological functioning'.[143] In this space, we find ourselves in a politically-charged intersection between European-inspired conservation and our interpretation of traditional practices. What it boils down to is this: did First Nations people use fire, and was the landscape changed by that fire? [143] There is deep-seated belief on both sides and this is not the book to unpack it all, other than to say that European-inspired conservation isn't going to work for this landscape moving forward. We have to do something different, and fast. Widespread clearing and burning during European settlement forced the natural vegetation into islands surrounded by farmlands. But the landscape includes grasslands too, whether conservationists believe these are the result of First Nations' land management or not is moot. First Nations people are part of the landscape, and if they changed it over the course of 10,000 years, that, in my mind, absolutely qualifies their interaction as natural. There is strong evidence that many of these grasslands disappeared with European settlement, likely because the dominant land users swapped from First Nations peoples to European settlers.[143] We've forgotten something important and fundamental about this landscape, and in many places we may be protecting a landscape type we created with our invasion.

The forested lands of Australia are dramatically different in their growth cycle to that of North American or European forests. Where those grow to be large, stable communities that gently renew over hundreds of years, Australia's forests are better described as a continued secession of destruction and renewal, and slow, creeping fire is a key part of that renewal.[143] We've changed that dynamic and, increasingly, the laws designed to protect have hampered efforts to reinstate careful, cool, mosaic burns.

In contrast to the might and force, the depth of heat and burning power of the mega-wildfires of our recent history and certainly the mega-fires of recent years, cool burns are conducted gently, slowly creeping along the ground through grasses, twigs, and fallen branches. The flames rarely reach higher than 40cm, and they begin from a central point, radiating out in a widening circle, giving time for many insects and animals to move away from harm. Birds often sit in nearby branches above the fire, so unthreatening is the process. Trees and tall shrubs are not impacted. The heat from these fires doesn't penetrate the soil or destroy the life-giving force of the soil's biodiversity, but they do provide immediate fertility back into that soil when the rains draw down nitrogen. Charcoal deposited during fire events stimulate the conversion of ammonia to nitrates, another important step in the nitrogen cycle. After these slow cool fires, the landscape bursts with renewed growth. Flowers not seen for decades suddenly appear. New grasses grow. And seeds of trees germinate *en masse*.[144-146]

Australia is a land of fire, containing plants long adapted to fires. But the very nature of the landscape is rapidly changing now, the nature of fires is changing too, and we have to accept that no plant is fireproof, given the right conditions. There are plants that have been either fire-retardant or fire-resistant, such as Australia's iconic banksia, part of the ancient Proteaceae family, with its distinctive candle-like cones that vary in colour from creamy white to reds and orange and yellow tones. Banksias have adapted to fire through their ability to re-sprout and retain seeds in woody cones that are released after the fire. 'If the plant dies from drought, it does not release its seeds – they just rot in the cone. Therefore, a fire is essential to melt the resin that keeps the woody fruits closed, in order to release the seeds onto the post-fire seed bed that is now ideal for germination'.[147] But, they need sufficient time between fire for plants to grow and produce viable seeds. These nuances are important to understand, because to arrive at an optimal fire management plan, each individual species has to be understood. Australia's eucalyptus are shade-intolerant species that adapted to exist within a fire regime, and species like the legendary alpine ash only germinate from seed on bare earth where leaf litter and shrubs have been burnt away. But even when these plants have reached maturity, intense fires can destroy any seeds on the ground and in the canopy and overcome nature's restorative powers.[147]

After a normal bushfire it is usual to see unburned patches that act as a reserve for seed trees that provide regeneration. But the new cycle of hotter, fiercer fires, created in drier conditions leave fewer unburned patches and fewer trees to spread seeds for regeneration. Ideally, patches of burned and unburned land create a mosaic. When these mosaic burns happen over a number of years the vegetation reaches different ages, supporting great biodiversity interactions. Intuitively, this simple strategy makes sense. But, changing climate has altered the rules irrevocably. 'We can no longer rest assured that nature will bounce back, and that knowledge should be a wake-up call for the world'.[148]

Shifting my Baseline

At the Extinction Crisis Inquiry, Kangaroo Island farmer and apiarist, Peter Davis, testified as a volunteer firefighter with more than 50 years of experience, but also as a landholder and farmer who had sat on the native vegetation board at its commencement in 1991. He raised a salient and deeply unpopular point. In South Australia's Native Vegetation legislation, burning is classed as land clearance. The unintended consequences of this legislation and the subsequent Wilderness Protection Act has been to restrict response to fire events.

> *'On 29 December there were two lightning strikes in Flinders Chase. The dozers sat for between six and eight hours waiting for approval to put a ring around it. We could have contained that first fire to less than 0.2 kilometres² if we hadn't had this Wilderness Protection Act that said you have to get the approval.'* [135]

As it turns out, those dozers did have approval, but interpretation of the Wilderness Protection Act delayed getting them moving. The legislation never intended an interpretation that would hamper emergency actions, but that is how it has evolved.

Beyond the emergency moment the Act still remains problematic. In South Australia at least, many landholders believe that getting permission to cool burn the twigs and branches, and woody perennials and grasses close to the ground in a stand of intact forest is so difficult that they have given up trying. I needed to understand for myself if this was just wilful dismissal, or if it was genuinely tough to do. So, I put myself through a mock process.

After visiting the South Australian Country Fire Service website that advised any burn-off application required council approval and compliance with Environment Protection Authority restrictions, I visited the next appropriate government website in the chain and waded through a lengthy guide about 'land clearing'. I am in the right place, but it is a little galling to read, because I didn't want to 'clear' my land. I wanted to protect it. I objected to fire hazard reduction coming under the negative judgement banner of 'land clearing'. Nonetheless, I soldier on.

Eventually I find a document intended to assist applicants to fill out an application for a Bush Fire Hazard Reduction Certificate, step-by-step. It doesn't help. After spending the best part of a morning trying to decipher what I could and couldn't do, I established I am permitted, on my own land, to 'clear a fuel break less than 20 metres wide' except if there is 'an area of land within 200 metres that is already sufficiently clear that would give comparable protection'. I can remove a big tree providing it had a trunk circumference of two metres or more (measured at a point one metre above the base of the tree) and it is growing within 20 metres of a building. Likewise, in this 200 metre space I can 'clear' vegetation 'to reduce the risk of combustible material ... for fire prevention and control'. But I don't want to 'clear' anything. I just want to gently burn the low growing vegetation and dry fuel to reduce fuel load.

As an academic, I read a lot of text. In my role as an international negotiator, I read even more 'government speak', but it took me several hours to navigate my way through the complexities of the application process to figure out that under the Act's definition, I do indeed need to apply to 'clear' my land. With a head full of peripheral information, I then learn that a successful outcome rests on hiring an Accredited Consultant, 'to undertake vegetation assessments to develop a Significant Environmental Benefit (SEB) Management Plan'. This Plan is a requirement. Scanning through a 112-page guide, I conclude that the 'science' of completing the application myself was beyond my academic capacity. This explains why consultants have to be accredited—receiving assessments with varying levels of information would make the assessment process problematic—and why there attracts a significant cost. But is all this deep detail necessary?

The next challenge is to establish what step follows the contracted Accredited Consultant and their completed Data Report.

At this point, I don't know whether a commissioned data report was the same as a SEB Management Plan. Frustrated, but determined to cross the finishing line, I remind myself that my goal is only to carry out a fire hazard reduction burn. The language that I am 'clearing' my land persists; an insinuation that implies my bushland will be gone rather than protected.

Next, I need to ascertain whether I need to submit the 'would-be' clearance application under the Native Vegetation Act 1991 or the Native Vegetation Regulations 2017. There is another guide to 'help'. Six pages in and I can't establish whether my case will be overseen by the Act or the Regulations—which is exactly the complications Peter Davis addressed in his evidence to the Senate Inquiry. It is far from a simple process.

No closer to understanding whether to apply under the Act or the Regulations, I am fast disappearing down a rabbit hole. I concede that in order to reduce the fire hazards on my land—which is implied as a wretched thing—I still need to employ the services of a consultant.

Although my case is hypothetical, it does illustrate a tangled, difficult, and impenetrable web that would take months of effort and cost thousands of dollars, which means the planning process would have to begin at least a year ahead of the actual burn.

My illustration is not to harm the conservation cause. Conservation will forever remain my passion. But fuelled by hope the sector has veered off a path that will help us survive in the coming climate chaos storm. Black Summer burned out of control, because of a balled-up, metric-driven interpretation of laws that suppressed cool, controlled fires which could have saved a significant portion of the species and habitats that were lost.

Conservation is also maintaining the dangerous, tribal divisions. Sadly, rather than seeing the world, for just a moment, through another person's eyes, members of the local conservation movement returned fire by labelling Davis' views as a '1950's land-clearance agenda'. It is possible they didn't recognise the fragility of connections after the fires. I heard more than once they had held their tongue in deference to the pain, but their lecturing tone does little to heal rifts and wounds. They agree we need to form a common understanding and agreement about how to manage fire for both community protection but also the maintenance of biodiversity. But saying must be followed by doing, and that means both sides need to compromise. Conservation has not ceded one inch of ground any more than the other side has. Something has to change.

From where I sit, with a foot in both camps, it feels clear that while the laws provide a framework, a problem lies in how these laws are interpreted and used. In this case, good laws have been twisted throughout the passage of time to exclude rather than embrace.

All because we 'hope' they will save the future. Hopium is a dangerous substance to abuse.

14

Cascading Failure

In the aftermath of the fire, Geoff and I walked across our farm assessing what was lost and what had been saved. We were tired and didn't look as closely as we might have, so it is not until now, as the winter winds are picking up, that we recognise the shed where we've been working—writing and trying to resurrect our business—is no longer as sturdy as we thought. We saw that the back wall had been charred black from the fire consuming nearby large trees, but the shed structure was still standing, so we didn't look closer. We knew, in time, the shed would need to be replaced. The heat buckled tin would rust quickly in the coming few years, but we moved on to assess other structures and fences as the list of rebuilding jobs was growing ever longer. Today wild winds draw our attention to the burnt and missing beams above our heads, to the nails intended to hold the tin roof in place that are now hanging in thin air.

I am watching a replay of the live-stream on my computer from the Bushfire Commission. Karl Braganza from the Australian Bureau of Meteorology is presenting with exquisite detail the climate drivers and weather predictions the Bureau had presented to the Australian government in 2019.

As I try to focus on my computer screen, I am aware the corner of the roof is lifting by a hand-span. It is difficult to miss, as flashing shards of bright light cross my desk. The tin rattles loudly and the few nails still attached to wood squeak and groan as the gusts pull against their tenacious grip. The clattering of metal draws Geoff back into the shed. He peers up at the roof, shaking his head about more repairs that need to be added to the now endless list and walks outside, phone in hand, to talk to the builder.

I watch him standing outside in the bright winter light, until my computer projects Mark Binskin, the Bushfire Commission Chair's question. 'About mid 2019 when you were starting to provide advice to those committees that look at what's coming up in the fire season, how did it play out in real time?' [149]

I turn back to watch Braganza's reply.

'Things really played out the way our forecast models, both in climate and weather, suggested they would'.[149]

My heart thumps hard against my rib-cage.

They knew.

Governments, at every level, knew. They were given the information by their own expert agency.

They knew and they did nothing.

Outside, the wind suddenly howls, lifting the corner of tin roof by an arm's length, before it crashes back down with shuddering force.

There are layers of governance above every community across the world. When we think about governance, or politics, we often bring to mind the visible, obvious layer of the governments we elect or that are appointed depending on how our societies are constructed. In Australia, this is our state and federal governments. Yet there is a supra-level above every nation state. It is not actually a separate body and has no means to force any country to do anything other than by peer pressure but is important nonetheless. The supra-level is the collective of nations who come together to decide matters of international importance—be that trade rules, or aviation rules, or how much biodiversity we should conserve and how. Since World War II this has mostly been done under the aegis of the United Nations (UN) as well as various regional bodies established for specific purposes—the North Atlantic Treaty Organization (NATO) for instance, or Asia-Pacific Economic Cooperation (APEC), or the North Atlantic Economic Community (NATEC). In this space live the climate change discussions that address emissions and adaptation. These supra meetings come to agreement about what each government should then do in their national jurisdiction. They also direct the work programme of any international agency staff that works under their mandate. For climate change this direction includes the science that is gathered by the Intergovernmental Panel on Climate Change (IPCC) created—by governments—to provide policymakers with regular scientific assessments on climate change, its implications and potential future risks, or the various projects that are funded to ease the impacts climate change, as well as a multitude of activities around arranging meetings, producing reports, and paving the ways for negotiations with other supra-level bodies. Nothing that happens in this space—and I really mean absolutely nothing—United Nations or otherwise, binds any government to do anything they do not choose to do. This also means that none of these bodies actually hold the responsibility for anything. The buck always stops with sovereign governments.

If you imagine the politics of the world in layers, sovereign governments operating in concert with each other are the top layer. Their national activities (laws, politics, agencies, and departments, in Australia these are divided between federal and state governments) sit beneath that. Under that big, complicated political space in many counties, sits another layer. In Australia, this is the local government space, otherwise known as councils—in some places, these are powerful and cashed-up entities of large cities, and elsewhere they are the stretched, beleaguered entities of rural communities. These bodies hold almost no law-making power. They are directed by the laws of the governments above them. The only power they hold is how they choose to respond. Well-funded councils in some Australian jurisdictions have taken brave and bold steps in climate adaptation. In many other regions, councils have followed the most conservative, passive roads, expecting everything to be managed and provided by state and federal governments. Yet, it is at this local level that the 'rubber hits the road'. This is where disaster is felt, and immediate response has to be coordinated. This is where the fine-grained actions that might lessen risk of disasters just around the corner can be actioned. This is also where there are no skilled staff to implement any mitigation or emergency response, and there are no realistic budgets to do anything unless the council has made a conscious effort to apply for a grant from the bodies above them.

This all means that where impact is actually felt, there is a gaping powerless wait for help, instituted by the very structure that governs our entire society. To a greater or lesser degree this is the same situation in pretty much every other political jurisdiction across the world. The labels applied may be different, but the powerlessness of actual people is the same.

Regardless of the leaning, to the political left or right, the governance of the world presumes all of these layers are working harmoniously together. On paper it looks great and reads something like this. Well-heeled government officials meet to hash out agreements between them about what they'll do. They each return home and task their mighty bureaucracies to write and implement laws. Everything in the vast and complex system of government within the country adapts to those laws and the thing that was agreed to is implemented. Problem solved. The well-heeled commend themselves for their brilliance, proudly patting themselves on the back in annual reports and strategy documents designed to explain to the rest of us that it is all fine—it is under control; there is a strategy. Their job done, they turn their attention to the next intractable problem.

However, the real world—the place where the rest of us live—is a far cry from that 'paper vision' process. Too often governance is disjointed, contradictory, isolated, and often frankly incompetent. One hand rarely knows what the other is doing. Decisions are made at the highest level that fall glaringly and carelessly short of what is needed. Then even those heedless decisions are poorly implemented. While frustrating and costly (economically, physically, and emotionally), there is a deeper problem this disjointed incompetence causes. It blocks the flow of decisions from one layer to the next, and in the worst case, gives wiggle room for agencies and big business interests to fundamentally ignore the implementation measures the nations of the world have agreed to pursue.

Climate Culpa

Obviously, the climate change negotiations feature high in the failure list. When the governments of the world met in Paris in 2015, they pledged (through their nationally determined contributions (NDCs)) to actions they each planned to take to reduce their greenhouse gas emissions and keep the global temperature rise below 1.5°C. They also committed to actions to build resilience to adapt to the impacts of rising temperatures. They agreed to report back in 2021. Five years after the adoption of the Paris Agreement, so little had actually been implemented, the emissions gap is as large as ever.[150, 151] This wilful disregard can be dressed up so many ways, but frankly there are no excuses that come even close to reasonable.

By the time governments all met again at the latest meeting in Glasgow (in 2021), they had achieved only a fraction of those pledges, and most were so far off-beam it is laughable to believe any of them will make good on their short term, 2030, pledges. By the end of the meeting, 151 countries had submitted new NDCs to slash their emissions in the following nine years. To keep the goal of limiting temperature rise to 1.5°C within reach, we need to cut global emissions in half within the coming short window. Clearly, that's not going to happen. The UN calculates that the NDCs, as they stand, put the world on track for 2.5°C of warming by the end of the century. Sure, that's better than the 4°C trajectory the world was on before the Paris Agreement was struck, but it is still extremely dangerous.[151]

The Glasgow meeting did have one good outcome. It finally put the critical issue of 'loss and damage' squarely on the main stage. Changing climate (for whatever reason) is already causing devastating losses of lives, land, and livelihoods. Some damages are permanent—from communities that are wiped out by fires, floods, cyclones, or landslides, to islands disappearing beneath the waves, to water resources that are drying up.[151, 152] The developing countries of the world—communities of people who have contributed the least to the world's woes, yet unfortunately face the earliest brunt of the folly—have been crying out for support to help them to adapt. Things such as building higher sea walls against flooding, capturing scarce rainwater for irrigation, and switching to drought-tolerant crops. The big and the powerful (in particular the US and Australia) have been resisting formal recognition of 'loss and damage' since the

Paris meeting, because they don't want to acknowledge the burden of responsibility they morally bear. Negotiators on the payroll of the great and the good in world affairs have been pushing for a clause that will require recipient countries to prove liability—that a big emitter's emission has directly caused the losses and damages they are experiencing. This negotiating position carries the stench of rotting flesh, to be frank.

However, during Glasgow, the big emitting governments reluctantly conceded loss and damage was an issue, and while they fell short of the agreement on how to fix it, they did consent to create a 'new dialogue' dedicated to discussing possible arrangements for loss and damage funding through to 2024.[152, 153] So far, the amounts voluntarily pledged to support at-risk countries remain egregiously below the annual $70 billion developing countries are thought to need now—a sum that could rise to $300 billion a year by 2030, according to the UN.[151] The Glasgow meeting agreed to launch a two-year effort to define a 'global goal on adaptation',[152] presumably so they can constrain how much the damage bill will amount to, even though by 2030, the economic costs in developing countries are expected to reach towards $580 billion.[153]

It is not as if this is a new issue. The need for this goal was included in the 2015 Paris Agreement, but six years on it remains—unbelievably and recklessly—still vague.

There is little positive I feel inclined to muster onto the page about the Glasgow meeting. I am resisting the solid 'hopium' push in some quarters to put an approving spin on the meeting; to focus on what was achieved and how 'difficult problems are now in view'. But we've been collectively spinning hope for decades now. Better we finally recognise the world's governments have demonstrated a reprehensible abrogation of duty to the entire living—human and nonhuman—community of the world. As I write, my close writing partner is heading south from her home that has been lashed by brutal storms, cut off and isolated for a whole week by flood, to be by her sister's side as she stands in the toxic mud that now surrounds her house destroyed in the Lismore flood. There is literally nothing but devastation. This is the same friend who has been the solid force helping me write this book since the wildfires, and now she faces the harrowing road of recovery too. If it was written into a movie script, it would be panned by the critics as too unbelievable. Yet, here we are. Away from the well-shod world of the governing elite, the reality is brutal.

I feel profound grief for all that will be lost by the time global warming passes at 2°C. And, I feel deep anxiety about the journey between now to the tragic endpoint, for so much. I have lost all respect for the self-servicing politicians and their willing minions negotiating a path between here and hell.

Slighting Sendai

Unfortunately, climate change is not the only international agreement that suffers from the duck and weave of power and politics. Until I started this specific writing journey, I was blissfully unaware that there had already been decades of UN discussion around disaster reduction and safeguarding communities when disaster strikes.[154] Had I stopped to think about it, the work would have been obvious. I would have noticed the lists of documents and agency work that was ongoing in my peripheral vision. But I was single-mindedly focused on the international biodiversity negotiations. I didn't even pause to look. Disasters happened to humans, and that wasn't my shtick.

Once I looked, it was clear that most of the world's national governments have signed up to this agenda, including Australia, through the UN General Assembly (UNGA). This work sits within an international process called the UN International Strategy for Disaster Reduction. There is a UN Office for Disaster Risk Reduction that supports it and the most recent of the negotiated position is the

Sendai Framework for Disaster Risk Reduction 2015-2030 (Sendai Framework).[155] The Sendai Framework intends to support member states with concrete actions to 'protect development gains from the risk of disaster'. It addresses drivers of increased disaster risk including: more frequent and intense natural hazards and exposure of interconnected and interdependent essential services; and forecast growing costs of natural disasters, both human and economic. It is designed to be applied holistically across four domains: built, social, natural, and economic.[156]

The Sendai Framework apparently works hand in hand with the other 2030 Agenda agreements, including The Paris Agreement on Climate Change, The Addis Ababa Action Agenda on Financing for Development, the New Urban Agenda, and ultimately the Sustainable Development Goals. It was endorsed by the UNGA following the 2015 Third UN World Conference on Disaster Risk Reduction[157] and replaces the Hyogo Framework for Action adopted in 2005, that in turn stood on the shoulders of the Yokohama Strategy for a Safer World: Guidelines for Natural Disaster Prevention, Preparedness and Mitigation from 1994. This is all I would expect from an international process. It means there is an agency charged with its process, and governments are reliably turning up to, at least, take participating in the discussions seriously.

Building on the Hyogo Framework for Action, the present Framework aims to achieve the following outcome before 2030:

> *'The substantial reduction of disaster risk and losses in lives, livelihoods and health and in the economic, physical, social, cultural and environmental assets of persons, businesses, communities and countries.'* [157]

To attain that declared outcome, the UNGA—which means every sovereign government across the world—agreed the following goal must be pursued:

> *'Prevent new and reduce existing disaster risk through the implementation of integrated and inclusive economic, structural, legal, social, health, cultural, educational,*

> *environmental, technological, political, and institutional measures that prevent and reduce hazard exposure and vulnerability to disaster, increase preparedness for response and recovery, and thus strengthen resilience.'* [157]

Nice words. 'Hopeful' even.

In March 2015, the then UN Secretary-General, Ban Ki-moon, stated that 'sustainability starts in Sendai'. In the UN year of opportunity for a universal vision and plan for sustainability, the Sendai Framework was recognised as the starting point, followed later in 2015 by the agreements on climate change (Paris) and a brand-new set of Sustainable Development Goals (SDGs). All three agreements share a 2015-2030 time-frame and articulate the same fundamental ethos of sustaining human life without harming the planet or humanity.[158]

Clearly the groundwork has been done. The 'paper path' is identified and commitments have been made. Yet, as I've already outlined, too often these lofty documents with their meaningful statements and goals remain little more than words. It is never written into the documents, nor spoken formally on the floor of meetings, but it is a barely veiled, widely understood secret assumption that when the developed world signs up to these measures, they generally presume these declarations are really just for the regions of the world's poor. Indeed, the UNGA Resolution makes firm statements about the responsibility of the wealthy and safe to protect the populations where risk was high and available funds to mitigate disaster are limited.

Nonetheless, the Sendai Framework is for everywhere and everyone in the world. Australia has signed up to this, so where was that ambition manifested in any of Australia's reactions to the Black Summer fires? Where was the Sendai Framework in the Prime Minister's perspective when he rebuffed the fire chiefs trying to get his attention in 2019? Where was the Sendai Framework in the Prime Minister's mind when he abrogated his moral responsibility and went on holidays mid-way through the catastrophe? And where is the

Sendai Framework in the government's reaction to Australia's current climate-driven flood crisis, and the unfathomable decision to wait a full week before declaring the mega-floods a national emergency.[159]

The federal government is committing tens of millions of dollars in support for local mental health support services, children's mental health, and emergency relief, food relief, and financial counselling services.[159] It is easy, from a distance, to see this as measured and enough, but it falls woefully short. People inside the flood zone feel the Australian defence force assistance has been too slow and too limited, and there hasn't been enough government help.[159, 160] Too many people are either being knocked back for aid and support, or are too weary to apply. Residents have resorted to funding their own helicopters for rescues and food drops, in the absence of more government-funded air support.[161]

Two years on from the devastation of the Black Summer fires, with a major Commission of Inquiry and clear recommendations, the internet is once again overflowing with stories of bureaucratic bungling and painful community isolation. Queensland and New South Wales were both hit hard in Black Summer. The federal government was in that fray too. It is not as if they have no collective experience to draw upon. Where is the learning? Where is the preparation? The Sendai Framework has four clear targets. One of these is 'Enhancing disaster preparedness for effective response'.[155] So where, most importantly, is the plan?

All these supra-level agreements—Sendai, Paris, SDGs—should be feeding into the directions, policies, and laws of every government that has agreed to them. Sadly, while this international work gently tilts the direction of the world, I don't know of any international agreement, beyond trade, that is even halfway implemented. Australia might be slighting Sendai, but so is everyone else. Twenty-eight years of UNGA level discussion, and while Australian government agencies have been building their work under the Sendai Framework, it seems this emerging, urgent situation has been totally ignored by Australia's political leaders.

That accusation isn't just levelled at federal and state government.

Our local council is small, with a tiny workforce tasked with managing a considerable land area. The ratepayer base of Kangaroo Island is also limited, and land values are low, so this small team also lacks financial resource. Nonetheless, the council carries considerable responsibility for the management of native vegetation in local parks and council lands, as well as around fourteen thousand kilometres of road, bordered by formally dense trees and shrubs that snake around the island on either side of every road. Lacking funding and hamstrung because of the same Native Vegetation Legislation that impedes private landowners to manage the risk of fires overtaking their natural landscape, the council has once again fallen woefully behind in any realistic schedule to manage this considerable native vegetation estate. Perhaps I am softer in my criticism of this failing because the council really are just members of our community who have the good fortune or bad luck to hold council jobs. Perhaps I am disinclined to assert the full-frontal attack I am comfortable to level at the international-, national-, and state-level failures because I personally know many of the people who are staff or elected councillors. I appreciate they are managing a complex system as best they can. When I set out to write this book, I committed to do no harm to my community.

But I will say this much. At the end of the day, our council was unprepared, and while there were solid, even noble, attempts to rise to the occasion, with the swift launch of the Mayoral Bushfire Fund and commitments to process rebuilding paperwork with speed, immediately before the fire and in the months afterwards the council failed the community. I understand that councils don't make laws. They respond to the laws handed to them by federal and state governments. The need for preparedness simply never trickled down, but council never forced the flow either and it should have. The Sendai Framework says so. We are an island isolated by our own short-sighted imagination of what can happen. What is perhaps more shocking to me is that since the fires, there has been no visible self-assessment of what went wrong and what to do next time. There are no visible steps being taken to plan for the future, let alone to even discuss what that future looks like. Our council sadly, has slipped back to a focus on 'rubbish and roads', following the lead of a limp and ineffective state government-led recovery process that has focused most of its effort on government agencies, and not helping the community to adapt for the future.

Government has abrogated any preparedness leadership, leaving it to manifest in the community at large.

The Bushfire Commission Speaks

The Royal Commission into National Natural Disaster Arrangements (the so-called Bushfire Commission) that was conducted following the Black Summer fires, but was expressly extended to include all national natural disasters (including, notably, floods), articulates an important road map for how the Australian federal government can better support state and local disaster responses.[156]

The Bushfire Commission's findings are not new. They build on a shocking 240 previous inquiries and reports about natural disasters.[156] These documents have been marginally implemented, at best. Still, the Black Summer catastrophe across Australia was so big, this latest Commission did carry more gravitas and weight than before. It has produced a brave report that takes a broad sweep of input from across the professional disaster community, as well as business interests, indigenous land managers, and the general community. Sadly, its 964 pages still reflect blinkers and blindsides.

There are important points the Commission highlights. Foremost the process brings to light that Australia adopted the Sendai Framework in 2015 and has responded by creating Australia's National Disaster Risk Reduction Framework (NDRRF) to implement the Sendai Framework in the Australian context.

Moreover, in 2017, the National Resilience Taskforce had already presented a strong case[156, 158] for Australia to enhance its national disaster preparedness:

> *'Evidence is mounting that Australia's natural hazards are intensifying, with growing exposure to numerous risks and increasing potential for severe to catastrophic impacts on the nation. ... A variable and changing climate is expected to further increase the severity and frequency (albeit not uniformly) of natural hazards in Australia. ... Globally, it is recognised that loss associated with weather related extremes is on the rise. ... [T]he number of people and assets exposed to natural hazards is continually growing, leading to the creation of new risks and a steady rise in disaster related losses, with significant economic, social, health, cultural, and environmental impact in the short, medium and long term—especially at the local and community levels.'* [158]

Those facts would suggest there must be a plan, but the Commission report reveals something different. Australia's national arrangements for coordinating disaster management is mind-numbingly complicated. Nineteen whole pages of the Commission report are dedicated to just describing the 'arrangements' and how they work together, at least on paper. The next 317 pages are a sad catalogue of all the things that don't work, with page after page of exasperated input from disaster experts, pleading for the system to be sorted out. It is alarming that something so important is in such disarray. A broken bureaucracy is one thing. There is something deeper missing in the mix that also worries me—a clear acknowledgement from government of responsibility. The National Strategy for Disaster Resilience (NSDR) from 2011 and everything that follows it, seems to assume that government's role before a disaster is to educate the community about resilience—as if telling us to be bushfire-safe or to take care around fast-moving water is the limit of their responsibility. I see little evidence of genuinely strategic, high-level intervention by governments to direct Australia's infrastructure and communities towards resilience, especially conversations around how critical rural communities are for food security, let alone biodiversity conservation. There are few plans to mitigate future risk. Putting aside emissions and climate change for one moment, I am referring specifically to all the adaptation actions we should be taking, right now, to protect ourselves and the aspects of our built and natural landscapes we hold dear. Houses are still being erected in flood plains. Dams and reservoirs risk breaching their capacity with no major works engineered to divert the overflow away from built environments. Building standards do not normalise bushfire-safe building materials and designs. National Parks still have their fuel load budgets slashed, year after punishing year, causing dangerous and unnatural fuel load levels to build in a heating and drying landscape. Telephone towers are only erected where telecommunication providers see an increase in commercial opportunity, not to plug the gaps of dangerous mobile black spots that need communications during natural disasters. Meanwhile, government agencies increasingly push communities towards a reliance on that same telecommunication's technology to stay informed during the disaster, even though most black spots are in disaster-prone areas. Australian governments, of all stripes and colours, seem content to leave the shape and direction of these important resilience measures to market forces. They restrict their 'involvement' to a limited hand in managing the disaster when it unfolds.

Partly, the National Resilience Taskforce says this is because the changing climate and disaster management stakeholder groups see the world in different ways, and the disaster management stakeholder groups, in particular, find it difficult to imagine risk until it has happened.[156]

To be fair, the Taskforce did successfully raise the case that more needs to be done.

> *'Through a facilitated process of 'imagining the*

> *unimaginable' in May 2016, it became apparent that—among all the challenges we faced—the scale of severe to catastrophic events has the capacity to shock the nation, its institutions and systems, placing stress on all aspects of society. It also became apparent that preparedness planning at all levels and across all sectors had not matured sufficiently to address severe to catastrophic events. Analysis of global and international risk statements revealed Australia's situation is not unique.'* [158]

Nestled into page 114 of the Bushfire Commission report is a telling illustration. It explains, graphically to the reader, the results of a data mapping exercise Deloitte Access Economics were commissioned to undertake in 2018. Although Australian governments recognise that information is critical to be able to prepare for and respond to natural disaster events, the Taskforce comments that 'official national information on hazard intensity, exposure trends, and underlying vulnerability is not available'. Interesting. And alarming. The reader then turns the page to the Deloitte graphic that highlights how the National Natural Disaster Arrangement agencies are unable to report on twenty-two of a total thirty-eight indicators across the seven Sendai Framework targets. That means there is data for the lean side of less than half of the agreed indicators that Australian governments use to guide themselves about how adequately they are protecting the Australian population and the things we collectively cherish.[156] Pause with that for a moment. They know only half the picture. Worse, they know they know only half the picture.

The Bushfire Commission has recommended some eighty important reforms. The majority of these relate to critical improvements needed in the way emergency services and a defence force interact during natural disasters. They highlight where more support is required (such as sovereign aerial firefighting capability) and where coordination bottlenecks should be addressed.

There is a recommendation for state and territory governments to improve public education and engagement programmes about disaster risks, yet there is no mention of the need for people to actually adapt to those risks, and how that adaptation should be directed. It is all focused on being vaguely 'prepared' to either defend or evacuate your home when the disaster hits. I am sure this is because recommending wide-scale adaptation—which is what is actually needed—would require considerable government investment. My lived experience is that the recovery end of the disaster is where the resilience rubber hits the road. You might learn to safely evacuate your home, but if you or your business can't survive the recovery process once it is destroyed, you are lost to society.

There are recommendations about better coordination and preparedness for post-disaster relief and recovery, including nationally consistent, pre-arranged recovery programmes, that address social needs, legal assistance, domestic violence, indirect impacts, and crucially environmental recovery. It highlights that agency staff should be pre-trained to reduce confusion, inconsistent decisions and advice, and enable agencies to respond with necessary speed, rather than appear like they are making everything up on the fly. Clearly, given what the residents in Richmond Valley, Lismore, and Clarence Valley, or in Brisbane, Fraser Coast, or Gladstone were experiencing in early 2022, that recommendation went into a box and got tucked under someone's desk. Two years on and Australia proved itself to be no better prepared than it was in 2019.

Early in 2022, the then Chief of the newly formed National Recovery and Resilience Agency, Shane Stone, in an interview with Nine Entertainment rightly said that flood plain development should end, but then destroyed his sensible point by victim blaming, as if those at risk are somehow responsible for their plight.

> *'You've got people who want to live among the gum trees – what do you think is going to happen? Their house falls in the river and they say it's the government's fault'*, he said. *'Australians need to have an honest conversation about where and how people build homes. The taxpayer and the ratepayer cannot continue to pick up the bill for these huge, catastrophic damage events.'* [162]

This was a transparent attempt to shift the media attention away from the agencies' failure and to place the responsibility for flood damage on the shoulders of people least able to defend themselves. Many of those homeowners purchased their homes long before climate chaos was an evident reality, and certainly without their council informing them of the scale of risks they might face. Many of these towns have histories of more than 100 years. The responsibility for those homes being newly in a catastrophic flood or fire zone remains at the feet of government who failed to take the changing climate seriously decades ago, when there was still time to reduce harm.

Moreover, those of us 'in the gum trees' are communities surrounding the farmers who put food on tables and fibre on backs. We are the teachers, and doctors, and nurses, and firefighters, and retail store workers who make rural life possible. We are the regions who feed and clothes the millions sequestered, with assumed safety, within the metropolis. The arrogance of Stone's statement, especially at such a fragile moment for so many individuals, is astonishing.

State, territory and local governments should be required to consider present and future natural disaster risk when planning new developments, but the Commission report itself is silent about how to address existing developments. At a minimum, the National building code should be updated to require new buildings to be more resilient to natural hazards. But that is merely the thin edge of the problem. We need to fundamentally change how we live.

There is much I admire about the Bushfire Commission process, including the willingness to look under the carpets for the problems. The Commission called for an Authoritative Disaster Advisory Body and a Standing resilience and recovery entity. This entity has been realised in the new National Recovery and Resilience Agency, even if it seems to have failed its first test.

The Commission report recognises the impact of disasters on human health, and makes important mental health recommendations, as well the need for a national air quality forecasting capability. It also identifies some tentative steps towards better engagement with traditional owners, but the brevity of the recommendations reveals that white Australia does not yet recognise the shallowness of our self-awareness in this respect.

There is a great deal of emphasis on the mismanagement of fuel loads in the Australian landscape, and that tracking management progress on government lands (National Parks, Wilderness Area etc) should be easily available to the public. Similarly, flood-related progress and strategies should be available for everyone to see. The Commission report also recommends that the process for managing fuel loads on private property should be urgently reviewed to allow land owners to undertake bushfire hazards reduction activities (notably, activities that are mis-termed 'land clearing').[156]

Crucially, the Commission report recommends information is better tuned to the scale it is needed, and for climate projections to be 'downscaled' to regional and local levels, so potential disaster extremes can be better understood. Currently, global climate modelling works to approximately 100 kilometre grid cells, providing a macro view of climate and weather.[156] Regional modelling could more helpfully be tuned to provide important insights to mountain ranges, coastlines, and yes .... islands.

While the Commission Report doesn't say this, what seems evident between the lines is a pressing need to rebuild community trust, because that has been devastatingly undermined in almost every community hit by wildfire during the Black Summer fires and now the 2022 catastrophic floods.

I am not alone in my gloomy assessment. In late 2021, twenty-one researchers, lead by Rachael H. Nolan, published a brutally honest assessment of where Australia sit, post Black Summer.

> *'While governmental inquiries produced broad-ranging recommendations, we argue that they have not resulted in a fundamental shift in the way in which fire will be managed in the future. Overwhelmingly, they reinforce the status quo of a centralised and technology focussed approach*

> *to the mitigation of risk, with greater strategic nuance and an expanded role for national level co-ordination. ... The fire–inquiry cycle, despite its strengthening of the mainstream of fire management (i.e., more suppression resources, technology and enhanced co-ordination) has not delivered the kind of transformation that would be needed to significantly alter the outcome of a fire season similar in magnitude to or exceeding 2019–20 in the near to medium term.'* [3]

To some extent, the Australian government appears to have recognised they were derelict in their duties in the lead-up to the Black Summer fires, while still not fully embracing the full extent of the responsibilities they hold for the collective welfare of the whole living—human and nonhuman—community. With the establishment of the new agency, there was an opportunity to shift national policy and disaster coordination forward. It has been sad to watch the next disaster unfold and see politics obfuscate, duck and weave, around first response capabilities and the provision of emergency food and water. It seems that government remains tone-deaf to what is actually happening across Australia.

Absolutely, we should all be well-prepared—bushfire aware and flood ready—but as individual tax payers we do not hold responsibility for the bigger picture of fuel load management and flood mitigation, nor of drought preparedness. It is simply negligent to assume that the country can lurch from one catastrophe to the next, with the communities in the epicentre of each tragedy handled a few baubles and beads and told to toughen up and rebuild themselves. I am grateful for the mental health support that has been gifted to my community. I appreciate the support from Minderoo, BlazeAid, and the Army. These sources of support were powerful, but they were also fleeting. The longer haul of rebuilding has been invisible to the world, and there is almost no energy to prepare for the next time. This is because the people at the coalface—those community members the government is so fond of praising for their 'can do' spirit—are exhausted and weary from battling bureaucratic stupor and bungling, on top of rebuilding their very lives.

Maybe fuel load management or flood mitigation should be in our hands.

Maybe climate chaos adaptation should be under our control.

15

Wicked is Not Good

The room is full, packed from one wall to the next, with angry, hurt, and frightened people. We are here to hear senior government officials tell us what has happened and what will unfold next. We've waited for months for this meeting and I can feel the fury radiating off one of our wise elders who sits directly in front of me. My dear friend sits a few rows behind me, her presence anchoring my spirit that desperately wants to flee the room. It is time to voice truth to power, something I've spent a lifetime doing, but today I feel sick with the collective pain in this room.

A government employee starts to speak. He stands confidently to say 'he knows our pain'. He shares it. A few years ago, he went through another fire and understands what we are feeling. He names it. We know it. There is a collective gasp as we all internalise his terrible comparison. That fire lasted two days, at best. It was started by machinery, not lightning. It was over grasslands, and entirely different. Yes, there were losses and those are terrible, but not at the scale we've experienced. Yes, there is ongoing hardship, but not at the scale we face. He smiles, oblivious to his gaff, and barrels on with this tone-deaf empathy. When he flippantly proclaims 'these things happen', I stop listening.

Another speaker stands to tell us all what the government thinks. His voice drones on. I don't hear what is said. I am falling into a deep inward reflection, trying to work out how we clamour from this hell.

Then I am snapped from my inward journey. The wise elder in front of me stands and, with the force of a mountain, shoots back, 'None of this is good enough. We don't need words or excuses. This fire was different from anything in my lifetime fighting fires. I didn't think we would survive. If this is climate change, let's call it that, and stop stuffing around'. His body shakes with rage.

He wants leadership that reflects our new reality and it is nowhere in this room.

Dangerous Divisions

In the months following the fire, there is a massive outpouring of care and compassion for the bushfire victims, biodiversity, and injured wildlife. Black Summer donations from Australians alone nudges $640 million[163] and there are significant international fundraising campaigns as well. This charity demonstrates the generosity of the human spirit and should be celebrated.

Yet, the scale has left a false impression. The implication has come to rest in many people's mind that the fire victims received handsome sums of money from government and public donations. I have heard from more than one person in my own community, in a barely concealed green-tinged tone, that 'the money' was enough to rebuild our home. How lucky we are, is the suggestion. We get a free house from the disaster. Clearly, they suggest, instead of having depression and bone weariness etched on our faces, 'we should be grateful'.

Deep, soul-moving gratitude is unquestionably part of my everyday wave of emotions. I am grateful for the profound support and care of my small community, and for the heroic commitment of a few individuals to carry us through our darkest days. I am grateful to the South Australian Country Fire Service for their acknowledgement of the losses of those who were on duty during the fire. I am grateful to every single Country Fire Service and farm fire unit for doing everything humanly possible to save what they could. I am grateful for the swift deployment of mental health support in my community. I am grateful our insurance company didn't contest our claim. After painful months of rebuilding structures, I am grateful to have a home again and for life to be reasserting a regular routine, even if my home is empty of anything that carries memories. I am grateful to the local businesses that discounted our big household purchases of fridges, ovens, and stoves, as well as the extraordinary amount of hardware that must be gathered together again to rebuild a rural life. Firewood doesn't chop itself. It needs chainsaws and axes. Gates don't magically jump off the ground and swing with ease. They need steel and chains. These local business 'donations' don't even factor in the reported $640 million of donated money. I am grateful for gifts of handmade quilts, stitched and knitted by beautiful strangers, that kept us warm in the pod and now rest at the end of my bed. And yes, I am grateful for the gift of those precious donations.

What seems misunderstood by many is the scale of what was actually received by the wildfire victims. And, sadly, this misunderstanding is happening all over again with the flood victims. Putting to one side the grants that became available to rebuild businesses heavily impacted by the fire and the generosity of the Country Fire Service Foundation for its serving, volunteer firefighters, the sums received by individual households were modest. At best, it purchases kitchen crockery and pans. It probably stretched to some clothes, or the contents of a normal pantry. Certainly, it was not enough to even refurnish a house, let alone build a new one. The rebuilding taking place is happening through bank loans, insurance claims, and personal savings. That our lives now include new buildings that shine in the sun and are free of damage is because it is only possible to rebuild what is lost with something new. And, many of us are making choices, changing the mixture of our assets with what is going to be fit for purpose in the future. Many are drawing on savings or throwing ourselves into debt to do so. Yes, it is an unexpected blessing to be able to choose, but I have yet to meet anyone who lost their world in the Black Summer fires who wouldn't turn the clock back in an instant to have their homes filled with life's memories again, or to have their bodies functioning without crippling anxiety, depression, and the myriad of ways that long-term stress and smoke exposure debilitate the human form.

What is less understood by people holding these misinformed views is that the lion-share of the public donations have been deployed into programmes for community mental health support, community-level infrastructure rebuilding, and community grants for sport clubs and other community bodies—funds directed at the whole community, not to specific individuals. Absolutely, we are beneficiaries of these programmes, but so is everyone else—including those who have lobbed the 'gratitude' actuation at my feet.

The help provided to the children in our community has become another point of division on Kangaroo Island. The fire physically impacted a third of the island and involved children in two separate school campuses, one inside the burn scar and another outside. While there was a conscious effort on the part of education professionals to ensure that there was equity in accessing mental health support for these young, vulnerable innocents, there was a public outpouring of goodwill that focused on the one school inside the burned zone. This goodwill was not sought by the school administrators. It came unbeckoned, but left the impression that one set of students mattered more than the other. This didn't help the parents of children at the other school feeling their children were left to the side.

Similarly, public meetings, events, workshops and the like have been routinely focused on the township inside the burn scar. This means that many people from across the island missed the embrace. They may have been impacted in other ways, either because their businesses were hurt with the closure of tourism during the fire, or because they had volunteered throughout the fire as either firefighters or in other capacities, or simply because they feel an empathy with their fellow islanders and shared the shock and pain. But they have missed being drawn into the care.

The rift between conservationists and the farming communities also grows deeper. Both sides are being bloody-minded and neither wants to hear the other, but it must be said the conservation sector has harmed its reputation at a significant level by focusing, wholesale and blindly, on the recovery of a few iconic wildlife species, while the surrounding community that fought the flames to protect those same species is still in deep pain. The phenomenal sums of money raised for conservation work are staggering and many, many times greater than the human community has received. I don't mind the focused conservation effort. I am grateful that attention is being directed to saving what we can. I just wish it was being done with a more self-aware footprint.

The other factor that is unsettling is the various committees and processes that were launched to effectively guide the rebuilding process for the community, without the community being invited into the tent, including those who had been directly impacted by the fire. Over time I've come to understand that, mostly, the people in these processes spent their time deciding how government agencies should direct their programmes. It was about infrastructure, and mental health services, and national parks, and roads. It wasn't about the community—about who we were then and who we needed to become. It was focused on how government agencies could shuffle their budgets around to do what they were always charged with doing.

Our firefighting community is also divided along a terrible fracture line of how the Ravine fire was fought. There is an established process and clear rules that the government-managed firefighters must adhere to and that includes a forensic inquiry post-fire about what happened, who was hurt, and the impact of different actions during the fire. Accepting this process is part of the contract paid in return for trucks and firefighting equipment. Nonetheless, there were months and months with no information. The pandemic rolling through has been used as an excuse to call off further public meetings and for the failure to report transparently to the community within a fair time period after the fire. A listening post process was eventually held, an internal report eventually written and released—*Lessons from the Island*—and finally the community given a single, informed opportunity to talk about the fires.

Released in March 2021, it makes sobering reading. Resource deficiencies, as well as fatigue, mismanagement, and incompetence led to serious communication breakdowns that hampered fire response efforts. Remembering that the CFS is crewed by volunteers from the community and provided with resources from the government, it is telling that the report found the problems identified after the 2007 were repeated in the government-funded side of the system during Black Summer.

> *'The CFS has a lessons management system, however it failed implementation for the [Kangaroo Island] fires, as the lessons [were] not translated into planning across coordinated firefighting agencies.'* [164]

In all, of the 77 lessons identified in the 2007 plan, 44 were repeated in 2019/20 and five were effectively ignored. That leaves 36 percent actually learned. Given the stakes are human lives, livelihoods, or the biodiversity on which we all depend it is staggering that the report card is such an epic fail.

Scant resources were poorly used. Shift changes were bungled and slow. Mistake after mistake made.

> *'The fires on [Kangaroo Island] needed every capability they could get. The insertion of the [Australian Defence Force] was a welcome one, however the tasking process took some time to adjust to and work through. The integration of the forestry industry was mixed between fully integrated and not at all. Understanding capabilities outside the general coordinated firefighting agencies was generally not applied.'* [164]

The report also found several instances of insubordination—by 'a culture of some not following, or actively working against, the chain of command'.[164] Investigating these cases has dragged on for an unacceptably cruel amount of time. All the while, our local firefighting force is in tatters. Debriefs have not been happening for some brigades. The mental health of members has been plummeting, caught in the vicious battle between the two camps of who was right and who was wrong.

It must be said, reading the state government report, *Independent Review into South Australia's 2019-20 Bushfire Season* (the so-called Keelty Report) alongside the independent CFS one, I am struck by how carefully the terms of reference must have been established for both investigations. Someone went to great pains to ensure some things were not investigated—specifically if the government was culpable. In the Keelty Report, released in June 2020, there is an account of a version of events, with stats and numbers about losses, an analysis of how government agencies cooperated or not, a nod that the lessons from the 2007 fire should be heeded and pretty much nothing else [80] The *Lessons from the Island* report provides a welcome forensic examination of how CFS performed.[164] Neither provide any analysis about the sufficiency of physical resources within the state, nor discussion about the adequacy of the standing budget, and there is no consideration if government needs to front up with more cash to keep its citizens safe. There is certainly no acknowledgement of the need for a government strategy for community adaptation in the face of future threat. And herein is, perhaps, the biggest of the dangerous divisions. The community is asked to stretch further and harder every time there is a major fire event, to a point where sinews and muscles break, yet the government coffers remain comfortably closed. Equipment in remote regions remains old and tired, prone to frequent breakage, and there are insufficient spare parts at hand. The well-heeled, elected-few feel none of this pain. The community is so beaten and worn, we've lost sight of the fact that trucks, and tracks, and equipment are not favours provided to us by a benevolent uncle. They are our resources and our needs. They are paid for by our taxes, and represent our rights for safety.

Ours.

And we need much more.

Suffering is, Actually, Optional

In 2011, Sharon Caudle and Ernest Broussard documented one community's proactive recovery from Hurricane Ike, in Cameron Parish, Louisiana, US. They wrote 'with a disaster pain is inevitable, but suffering is optional'.[165] I came across their paper not long after the fire, and as my writing worked through the journey of time the Cameron Parish case study became a blueprint in my mind for how my community might untangle the Gordian knot of our wicked problem.

In the early months of 2020, I had high hopes the trajectory of my community would follow Cameron Parish. I honestly started writing this book thinking I would be documenting something entirely different. If the information was out there, and I could find it, surely government agencies would be tapped in as well, right? Wrong. If you've lasted this far, you know this book charts two years of disappointment, desperation, and emotional devastation.

Caudle and Broussard synthesise the characteristics of effective recovery and resilience building down into a fairly simple—and once stated, blindingly obvious—list.

> 1. **Vision and Planning**: Is there as compelling vision of the future shared within the community and does the planning reflect that vision in the face of likely recurrence of the disaster? Are the phases of relief, rehabilitation, and reconstruction used as windows of opportunity to build community resilience to future disaster risks?
> 2. **Institutional, Economic, and Environmental Vitality**: Are critical infrastructure, ecosystems, and ecological infrastructure, as well as the community's culture resources able to be preserved, restored, and protected?
> 3. **Leadership and Management Capacity and Policies**: Is there informed, coordinated, and facilitative leadership in all sectors and throughout phases of the recovery process? Is this leadership able to facilitate the community's vision and provide adequate resources to reducing future risk, including investment in risk assessment and early warning systems?
> 4. **Individual, Family, Community, and Regional Impact and Capacities**: Is there a holistic view of the disaster's impact on the daily environment, society, economy, and social networks and institutions of the community? And, is there an equal chance of recovery for all?
> 5. **Engagement, Communication, and Learning Processes**: Can the community and local authorities

access and share necessary information, technology, lessons learned, expertise, best practices, resources, and authority? And, is there meaningful participation of all stakeholders in planning and recovery process?

Objectively, I have to write that while there has certainly been good-intent, the process so far has failed my community on all five of Caudle and Broussard's characteristics of effective recovery and resilience building. And we have suffered because of it. That we are still standing is more because of the inherent tenacity of individuals in our community than the government-led recovery process. That this book is likely the first time many people have even heard the process hasn't been 'rainbows and roses' is down to a deeply-held desire of those tenacious individuals not to disappoint people around them who care. We've sucked it up, held it in, bent our heads, and ploughed on. But this in itself is dangerous and the ramifications will come back to haunt us all.

Untangling the Gordian Knot

This book, so infused with the mental health and resilience of my community, has been the hardest writing I have ever done. I am suffering the twin impediment that I am out of my normal sphere of writing and touching on a serious subject about my community's welfare that I know needs to be handled with care. At the same time, I feel a responsibility to represent the gravitational force of my community's experience and the tangled layers of what we face. It is not easy territory to write in, so when I discovered the term 'wicked problems', I willingly dove into the rabbit hole.

After trawling through academic journals and policy papers, Ana Carolina de Almeida Kumlien and Paul Coughlan surfaced to the top of my pile. They beautifully and eloquently provided an entry for me.

'Wicked problems are issues so complex and dependent on

> *so many factors that it is hard to grasp what exactly the problem is, or how to tackle it. Wicked problems are like a tangled mess of thread—it's difficult to know which to pull first.'* [166]

And there it was. The 'resilience' equivalent to understanding 'quantum mathematics'. With that sentence I was able to unpick what I was trying to write. My community's resilience is in tatters because we face a wicked problem, have no disaster and resilience leadership at our helm, and we don't know where to start.

Typically, wicked problems have multiple causes. Their dynamics are not easy to plot in the linear way most of us like to think, and they have negative consequences for society or a community if they are not addressed. Their characteristics are often difficult to define, and usually have no stopping rule. Generally, solutions are not 'true or false', but 'good or bad'. Every wicked problem may be a symptom of another problem and there are often multiple explanations for the wicked problem. Attempts at solutions can impact events in ways that may not be reversible. And, there is a time element, too—time is often running out on the capacity to solve the problem, and there is a radical discounting of the future in solution attempts, meaning people tend to focus on today rather than think about what tomorrow might bring.[167-169]

Kelly Levin, Benjamin Cashore, Steven Bernstein, and Graeme Auld actually call climate chaos a super-wicked problem:

> *'[C]limate change, which we characterize as a "super wicked" problem compris[es] four key features: time is running out; those who cause the problem also seek to provide a solution; the central authority needed to address it is weak or non-existent; and, partly as a result, policy responses discount the future irrationally.'* [168]

I hear a hallelujah chorus. Wicked problems are genuinely wicked.

It took me awhile, and I came back to this Gordian knot many times during the writing. Finally, I settled on a definition for my community's specific wicked problem.

> ***We are a community who faces grave changing climate impacts, without the autonomy to adapt to these impacts because we are shackled to a political system that does not respect our community.***

On reflection, I think this definition would fit many communities across the world. Our lack of autonomy is demonstrated in the cascading failures I've already outlined. At no stage did anyone ask us what we want and who we want to become. The reports released by our state government spoke to their own, internal audience and to their processes, not to us and what we needed then or now. With the benefit of hindsight, I can see the lack of respect begins in the early stages of recovery. I have detailed our journey in the previous chapters and I am watching it happen all again in the 2022 catastrophic floods.

John Drury and his colleagues produced a salient review in 2019 of disasters across the developed world, from the 9/11 attacks on the World Trade Centre through to floods in the UK. Their review blows away a few myths that are perpetuated by the media about really who is involved and who does the heavy lifting of recovery. The public, they remind us, are often first responders to disasters, and rather than acting with 'mass panic' or 'self-interest', the evidence suggests the general public more often operate with mutual concern and altruism. A social identity forms during the disaster that authorities can either foster or erode. Fostering it requires understanding the community involved, their norms and their perceptions, and then communicating to the community through trusted messengers. The evidence also suggests human voices, rather than bells and sirens, are more effective and that information should be regular and consistent, and to openly communicate what is known and not known, rather than silence and telling people to 'keep calm', it is under control. In the recovery phase, after the disaster, timely and accurate information remains crucial, as does actively listening to the community and acting on the concerns they raise. Disaster communities run out of energy quickly and Drury's work suggests they are frequently robbed of their agency and undermined by interventions of authorities keen to restore top-down, command, and control. Governments often fail to recognise the secondary stressors in the recovery phase—like chasing insurance, rebuilding homes, the pressure of continued dislocation—and falsely believe their support is only needed for a short period. Members of a disaster community also need to keep talking to each other as they recover. Spaces and places for this should be facilitated before the sense of group cohesion breaks down. And, a pandemic is no excuse either. There are ways 'place' can be fostered without people having to be in the same room. Finally, Drury's recommendations also highlight that disasters often bring to light the need for radical change—disaster communities should be actively engaged in re-purposing themselves for long term survival.[170-172]

Working my way through this published literature, I find myself stunned by the low level of government awareness of the bear traps that are seemingly well known by disaster recovery specialists. These patterns are clearly documented in the science, social science, and psychology literature and yet our community has been largely left to blunder from one upset to the next. I am left with an urgent sense that communities can't rely on governments for this crucial recovery support. It failed too many times to be trusted. We must build our sense of togetherness on our own.

Those wishing to address the wicked problems of a changing climate don't have the luxury of 'coming back' to the political system for a retry once the impacts take hold. The impact of wildfires and fire storms, or catastrophic flood and rain bombs here in Australia have been forecast for more than a decade. Government inquiries after each event have warned us that we must better prepare, both to reduce the risk and the post-event impact. Mostly, those warnings have gone unheeded either because our governments have lacked the leadership and vision necessary to put adequate measures in place, or because the changing climate campaign ran away with the debate too quickly and refocused everyone's attention back on mitigation and 'net zero', and away from adaptation. It was an easy sleight of hand, because almost everyone, myself included, believed that a changing climate was going to bite somewhere else first. Many of us 'hoped' common sense would creep in and our societies would adapt in time into some utopic version of the future.

Regardless, we were ill-prepared and we are now caught in a complicated mess that is hampering our immediate recovery and risking our future.

For the first six months, our government-led recovery process was focused on itself, its internal jobs, and the red tape between government departments. Government officials with little or no disaster experience told us what we needed, forced a schedule on us without our input, and decided what priorities should be processed without stopping to ask us what we thought. The hubris has been outrageous. And many individuals responsible for that galling superiority have now been returned to their previous government duties that caused us this pain in the first place.

Now, as we stand in our verdant green paddocks, many in our community are anxiously anticipating the fire seasons to come. What is the plan? How will we manage? Can we do it? I have not spoken with one person in our community who believes the Black Summer fires were a once in a lifetime event. We know wildfire at a mega-scale will be back again, and likely within the decade. We have precious little time.

I have come to recognise that starting that vitally important community discussion means understanding how all our problems relate to each other, how we can take control of our future and what that control will mean. We have to unpick the wicked Gordian knot by ourselves. We have to reorient ourselves to respond to our long-term collective interests so that this tragedy can be overcome. We need to collectively accept the inevitability of disaster; to understand our limitations, improve our existing capabilities, and develop innovative, creative solutions well ahead of future events. 'Loss can be planned for better, or ignored for worse'.[173]

REVOLUTION

January 1 - November 2, 2021

16

First a Vision

Her eyes sparkle now that she thinks about what might be possible. We've just talked through the pain of the event, but there is enough time between its physical influence and the bright sun shining on us today not to dampen quiet dreams. 'Imagine how cool it would be' she says, 'if we were really in control; if we really got to decide for ourselves. No-one from the city telling us how it'll be. Just us. Just all of us here'.

She sinks into her seat, with a inward smile, and turns to face the window and the bright sky.

I sit, watching her quietly for awhile before I answer, soaking in the perfect moment when someone else, without knowing it, has reaffirmed your deepest wish and dream.

'It would be beautiful' I quietly reply.

'Maybe we can'.

If we allow that we are community, like many across the world, who faces grave changing climate impacts but without autonomy to adapt to these impacts, we must also accept we need to carve a brave new path—to identify our own long-term community interests and build our own solutions. We need a vision.

Words are simple. Actions are tough, especially when they mean we must rewrite the pattern of our lives. Yet, there are simple truths we have to face. No central authority can see the whole picture, and when disaster strikes it is felt at the local level, not in the state or federal capital of any country. As disasters unfold across the world, communities are discovering that all governments want to do is put a band-aid on the problem. The recovery 'aid' is short term, and embarrassingly small compared to how much we all pay in taxes over our lifetimes. As the immediate danger fades, there is little or no systemic thinking about what needs to radically change to protect people and nature the next time.

Also, we all have to understand that decision makers within different government departments do not control all the choices required to alleviate pressures on the layered problems we face. Often these internal government choices pull against each other. More often than not the international commitments a country makes are simply not carried out in the way that they appear on paper.

For decades this is the system we've accepted and for decades it has been liveable. Injustice in the world has haunted the recesses of our minds, but in the mainstream, privileged, wealthy western world our lives have been safe and had the appearance of security. The developed world now faces a future that looks and feels very much like the future we've willingly contributed to but ignored in indigenous communities especially, but at scale across the developing world, too. Our hubris has come home to roost.

Now we face a future with more apocalyptic wildfires, killer heat domes, catastrophic rain bombs, lethal floods and mudslides, deadly droughts, and violent wind and sandstorms that exceed our capacity to fight these forces the way we have in the past. Each of our communities is unable to direct science to help us, because decisions about mitigating big catastrophic events rest in places of political power, not where we live. This sad truth is not just for my community. It is a truth across the world. I cannot imagine anywhere where this is not the case.

To change our status quo, we need to be prepared to step outside the system. To chase clarity about the reality of our situation and then take the necessary steps to protect our future. Think for just a moment about how much of society is built on a foundation of rules, regulations, and economic capacity that directs who can do what and when. I've already expanded on the example of farms that must submit costly, complex, scientific applications to seek approval to conduct controlled winter burns to reduce fuel loads on their properties. Forestry is likewise constrained. Our local council, that barely has enough funds to collect our rubbish, manage our road surfaces, and act as the approval body for the state government building regulations, is responsible for management of the same in the vegetation so beloved by our tourists and conservationists, that snakes around the island in a connected mosaic of roadside corridors and habits. The system of threat mitigation is so deeply bureaucratic and centralised in its thinking, that neither farms, or forestry, or our local agencies have the money, skills, or head space to seek, then plan, and execute the blindingly obvious tasks of reducing threats and protecting biodiversity. As a result, year in and year out, disaster mitigation does not get done. And while we grumble about this failing, we do nothing about it because we remain captured inside the systems ourselves.

And, during a fire, there are rules about who can be where. Fire trucks must obey their chain of command, even when the directions of that chain are clearly, obviously wrong. To veer off and do what they know is right risks criminal responsibility falling on their heads. The legendary farm fire units, sitting as mavericks outside that command system are a secret weapon employed and cherished by our home-grown firefighting force. They are nimble and go where larger fire trucks cannot. But here is a deep secret laid bare. Most of the farm fire fighters are also our professional fire fighters, active in their own utes on the days they have been rostered off from their firefighting duties. Most took no more than two or three days of rest throughout the full two months of wildfire on Kangaroo Island. Yet, to my knowledge, not one farm fire unit was consulted in the two government enquiries about this fire season. Because, the system doesn't really want them there.

Each of the community tragedies unfolding across the world over the past few fateful years are small brush strokes of detailed canvas where, once viewed as a whole picture, reveal the extent to which we have no control over our own futures.

Dependant, and Weakened

The brutal truth is that decision makers when faced with wicked problems—even in the face of overwhelming evidence of significant risks or catastrophic impact—make decisions that disregard future and instead reflect very short time horizons. Our entire system of governance irrationally discounts our future needs.

Soon after the fire, governments should have reviewed building regulations and supported our building industry to provide affordable fire-resistant housing. They didn't. Instead, government and 'the market' have left the responsibility to each individual home builder—the beleaguered individuals who face a building industry firmly grounded in the existing, insufficient building codes, with absolutely no incentive to change. In fact, the building industry is forced, for their very survival, to stay entrenched in their current codes because they are too easily undercut by their competitors. As a result, homes are going up that will be no more secure than the ones that were destroyed.

Governments should have facilitated discussion about how we survive the next big disaster that closes our transport and stops our income. There has been nothing, even though disasters have continued rolling across communities all over Australia over the past twenty-four months. In truth, we might be tough. We might be tenacious, but here on Kangaroo Island we are not resilient because we are not self-sufficient. We have no mill. We have no abattoir. Although we have the soil, space, climate, and water, we no longer produce dairy, fruit, nuts, and vegetables except for family consumption if we have farms. There is no incentive to have others come to the island to start these enterprises because transport and infrastructure cost make the exercise unviable. Although we produce enough grain and meat to feed ourselves many times over, we cannot access any of it because the Australia-wide farming model forces farms into a deep dependence on supermarket chains and overseas markets. We have allowed our community to develop as a service provider to big cities across the world, with little internal economic resilience. This situation is replicated across almost every community across Australia, and across the developed world. We are all dependent and, when disaster hits, we are broken.

As if that is not enough, there is another layer to the wickedness of the problems we face. One that we share with other communities struggling to rebuild their resilience following large scale disasters.

We are a community battling the gripping mental and physical health impacts from the fire and its consequences—the overwhelming loss of security, that is not easily patched over again.

On average, there is at least one disaster every day worldwide, affecting millions of people around the world every year. And the frequency is increasing because of a changing climate and growing population density. This means that every day more and more people are stepping across the threshold that my community has stepped, and are looking at the world anew.[174, 175] It is not a surprise that mental health science is looking at these risks with some alarm. These disasters leave deep scars that we have to heal. Where survivors have feared for their life, there is an increased prevalence of depression, anxiety, and post-traumatic stress disorder.[176]

Mental health science knows that post-disaster, life stresses and social support have an impact on people's long-term recovery. Ongoing stressors such as property damage, marital stress, job loss, physical health conditions related to the disaster, and displacement can increase vulnerability to post-disaster mental health conditions. This information brings some consolation that our anger and depression about looking at our homes as piles of rubble for months and months has been justifiable. That those who lost their entire income streams are not being selfish when they fight with their demons about the directions of their farms, forests, or tourism businesses.[176]

To the government's credit, mental health support was swiftly imported to the island, through the funding of deeper, wider services. Our local medical teams also swung into action to monitor our smoke-related health impacts. Many of us have become regular patients of skilled disaster counsellors, seeking to stave the longer-term impacts of depression, anxiety, and fear. For this gift I have nothing but praise. It is still too early to really tell what the physical heath toll has been on my community, but the national figures suggest it is going to be high.

Waking to Reality

The baseline for the way we think, we plan, and the actions we prepare for has shifted, but government process have not shifted with it. We are waking to the reality that we cannot allow government to hoard decisions any longer. As a community we sense this. We want empowerment to manage our fire risk and our island's sufficiency from a local perspective through a landscape wide plan that brings everyone to the table. We've lost confidence in bureaucrats who are empowered to make decisions about adaptation or about how to handle extreme events, while sitting on the 12th floor of an office building in a major city. They have demonstrated, very clearly, that their decisions let us down when their objectives conflict, even when it is clear to us all the world has fundamentally shifted. In my wide-ranging discussions with people across the island, our community is crying out for greater local empowerment.

The Ravine fire started deep inside a wilderness protection area. It didn't start on a farm, or in a plantation. It was in a park, and during the fire senior levels of government made the decision to wait for the fire to come out of the park before it could be fought. Such a fateful decision sits on the shoulders of previous government decisions to scrap budgets and delay mosaic burns over the previous decade. And those decisions sit on the shoulders of another two decades of scrapped budgets and delayed burns. The documented recent fire history of the eucalyptus forests of south-eastern Australia most of all demonstrates that leaving fire-adapted forests unattended, unburned has long-term social, economic, and especially environmental consequences.[47, 48, 177-179]

Budgets were easy to scrap. Fire in parks is unpopular. It looks frightening for tourists. Suggesting it solicits reams of protest letters. What bureaucrat wouldn't dust their hands of the trouble, divert the budget into something more compatible, and pay the problem forward into the future. Yet it is these decades of decisions that have suppressed natural fire, and failed to safely replicate its life-generating power, that brought devastation to our community's doorstep. I've chosen those words carefully and lay them on the page aware they will shock some and generate howls of indignation from others. I defend my right to say them because it highlights how tangled and gnarled the thinking around fire in our forests has become.

Australia is a fire-prone continent, but we have followed the lead of our European colonial ancestry and dismissed the firestick knowledge and traditions of people who—frankly—hold far more wisdom. We took our cues about fire from a continent of people with no experience of wet-dry seasons and no knowledge of dry lightning. We culturally embraced the idea of fire as bad and to be conquered. It was a 'social disorder' and that failure of understanding has driven the direction of our landscape, science, policies, and laws ever since. We failed to recognise that fire is a coin with two sides and our landscape has evolved under the careful hand of First Nations people who managed good fire to prevent the escalation of bad fire.[73, 180]

Fire has played a prominent role in the evolution of biodiversity and is a natural factor shaping many ecological communities across Australia and other parts of the world.[179] However, the modern incidence of mega-wildfire across the world is now threatening ecosystems and habitats that have never been fire-prone or fire-adapted, as well as impacting fire-adapted ecological communities by burning too big and too often.

Of the 29,201 terrestrial and freshwater species categorised as threatened with extinction by the International Union for the Conservation of Nature (IUCN) researchers have uncovered that at least 4,391 (15 percent) of these already threatened species are further threatened by the dramatic changes in fire regimes across the world.[179] If you consider how many species are not yet assessed and that the assessments pre-dates the devastation of 2019, 2020, 2021, and 2022, it doesn't take too much imagination to see that number grow, exponentially. Assessments undertaken through the IUCN Red List of Ecosystems show that altered fire regimes, in combination with other drivers, threaten whole ecosystems with collapse, including the Cape Flats Sand Fynbos of South Africa and Mountain Ash forests of Australia.

> *'The endless [Black] Summer fires of 2019/20 had a monstrous drought to ready fuels, dry lightning to kindle blazes, and a mosaic of quasi-natural fuels in protected lands and dispersed settlement vulnerable to ember storms. Climate change and land use change, both underwritten by fossil fuels, readied plentiful tinder. Against such forces – ignitions so abundant, fuels so profuse – human countermeasures were inevitably inadequate.'* [73]

No one with boots on the ground, in parks or on the farms and forestry land that surrounds parks, believes that these great stands of woodland are totally in nature's care. That time passed a century ago. We've put boundaries around them and delayed fire so we don't turn tourists away. We leave dense vegetation to grow unnaturally deep under the branches of towering trees because they are beautiful for tourists. The behaviour of the wildlife within these areas is changed by the surrounding landscape, yet we stay silent about this, less it detracts from a visitor experience. We tie landholders and local agencies in knots to prevent them burning the woodlands on their own land or roadside vegetation, because we don't trust their motivations. We lock other privately owned land in conservation heritage agreements, and then all but walk away from a responsibility for them to burn. We have embraced a norm from another land that 'endlessly finds ways to delay, denounce, and render difficult landscape burning in all and any forms'. Yes, parks and wilderness areas, as well as the roadside vegetation that snakes around our island, and the gorgeous stands of woodland on private land, are vital, important repositories of biodiversity. I will defend their protection until my dying breath. But because we want these areas safely accessible to people, we must recognise that we are already changing them to suit our recreation and to grow the food that sustains us all. We know they need to burn, and when we don't let that happen—gently, slowly, calmly as nature and First Nations peoples would do, creating a huge patchwork of different aged burnt ground—because it offends us, or scares us, or reduces government income, or requires more government spending than bureaucrats in cities think these areas are worth. When we cause large areas to grow at the same rate and build with the same catastrophic and unnatural fuel load, we have abrogated our responsibility to the biodiversity we seek to preserve and to the communities nearby. When we choose to build our management around human desires, we suffer the consequences of mega-fires.

I am not exaggerating with that statement.

> *'... [P]opulations in southeast Australia are among the most exposed in the world to economically or socially disastrous fires, and it is important to recognise that limits to adaptation exist. Disaster risk management is expected to become increasingly challenging and less effective as ongoing climate change moves regional climate and fire regimes outside of the range of human experience. ... Pursuing ambitious global mitigation efforts alongside national and local adaptation measures would provide the best strategy for limiting further increases in fire risk in southeast Australia.'* [181]

It is sobering to read a scientific statement such as this about the place you call home, but the reality of firestorms is one my community must face. For other communities it will be killer heat domes. Some poor souls must look towards a future of toxic clouds or violent sandstorms. Others will have catastrophic rain bombs spawning lethal floods and mudslides, while people a world away will be deep in deadly droughts, dreaming of a time when there is water to drink. This is climate change.

Who Will Adapt?

Community resilience has become a catch phrase trotted out by many, but understood by few. Yet, it is an important concept for characterising and measuring the ability of populations or groups of people to anticipate, absorb, accommodate, or recover from the effects of national disasters. Who is it that needs to adapt? And, what do we need to adapt to? Resilience stems from a shared vision, and that is a conversation my community has not had.

There was a process, and many meetings, about building a 'Community Recovery Plan' that purported to be 'community-led and collaborative', built on the basis of 'genuine community engagement that would maximise successful outcomes', yet the people involved were for the most part government agency staff or contractors to large government-managed grants.[182] Even our local government, the Kangaroo Island Council, recognises '[t]he future of the Island is at a crossroads and our response over the next few years will determine how well we collectively re-emerge and restore the Island's economy, environment and well-being', and yet their four-year plan is suspiciously absent of a community-generated vision too. The words on paper speak of the world-view of a few people, guessing that the rest actually want to maintain things exactly as they are—'A confident and cohesive Community supported to rebuild our unique Island environment, with a strengthening economy led by primary production and tourism'.[183] But, is that true?

The Community Recovery Plan was top down, managerial, and designed to maintain the status quo. The council's insular interpretation was simply followed. The Community Recovery Plan table of actions and outputs reveals who it really serves—government departments. For almost every action the lead is a government agency.[182] The other fatal flaw is the Community Recovery Plan focused on the two years after Black Summer, without any trigger for what comes next. We are now well inside that 'after' period, and pretty much all we can hear is crickets.

My community has just been through a profound, destabilising, and frightening disaster. One that other communities across the world are also experiencing. The least that can be asked for is the development of a genuine community vision. Once the direction we decide to head is understood, everyone can bring their knowledge and perspective to the table to construct the path for how we get there. For my community that might be that we want to own our fire management process. We might want to ensure that our internal economy is robust enough to weather the coming changes and threats we know we face. Perhaps we will want to increase our capacity in some areas (maybe food production, or communications infrastructure, or educating the next generation about our past, present, and future). Maybe we want everything to stay exactly the same as it is now. I honestly don't know, and that's the point. None of us does until we genuinely ask. We need to discuss who we want to be.

I have called our wicked problem here on Kangaroo Island, a Gordian knot of government ineptitude, land-management and fire planning regulations that is unfit for purpose; firefighting that empowers decisions not in the interest of our community or the nature we live within; an economic dependence on markets that are no longer reliable; almost no internal economy; and a deep mental and physical health tsunami yet to come. I have characterised us as a service provider—a work horse wearing blinkers—to cities across Australia and the world, without work cover, sick leave, or holiday pay. We've never recognised the precarious existence of the harness we wear. Until now.

We need to break this abusive cycle. Only when we've agreed on our vision can we honestly audit ourselves against that ideal destination. Only then can we see where our gaps are, and understand what we need to grow, change, or adapt to get there. This will need a deep, clear-sighted look at the resources and capacities of the community; and the role of land, water, forests, and oceans for food, fibre, and the personal well-being of community members. Socio-political capabilities, including power dynamics within the community and the capacity of the community to genuinely influence political decision-making, need to be understood. There are financial capabilities and resources that also must be objectively considered, including how well the community's infrastructure works (roads, water and sanitation, transport, communications, and housing). This can also incorporate the availability and access to hazard mitigation equipment such as fire trucks, or earth movers. Finally, there are human capabilities and resources that need to take into consideration things such as gender, health and well-being, education, as well as how much people feel they belong or are connected to their community.[184]

In case you think this idea is radical, be assured it is not. As the impacts of Earth's changing climate to escalate, resilience is becoming a hot topic among disaster researchers. There is a strong consensus that resilience needs to be built at the community scale, rather than at a bigger more diffuse population level.[184, 218-221] Researchers are now suggesting that communities everywhere self-audit to see how they fare. The process reveals gaps and areas that need adjustment, but also reveals cultural and governance problems that might be ingrained and unconscious. Even the Australian federal government knows this. While the *First National Action Plan to Implement the National Disaster Risk Reduction Framework*, endorsed by all Australia's Emergency Management Ministers on 22 May 2020, is a similarly hollow document to Kangaroo Island's local plans, the foreword makes an important point. David Littleproud, the then Minister for Agriculture, Drought and Emergency Management, stated:

> *'We need to change the way we think about our vulnerability and resilience to natural hazards. We must address our risks before disasters strike, and prepare for future changes to climate we know are happening, so that we never see suffering on the scale of this season ever again.... Our world-leading researchers have told us that we can expect more climate extremes into the future. Events such as drought, bushfires, floods, and storms will become more severe.'*

Business as usual won't cut it. Everyone knows it. But while government is comfortable to mouth the words, they have demonstrated they are incapable or unwilling to change.

So here is my community's wicked problem and here is what we can show the world. We are already a tough, bonded group, with inherent tenacity from having lived beyond the cotton wool of a city where life is curated for its inhabitants. Our path is a journey that will be trod by more and more communities as the changing climate takes hold. Many more will step through the threshold we have passed, and move from the softer, more hopeful world of 'mitigation' into the sharper, harsher world of 'adaptation'.

Our journey, our path, is one that can be followed.

17

Embrace Connection

The sun streams into the room from a tall window behind his chair. He is a gentle, quiet, and slightly mischievous soul, who doesn't waste words or fill empty space with chatter. When he does speak, each word has intention. His eyes radiate deference when he talks about the knowledge and sense of duty his father passed to him. His was a childhood standing by his father's side, watching and learning the wind, the clouds, smelling the air, and when the time was right, and rain was coming, burning patches of bushland, to keep everything safe.

'Dropping a match' is the phrase he and many others use, and you can hear the generations of fire lore behind the words. Understanding developed in a time when reading weather was a skill, not an app on your phone. A time when changes in wind were important subtle local signals, too easily overlooked at the distant view of modern meteorological maps. A time when the people living in a place were the first point of call for local know-how. When things were done when the conditions were right, with a decision made on the day, not weeks or months before.

I've heard from others that his 'old man' was a legend, knowing fire and the bush as an intimate friend. He is proud of the skill he has inherited. You can feel it in the soft way he tells the tales. Spare with words, and heavy with pauses, as if in the telling the tales might be lost.

I am struck in the moment that we should treasure this knowledge.

***

The sky is bright cobalt blue today, and the sun's heat radiating through the shed's tin keeps the inside warm. Only a month ago the louvred windows were shuttered to keep out the rain, now they are open to welcome a gentle breeze. A young magpie stands on the roof and its comical-sounding warble—broken and disjointed, a teenager learning this iconic call—is amplified through the roof, as if I am sitting inside nature's own speaker.

In the peace of this moment, I find myself drawn in by goodwill. Perhaps this is what the bird has communicated to me—my writing journey through two years of pain is nearly done and perhaps it is time to be open to learning.

For weeks I have been scrolling through the witness statements of the Bushfire Commission on June 28, 2020. Today, I watch the video of the Commission Chair inviting the wisdom of seven generous First Nations men to be heard—all land and fire practitioners—with grace and humility.

In the ninety minutes of their testimony, they overturn thirty years of my western learning.

What is New is Old

As I interviewed people across Kangaroo Island, and in the myriad of informal discussions I was privileged to have directly following the fire, it was notable how often people brought up a need to embrace something totally new. The phrase often used was 'cultural burning'. A new thing that is actually deeply ancient. It is the reconstruction of everything back to connection with the land. The desire to embrace this ancient wisdom is not really a surprise, given Black Summer was painfully rewriting all our assumptions about how safe and secure we were, who would protect us, and how we were caught so devastatingly off-guard. It was a sentiment also echoed superficially across Australia's media.

In the discussions within my community, it felt like people were tapping a desire to return to something rich and deep; an older, wiser way of approaching our land management that was invested in localised knowledge and understanding rather than the centralised planning we'd ceased to trust.

I knew simply reporting the 'cultural burning' statement without doing the homework would be trite. I also knew it wasn't simply a solution 'to apply' without significant change in the entire construct of our society. So, I spent a few months in a deep dive to gather better understanding about what cultural burning really means, as far as someone with my cultural background can. I discovered it is about humanity being wise again.

In the cut and thrust of life we often forget that history intersects with the present in tangled, deep ways. One damaging truth of present-day Australia is that its dominant identity and story—indeed the identity and story of most colonized lands—is born of another land. Modern, 'white' Australia is a place that fears fire. This fear stems from the imported visions of fire as a demon brought to these shores by the invading colonial fleets. When European sheep farming moved onto the inland plains, the danger of grass fires or bushfires became more evident to the inexperienced colonists.[217] Threatened by the perceived hostility of a place they didn't understand and didn't belong to, European usurpation began a process of colonising and suppressing the custom of a mosaic of peoples who had an entirely different perspective of fire—the ancient First Nations practice of using fire to manage lands (Country) commonly known in modern Australia as cultural burning.[143, 180, 185]

> *'Fire has played a significant role in the shaping of the Australian landmass and its biota. It is an ancient elemental force, constructed as a powerful cultural and religious symbol by Aboriginal peoples in Australia, and a key tool for the reproduction of landscapes. .... Since the arrival of settler Australians and their confrontation with the 'burning rage' of the Australian landscape, fear of wildfire has motivated a repression of Aboriginal burning practices in most parts of Australia.'* [186]

Like many places beyond Europe, fire has been a tool in the human repertoire maintaining habitats and populations that are fire-dependent or fire-sensitive. When early human groups settled Australia on the distant side of 60,000 years ago, the natural fire regime was altered from lightning-induced fires to human-induced fires.[186] Fire ensured that fire-dependent landscapes were able to support the plants and animals upon which these people relied. The gradual and careful collection of traditional knowledge taught people that early season burning prevented the accumulation of vegetation that fed destructive late season wildfires which would also have decimated the local biodiversity on which they depended. [143, 180, 185] The modern notion that pristine nature exists anywhere is a misnomer, except perhaps the peaks of the Himalayas and Antarctica. Everywhere else, humans have shaped nature as much as we have been shaped by nature. People—humans—have been inside the evolution of nature and landscapes all along. It is only in relatively modern times, as we collect in vast cities, that we have come to think of nature as something external to humans.

When the invading settlers arrived in Australia they imported their entitled belief of their superior knowledge that was coupled with a deep fear of wildfire.[143, 187] Oliver Costello, founding director of Firesticks Alliance, an Indigenous-led initiative for Indigenous and non-Indigenous people to look after Country, says,

> *'Since colonisation, many Indigenous people have been removed from their land, and their cultural fire management practices have been constrained by authorities, informed by Western views of fire and land management.'* [188]

The Firesticks Alliance uses the term cultural burning to describe burning practices developed by Australia's First Nations people to manage the health of the land and its people.

> *'Cultural burning can include burning or prevention of burning of Country for the health of particular plants and animals such as native grasses, emu, black grevillea, potoroo, bushfoods, threatened species or biodiversity in general. It may involve patch burning to create different fire intervals across the landscape or it could be used for fuel and hazard reduction. Fire may be used to gain better access to Country, to clean up important pathways, maintain cultural responsibilities and as part of culture heritage management. It is ceremony to welcome people to*

> *Country or it could also be as simple as a campfire around which people gather to share, learn, and celebrate.'* [189]

The Bushfire Commission recognised that First Nations land management in Australia—*Caring for Country*—had successfully informed land management for tens of thousands of years; long before Europeans arrived on Australia's shores. This is place-based knowledge developed from observation, ongoing interaction, active custodianship, and adaptation to changing circumstances. Because this is knowledge born of place, it also differs widely across Australia. It is only recently that science has confirmed what this ancient wisdom already knew—different landscapes across Australia require different regimes depending on the requirements of Country. And this knowledge is not fixed in time either. It is adapting its traditional and cultural practice to changing ecosystems and new technologies.[149]

I need to emphasise in the clearest words possible, I have no personal claim to this knowledge, and nor do I have cultural connection to the ancient wisdom that stems from the land on which I live. I am a modern stranger to my home, so my interpretation is shallow and needs significant guidance. From reading and listening, the best understanding I can formulate is that cultural fire management involves lighting low, cool fires that are good and healthy for the land, under controlled conditions, to lower the risk of future 'bad' or damaging fires. This is done on the basis of deep, multi-generational knowledge about place and all that lives within it. Western fire practices involve hazard reduction burns, which are similarly aimed at burning out litter (but often with far more heat and ferocity), but this is guided by western science rather than generations of traditional knowledge (now recognised in many UN spaces as equally legitimate 'science'). Aside from the fire intensity, where things differ is western fire practices are then determined by the modern calendar and clock that governs all decisions made by bureaucracies.

I don't mean to suggest that science has no place. I believe it does. What is missing is the golden insight of cultural burning that starts from a holistic position of understanding everything is interconnected: plants, animals, insects, humans, the weather, and that we must learn to operate organically within that knowledge space. Cultural burns are just as specific as scientific ones: timed to coordinate with the seasons, animal breeding times, plant seeding times. Burning is similarly done at the right times and in the right manner to encourage the right native vegetation in each micro-region to grow, which ultimately proves far less flammable during bushfires than invasive species.[190] Where the two forms diverge, I think dramatically, is that one is decided and controlled by an agency many hundreds of kilometres away, and the other is a connected, spiritual path that has made an investment to make sure the right people are involved in planning and implementing fire, based on their cultural connections to the land and also the opportunity to actively pass knowledge to the next generation. This is a process born of respect for being on 'Country', and learning by observation and sharing.[189]

Yet, we must take care not to simplify First Nations fire management as simply another form of 'prescribed burning', 'hazard reduction', or 'mosaic burning'.[149] *Caring for Country* must come first. Only when we follow that path, can we look towards embracing cultural burning.

This deep cultural practice is not restricted to Australia. The First Nations peoples of the Klamath-Siskiyou bioregion in the Pacific West of the US are reinstating First Nations fire stewardship practices across private and public jurisdictions. First Nations fire practitioners in British Columbia, Canada, are returning to cultural burning practices in their traditional territories. Fire is used by the Wapishana and Makushi people of the South Rupununi in Guyana to prevent the build-up of flammable fuel in the Wildland-Urban Interface.[185] First Nations peoples have also been using fire in the cerrado (savannahs) of Brazil as a form of management for thousands of years.[191] The First Nations Pemon peoples of Venezuela have shown that savannah burning is an important tool in indigenous land management and plays a key role in preventing large catastrophic fires.[192] The rural peoples of southern Mali begin an annual burning regime early in the dry season in order to fragment the landscape, with the goal of preventing later fires that can damage natural resources.[193] Studies in West Africa show that rather than converting forest or shrub vegetation to savannah, First Nations fire practices are often vital for maintaining dynamic forest–savannah and savannah mosaics.[192]

Such deep involvement of a community—across generations and interests—is the antithesis of modern management practice. There is so much science doesn't know and so much government agencies can't see nor understand. There is so much knowledge held in the wisdom of peoples that have been connected to land for thousands of generations. In case a higher authority is needed, even the United Nations Declaration on the Rights of Indigenous Peoples supports cultural practices like burning.[194] It is time we recognised this wealth and *let it lead us*.

As if woken from an evil dream, the Australian public suddenly emerged from the Black Summer fires eager to hear and understand more about First Nations fire management, to embrace the news of Indigenous rangers working with government agencies and scientists to introduce cultural burning to a large part of Arnhem Land and across northern Australia where the majority of Indigenous fire management in Australia currently occurs.[149]

This enthusiasm to apply cultural knowledge to fire is a huge step, but it is an incomplete and superficial one, and risks yet again appropriating knowledge from First Nations people. Dominant European-based culture needs to change how we operate—to embrace patience and commit to listening and learning outside of the narrow lens of western learning we tenaciously cling too. First Nations fire practitioner Victor Steffensen uses the analogy of a car to describe the change required. We can all travel together, he suggests, but it is time for non-Indigenous peoples to get out of the driver's seat and into the passenger seat, letting First Nations peoples take the wheel. To extend the analogy, it shouldn't simply be a matter of handing over the keys and walking away, lumping First Nations peoples with a vehicle with a lot of problems.[195] Foremost, realistic expectations are crucial. It has taken hundreds of years of 'white-fella' mismanagement to get us to this point. We now have weeds and deep unnatural levels of lethal fuel loads, widespread across the landscape changing the fire dynamics in new and unpredictable ways. We have to recognise we have changed the landscape.[196]

Before non-Indigenous peoples can prove themselves receptive of receiving First Nations knowledge, we need to consciously reverse our default to exploit. For generations the perspective of the dominant society has side-lined and ignored, ancient First Nations knowledge in public debates and policy decision.[195] Amidst this anguished plea for help from the Australian public, this marginalisation continues. At the beginning of 2020 Reconciliation Week in Australia, in the depths of the pandemic, and as race riots escalated in the US, the corporate mining giant Rio Tinto detonated 46,000 years of human history at Juukan Gorge in the Pilbara. Chris Salisbury, Rio Tinto's chief executive of iron ore, apologised for 'the distress' caused by the destruction of the site, but not for the act itself, which he defended.[197] This is one of millions of infractions made every year. It is this type of attitude and priority that we need to abolish. We'll never make amends, nor redress the past if we don't. And until we've taken those steps, we have no right to ask to be taught a new way.

A profound unique grief rippled through Australia's First Nations people after Black Summer. They watched the decimation of native food sources, burning raged through ancient sacred trees, and destruction of ancestral and totemic plants and animals. As *The Guardian's* Indigenous Affairs Editor, Lorena Allam, wrote:

> *'Like you, I've watched in anguish and horror as fire lays waste to precious Yuin land, taking everything with it—lives, homes, animals, trees—but for First Nations people it is also burning up our memories, our sacred places, all the things which make us who we are.*
>
> *... It's a particular grief, to lose forever what connects you to a place in the landscape. Our ancestors felt it, our elders felt it, and now we are feeling it all over again as we watch*

> *how the mistreatment and neglect of our land and waters for generations, and the pig-headed foolishness of coal-obsessed climate change denialists turn everything and everyone to ash.'* [198]

Amidst the pain that surrounds me now, I have stopped and paused often these past two years to remember that for those who live with the trauma of dispossession and neglect, and now the trauma of catastrophic fire, their grief is immeasurably deeper than mine.

Australia is not alone in this long overdue cultural awakening. In the face of increasingly catastrophic fires in the US, fire authorities are taking cultural burning—a once outlawed practice—more seriously. In California, First Nations peoples are finally gaining recognition for their land management practices, particularly after devastating seasons in the past five years. Across California this year alone, wildfires burned a record 16,000 kilometres^2, including California's largest fire in history, damaging or destroying 10,500 structures and killing 31 people.[199] As this book goes to press North America (including areas of the sub-Arctic), Europe, and Asia are on fire. Pakistan is flooded. Severe storms threaten both sides of the North Pacific, with two million people in Japan warned to take safe shelter from Typhoon Nanmadol. Perhaps a world battered by catastrophic fire, wind and, water will be the tipping point needed to shift our attitudes and perspectives in a new direction.

But what is the dominant European-based culture trying to achieve in seeking to support cultural burning? Are we, the beneficiaries of colonial dispossession, simply trying to make our lifestyles, houses, and property safer from the increasingly combustible landscapes we have helped create? After everything, are we still looking for help without reciprocity? [195] As Timothy Neale wrote for *Inside Story*,

> *'It is pretty galling, if you think about it, to see centuries of dispossession simply followed by requests for more. We should treat [the Black Summer] fires as a chance to support Aboriginal peoples' rights to Country and, thereby, their*

capacity to care for it. My hope is that, quite soon, when we whitefellas talk about cultural burning, we won't be talking about an idealised traditional technique that might have helped us with our problems if only we'd been able to get our hands on it. We will be talking about a vital and vibrant network of groups making decisions about their Country.' [195]

It is time to demand more from ourselves. We need to learn to live with fire—to become a fire-dependent culture [185] and we can get there by learning from and following the lead of our First Nations peoples.

Wisdom's Lead

Two years on from the Black Summer fires and I am a pupil again re-learning that society must embrace a future of connectedness and communication, to build decentralised landscape management plans that are invested in people who are part of a landscape; and empowering decisions at that level. To get there we need to listen to deep knowledge. We need to learn the indicators of healthy Country as seen through the lens of traditional owners—our First Nations peoples speaking with authority about our landscape—as well as the wisdom held in the heads of people who have lived their whole lives in a place and genuinely understand the passing of the seasons, the hills and valleys, where and when the wind blows. This is not to say that science and technology are not useful. They are vital, but they should serve, not lead.

It is not near enough, and the Bushfire Commission recommendations still place traditional knowledge below 'western wisdom' but I am grateful that five cameras beamed seven enthusiastic First Nations men—Victor Steffensen, Oliver Costello, Tyronne Garstone, Dean Munuggullumurr Yibarbuk, Shaun Ansell, Daniel Miller, and Russell Mullet to my computer screen. It struck me as a historic moment, listening to these gracious souls speaking truth to the halls of power, *and being heard.*

Victor Steffensen made the important point that the landscape has changed and there won't be quick fixes.

> *'There's a lot of sick Country out there. And just today I was out on sick Country again where the wildfires were and [it was] just full of weeds everywhere, since that fire, and there's not even a native plant in there for many hectares and the community is sad. The trees [have] got no leaves on [them], they are stressed. And there's a lot of work to do ... applying the fire at the right times to bring back the native vegetation. The Indigenous fire knowledge is the baseline for healing, and that's based on the law of fire and the law of landscapes; and the law never changes and that's why it's really important baseline to work with modern problems and challenges within our environment and our community.'* [149]

Dean Yibarbuk explained how from the beginning First Nations peoples moved around and set fires in their own landscape, early in the dry season, specifically to protect Country from wildfires later in the dry season.

> *'But we've come a long way from traditional practices now, and [we are] using modern technologies. There is two ways of appreciation, we believe, using our traditional knowledge and combining [this] with the western scientific knowledge as well.'* [149]

Oliver Costello added that 'different plants [and] animals have different values to different people and different cultural groups'. These are the indicators that need to become the roadmap for communities. But,

> *'... in these areas that have been heavily impacted by the bushfire season, we've been looking at ..... and seeing huge layers of shrub and regrowth. You know, some of those species belong there, but they're overly abundant and they're*

> *dominating, so they're taking away life from the grass, they're taking away water and nutrients. They're creating ladder fuels so when the wildfires will come through [again] they burn the canopies through. ... Look at those indicators. What are those values that are important?'*
>
> *'... the key things about cultural burning is that we're talking about people's connection to Country and their authority to be able to implement fire. ... We work with people that have that connection and that knowledge of [traditional law]. So people understand if they can talk about the special places, the cultural indicators, and if they have that knowledge, well, then they have those connections. So you work under that authority around the knowledge that they have.'* [149]

Russell Mullet told of his experiences living in the Gippsland mountains for over a decade and respecting the knowledge the older farmers in the region had for that land.

> *'[They are] not our people but they have knowledge about these landscapes. And there is a strong frustration from those folk that their knowledge isn't fed into incident control centres when bushfires are running; you know, which way the wind blows from at certain times of the summer, where the risk areas that they would have identified are not fed into that system, it's controlled from the incident control centre. And quite often that knowledge is totally ignored.'*

As Mullet explains, if we're going down this path of cool burning regimes, or cultural burns, relationships with the people who have knowledge is crucial.

> *'[We need] to talk to them about what they would like to see on that landscape as far as cool burning regime to reduce their risk for being harmed by bushfires. ... we've got to use the knowledge that's out there, whether that's coming from our community or whether it's coming from the non-Indigenous community.'* [149]

Mullet's insights about the Gippsland were important.

> *'... a national park, it's managed [differently] from a state park, as opposed to a coastal one. And so, you have all these rules to the landscape, but the land is still the land and it needs to be managed totally, not by this idea of tenure, but by helping places, safe places, for our communities.'* [149]

In the aftermath of the fire the First Nations people spoke up and many non-indigenous people listened.

> *'Maybe [Black Summer] is the turning point',* said The Guardian's Lorena Allam, *'where our collective grief turns to action and we recognise the knowledge that First Nations people want to share, to make sure these horrors are never repeated. Our precious Country needs us.'* [198]

A question remains whether Australian politics is sophisticated enough to listen and learn; to navigate us down a new, inclusive path. But maybe that is not the focus, now, in this dangerous climate chaos space. Politics remains important for generating the directions we travel as a country, in assigning the tax payers money towards the collective things we believe are important, in investing in big picture, large scale solutions to our problems, but I have learned something important since Black Summer. Resilience to weather terrible storms only comes from within community. Science can educate us, and has lots of wisdom to share, but that information needs to be put in the hands of people, not faceless bureaucrats, because resilience is formed in the tangible relationships between people and the land where they live.

We all need to learn to learn.

My immersion journey into cultural burning has not made me an expert. I will never be that. My ancestors did not walk on this land,

and if I could hear them speaking, they would whisper wisdom to me about a place very far away. My view is a precariously short snapshot in time. But the journey has woken a voice deep inside. It is a voice within each of us, because we all come from somewhere, and before the industrial revolution when many of our ancestors were herded into factories, and cites, and onto ships, all in service of making money for a small handful of wealthy elites, we all came from communities connected to their land.

This is about so much more than surviving the next fire. It is about surviving climate chaos and everything coming down the pipe—biodiversity collapse, ecosystems flips, food shortages, power infrastructure crumbling, transport logjams, education failures, health emergencies. Communities need to take back control of their own destinies, to look the future squarely in the face and decide what threats are on the near and far horizons and takes steps—collectively—to protect themselves and whatever they hold dear. This isn't something we can abrogate to others in distant places. We can't presume that government agencies have the answers, because they have proven to us that they don't. Our future can only be secured through an honest and respectful relationship with each other and the land where we live.

This is a profoundly local exercise, one that echoes in the pain-filled words of my own community since the Black Summer fires tore through the fabric of who we are.

18

Radically Local

After the fire, while I was still performing my disconnected pantomime to life, I sat eye to eye with young and old across our community listening to their souls. In leather-bound notebooks I recorded their thoughts, preserved quotes, captured revelations. Even though I have not written for months, as a second winter wanes I open these records. Each page is a person. With different words but consistently shadowed expressions, these precious people speak of three things—empowerment, change, trust.

To face the future, we must control our own destiny, they tell me. We no longer have faith that agencies hundreds of kilometres away will put our collective welfare—human and nature—first.

Something big has changed, they say. Some want to believe it might be a natural cycle. Others, including me, are confident it is climate change. It doesn't matter. As I sit here now listening to the songs of summer begin the 'why' feels profoundly irrelevant. Everyone said the world has shifted—we are entering a period of climate chaos and we need to think differently.

In their eyes I remember pools of pain that rippled with love. In their handshakes, that clung harder and longer than before, I felt deep commune. In their embrace, that was tighter and closer, was belonging. With words and without they tell me they know. We need to trust our neighbours, to better understand all the members of our community, not just our tribes, because alone we are condemned.

For nearly a year, as I struggled against demons in my mind, their messages floated around me, piercing my dreams, chafing my mind while I was awake. Gradually, now I grab each in-congruent thread and begin to twine the three together.

A rope far stronger than the sum of its strands emerges.

During the long periods of contemplating words and thoughts, I've felt something formative underneath the words I've typed. It is something that takes its texture and heft from those notebooks of community insight and feelings.

I've spent hours wandering around in my mind in between bouts of writing. Understanding **we are a community who faces grave changing climate impacts, without the autonomy to adapt to these impacts because we are shackled to a political system that does not respect our community**, it has been difficult to pin down a solution until I reached this final mile.

When asked what we do to protect our future, in a hundred different ways, my community told me three things:

> **We must control our own destiny.**
>
> **We are entering a period of change and we need to think differently; to embrace our land connection and wisdom.**
>
> **We need to trust each other because alone we are condemned.**

I am at that end point now and their voices come forward with clarity. I believe they are right.

While I have tried to faithfully not place a 'climate change' spin into the words of this book, in this final stretch I need to put my own cards on the table. Humanity, *everywhere*, faces a grave future. We are not adapting at near the speed we must to survive what's coming down the pipe. I am not being political or indulging in hyperbole in saying that. It is fact. The latest of the IPCC report states it with brutal clarity, even with the influence of big oil watering down the briefing for politicians.

The climate scientists have spoken. Inside my lifetime—and I am not young—at the most conservative of estimates, there will be profound impacts to ecosystems on which humanity depends. If we limit global warming to 1.5°C, there will still be a massive decline of coral reef and Arctic Sea ice-dependent ecosystems. Insect life will decline by more than fifty percent. There will be endemic species extinctions in important biodiversity hotspots. That alone causes me extreme levels of grief.[7]

Human society also has much to face, including a dramatic uptick in heat-related mortality, catastrophic wildfires, rain and wind storms, agricultural and ecological droughts, water scarcity; food shortages and impacts on food security and safety, and price spikes. If we limit to 1.5°C, most major cities will experience dangerous heat waves, while in our agricultural regions soil-moisture droughts will double in length and be more widespread, causing simultaneous crop failure across the world's breadbasket—all in the next few decades. What is waiting for humanity at the tail end of this century is likely far worse, including devastating sea level rise. If humanity continues as now, and we go above 2.5°C of global warming, sea level rise will be catastrophic with all the whiplash-level changes to weather and storms.[7] In all probability, humanity as we now see ourselves, will be gone.

Meanwhile, the levels of adaptation currently being planned and implemented across the world are woefully incremental. In some natural systems, hard limits of adaptation have already slammed against the wall. More hard limits will be reached beyond 1.5°C.[7]

Adaptation options , lead by governments, that are feasible and effective to the 3.4 billion people living in rural areas around the world, and who are especially vulnerable to climate change, are just not there. Nothing is happening with anywhere near quick enough pace. The 'solution space' is shrinking fast. At the release of the Working Group II report, U.N. Secretary-General António Guterres said the release of the latest IPCC report was nothing less than a 'code red for humanity'.[200]

> *'The alarm bells are deafening, and the evidence is irrefutable: greenhouse gas emissions from fossil fuel burning and deforestation are choking our planet and putting billions of people at immediate risk. ... We are already at 1.2°C and rising. Warming has accelerated in recent decades. Every fraction of a degree counts. ... This report must sound a death knell for coal and fossil fuels, before they destroy our planet.'* [200]

Guterres has eyes across the world like few others. He knows the humanitarian costs of what is taking place already. He is briefed, probably daily, on the extreme weather events annihilating ecosystems and human communities. He knows the already locked in climate change impacts are rolling at us, but still governments are dithering around hoping it will all stabilise and be a bad dream. Every chance he gets, he stands at the pulpit and implores governments to step up to prevent it getting much worse.

It won't stabilise. It can't. We can expect more and worse heatwaves, hurricanes, floods, droughts, and wildfires next month, next year, next decade and beyond.

Those inside the science tent are equally pragmatic about the state of the world. At the release of the IPCC WGIII report the Working Group Co-Chair, Jim Skea, said

> *'It's now or never, if we want to limit global warming to 1.5°C (2.7°F). Without immediate and deep emissions reductions across all sectors, it will be impossible.'* [201]

The IPCC WGIII report itself states:

> *'Global [greenhouse gas] emissions in 2030 associated with the implementation of nationally determined contributions (NDCs) announced prior to [the 26th climate meeting] make it likely that warming will exceed 1.5°C during the 21st century. ... All global modelled pathways that limit warming to 1.5°C with no or limited overshoot ... involve rapid and deep and in most cases immediate [greenhouse gas] emission reductions in all sectors.'* [8]

If you see evidence that governments are responding with the needed urgency, please point it out to me, because I don't; not at anywhere near the scale that is necessary.

Still Guterres and Skea's statements are about concern for the future and this book is about concern for now. The effects of human activities on Earth's climate to date are already irreversible on the time-scale of humans alive today.[202] The full impacts of current warming have not yet been seen. Ice sheets and oceans take many decades to fully react to higher temperatures,[203] but be assured tomorrow is looking much, much tougher than today.

Ten years ago, writer Paul Chefurka penned an important essay, *Climbing the Ladder of Awareness*, about how each of us understands the unfolding global crisis. His essay proposes most of us fit somewhere along a continuum of awareness that can be roughly divided into five levels or stages.[204] I have yet to find anything that captures the continuum better.

1. **Dead asleep:** where the individual believes there are no fundamental problems, just some shortcomings that can be fixed with the proper attention to rule-making. People at this stage tend to live their lives happily, with occasional outbursts of annoyance around election times or the quarterly corporate earnings seasons.
2. **Awareness of one fundamental problem:** the individual becomes engaged in one issue (climate change, overpopulation, peak oil, chemical pollution, over-fishing, socio-political injustice) and tends to become an ardent, vocal activist for their chosen cause, while being blind to any others.
3. **Awareness of many problems**: individuals become aware of information from different places and their awareness of complexity grows. They worry about the prioritisation of problems in terms of their immediacy and degree of impact, and can be reluctant to acknowledge new problems because the problem space is already complex enough.
4. **Awareness of the interconnections**: where individuals see the connections between the many problems and the grave risks of solutions in one domain worsening problems in another. Their thinking has moved to the large-scale system-level thinking. It is at this stage

the possibility that there may not be a solution begins to creep into their consciousness. Individuals in this space often withdraw into tight circles of like-minded individuals.

5. Awareness that the predicament encompasses all aspects of life: where the knowledge that everything we do, how we do it, our relationships with each other, as well as our treatment of the rest of the biosphere and the physical planet is actually the core problem. At this stage the floodgates open and despair and depression can take root.

Chefurka suggests that people at stage five have two choices.[204] I think, after pondering this ladder of awareness for most of the past year, I agree with him. There is an inner and an outer path. I'd add, it is possible to walk on both at the same time.

The inner path involves re-framing how you see and function in the world in terms of your consciousness and self-awareness. For someone on this path, it is seen as an attempt to manifest Gandhi's message, 'Become the change you wish to see in the world', on the most profoundly personal level. Those who have arrived at this point have no interest in hiding from or easing the painful truth, rather they wish to create a coherent personal context for it. Personal spirituality is a path often followed.

The outer path is one of adaptation and local resilience, of community-building and local sustainability, while never denying the grave consequences for Earth. Organized politics seems to be less attractive, because it is seen as part of the problem, and there is not enough time to reform it.

> *'From my observations, each successive stage contains roughly a tenth of the number of people as the one before it. So, while perhaps 90 percent of humanity is in Stage 1, less than one person in ten thousand will be at Stage five (and none of them are likely to be politicians). The number of those who have chosen the inner path in Stage five also*

> *seems to be an order of magnitude smaller than the number who are on the outer path.'* [204]

After the experience of a lifetime, and through the focus of a deep wound in painful moment, I have reached a point where I am done with my life before. I am standing with my feet firmly in the fifth stage. As I've travelled through my pain, I have learned from my community, listening to what has been said, but also to the wisdom held between the words; to the meaning deep within people's eyes or in the catch of their voice as they hold something back and quickly look away.

I believe in my soul that my community has an opportunity. We are armed with knowledge like never before in human history. All our elders live longer and their words can be captured and shared like never before. Science can speak to us with real-time revelations and advice. We are connected and literate and we have all experienced or witnessed profound trauma.

We have a rare, precious moment left to develop a shared community-owned vision about who we want to be and how we want to face the future, and to start building our internal community resilience around that vision.

We don't have to walk the path blindly. The field of community resilience building is, ironically, booming. Social scientists are deep inside studies building programmes around the concept. In 2017, Sonny Patel and colleagues released an academic review that sought to define what is needed for community resilience. They found nine core elements: local knowledge, community networks and relationships, communication, health, governance and leadership, resources, economic investment, preparedness, and mental outlook.[205] Other researchers and scholars agree as they turn their gaze to the roll out of climate-driven disasters across the world.[3, 206-212]

If I audit my own community, after the experience of Black Summer, against these nine elements we don't fare too well. At least not right now.

1. **Local knowledge:** To a degree, my community brings a wealth of local knowledge to the table, both from those who have lived for generations on the land and those

who have studied the ecology of this island. Yet, we don't feel that knowledge plays much part in decisions, the knowledge doesn't often interact enough to find shared ground, and as a consequence my community does not really understand our existing vulnerabilities. This could so easily be overcome though, if we learn to talk and listen.

2. **Community networks and relationships**: On this score we rate high compared to communities elsewhere in the developed world. We are small enough to know our neighbours and have discovered, through the Black Summer experience, that our tribes are not the whole community. We are well-connected even if we are not yet a cohesive whole. We've done terrible damage to each other since the fires, but if we were to walk away from our tribalism, we'd fare far better than many other communities I have lived in.

3. **Community communication**: This is not only about the functionality of phones working or internet connections being stable. Those are easily identifiable problems we've faced for a long time. This is about the tenor and tone of communication before, during, and after an emergency. I think we will do better with our education so hard won. That said, community communication is really about the creation of common meanings and understandings and about opportunities for people to safely articulate needs, views, and attitudes. This is a layer of communication my community does not naturally embrace, but I've seen strong signs since the fires that sections of our community are bravely stepping out to change that.

4. **Community health**: The pre-existing health of a community and delivery of both physical and mental health services after a disaster are important for community resilience. But, understanding and addressing health vulnerabilities can build resilience

before a disaster and mitigate long-term issues after a disaster. On balance, I think we're working on this, but we struggle without the health resources at our fingertips. We need to find ways to integrate our shared health into our common sphere.

5. **Resources**: We have tangible supplies of some things and almost none of others. We should have, in our own 'community bank', food, water, emergency shelter, sufficient medical supplies, transport, and essential machinery. The higher the level of resources exist within our community, the higher levels of our resilience. But, merely possessing these resources is insufficient; a resilient community must be able to harness these resources and justly allocate them within the community.

6. **Economic investment**: If not addressed, the direct and indirect economic costs of a disaster can plague an affected community long after it has occurred. And, the economic development of post-disaster infrastructure and increasing the diversity of economic resources are key elements that must be objectively considered. To date, no such discussion has been had, that I am aware of. We are blindly reinvesting in doing exactly what we were before the fire, without any consideration of internal community resilience. What the research says is crystal clear—a community's post-disaster economy is vital not just for recovery, but also for mitigating future disaster risks.

7. **Preparedness**: This has mixed elements for my community. Some people are hyper-prepared. Others are not. But because of politics and a pandemic, we have no community-wide plan in place about how another disaster can be mitigated and how an internally-governed disaster response process would work. National Parks have a plan for their lands. Council has something in place that vaguely resembles a good plan created in 2007, but

that has largely been left to collect dust on the shelf. Very little is actually being done, and there is no community-wide discussion about what we actually need. Everything is stuck in the silos of parks, council, and private land. Despite the landscape, nothing is shared at anything close to the ecological connectivity we need.

8. Mental outlook: These are the attitudes, feelings and views when facing the uncertainty that typically occurs after a disaster or when contemplating a future one. After a disaster, uncertainty is a common feeling among the affected population. The search for meaning and the quality of the meaning attached to the disaster can also affect a community's outlook. In this respect, we are a community suffering arrested development. Belatedly, a few careful conversations have begun, specifically around individual mental health and also about climate chaos adaptation and our community's ability and willingness to change after the disaster, both discussions accepting that the future will be different and unpredictable. But these are nowhere near enough, and the people involved are far too few.

9. Governance and leadership: The final, and perhaps, most crucial element, governance and leadership, shapes how communities handle crises and they shape how a community recovers, too. On this score, and with the greatest respect to our local council, this area is an epic fail. In Australia, like almost everywhere else in the world, we are so enmeshed in a governance system that abrogates responsibility and decision-making to faceless bureaucrats hundreds of kilometres away, we only see how low on the priority ladder we really are when the crisis hits the wall. We have a woefully low level of genuine community involvement in the major plans that chart our destinies. We have not empowered ourselves.

I hesitate to go further than this brief audit, because I recognise this is something that must be done with skill, access to detailed information, and direct community involvement. My role is merely to raise the questions and open the door for a genuine process to begin.

We must:

- control our own destiny;

- embrace our land connection and wisdom; and

- trust each other. Alone we are condemned.

By necessity my community needs to plan for fire risk, prepare for fire seasons, and address fire events. That is our grave climate chaos threat. Others will face floods, or droughts, or heat, or sand, or inundation from the sea. In mid-2022 the UN released another in its series of ever more alarming reports. Extreme weather, which the WMO now calls the 'day-to-day face of the climate emergency', is already exacting a heavy toll on human lives, leading to hundreds of billions of dollars in damages, and the a speeding loss of even more biodiversity.[213] Another UN study warns us that even previously unaffected countries are likely to see uncontrollable blazes inside the next 20 years. They make the sobering point that we can minimise the risk of extreme wildfires by being better prepared and building back better in their aftermath.[214, 215] That news makes the failure of the past two years all the more heartbreaking. There are people in my own community and elsewhere across Australia that are still not in homes,[216] and the current political focus on a bright and shiny future of targets and emissions, on technologies and the transfer of economies, fatefully overlooks the terrible human and biodiversity cost being paid right now.

We all need to become internally stronger to face a world that might not be able to support us as it does now. We all need to adapt.

My community learnt how vulnerable we were during Black Summer and that lesson was rammed home during the pandemic. We are a community that bears scars now and we've learned some harsh lessons about the journey of so-called recovery. We now clearly understand we have no autonomy and exist to service the needs of a system that is blind to ours. That imbalance must change. As disasters increase, the outpouring of goodwill and largess across the world will decrease.

I've made the case, because I believe it in my soul, that humanity's survival pivots on our connection with the land on which we live; embracing the wisdom of our own ancestors and that of the First Nations peoples of this land—of learning to learn.

I also believe, passionately, that we must move forward in agreement, and I know that agreement becomes harder the bigger a group of people is. This means we need to turn back to the human scale of community—groups of people whose names and faces are subconsciously recognisable, even if not personally known. A local community is typically defined as a group of people physically living and interacting in a common location. That place might have 300 people. It might have 3,000. The point is it is local and small enough to share norms and knowledge, to have regular overlapping interplay, and a sense of shared identity that means people can understand each other. It is smaller than a city, and cares not for political boundaries.

Beyond the agenda and directives of government agencies, I believe our community should come together to discuss the nine elements of community resilience, and to look, objectively, at the landscape where we live. We should define who we want to be, and how we want to survive here, and then we should overlay the ecological, typographic, fire climate science and other grave risks we face, with the social values, places and things assets we cherish.

Together we should develop a road map that has no concern for the boundaries of tenure and fence-lines, or political alignments and the power-plays of government agencies a world away. Instead, our road map should respond to rivers and gullies, to wind and to rainfall. It can protect what we value from tools and crops, to trees and creeks lines. It can capture all the expressions of our community and the wisdom held in its many forms. It might be a plan with bold frankness that identifies our vulnerability, like health, or income, or food security. It might stand on the shoulders of our inherent strength like firefighting lore, hard physical labour, and a community that fixes and makes things, that experiments and tries. It need not cut us off from the world, but empower us to face that world on the foundation of our internal strength.

I don't write these words lightly. I know it will require a significant investment of time and trust from all community members. It will need skilled facilitation and quality information to support it because we must also overcome decades of mistrust and tribal belligerence. It will fail if the 'vocal few' scrap and fight from the outside, against the will of the majority.

Most contentiously, it will need in-principle commitment from all layers of government that community investment and commitment will be respected, supported, and given fair and reasonable consideration.

But it can be done. Bigger, braver, bolder plans have succeeded throughout human history. It is only fear of change that holds us back.

Our road map may become a message for the world, but that road map is yet to be written. Today my community has a more fundamental message to tell. The time for pretty words and hollow targets is over. Communities everywhere must adapt to survive and save what we can before it is too late. We have experienced the beginning of the climate change curve and we cannot bequeath this hell to tomorrow.

We sit on our front porch with thunder rolling overhead and the illumination of lightning penetrating the dim interior of our new home. An hour ago, the air was alive with birdsong. Everyone—humans and birds alike—are now talking about the energy we feel in the air; the heavy tension that appears just before a storm rolls towards us off the ocean. Somehow, the birds know better than we do.

Thunder rumbles in the distance, still some kilometres away. Geoff begins a gentle count. A crack of bright lightning flashes nearby. The birds and I fall silent.

Geoff scans the horizon and feels the wind.

'That was over us and to the east', he says, and then pulls his mobile phone from his pocket to check the lightning strikes with the tracker app we all now have.

He is confident in his assessment. This one will pass us.

An hour later, sitting at our shared desk, I raise my eyes to glance over his shoulder. Green grass and yellow flowers blanket the ground outside. We are not frightened of fire, specifically. We are frightened we don't have the energy to battle through the aftermath, again.

We are not safe. We know that. We now live in a climate-changed world and none of the rules from before apply.

But we are learning our landscape anew and charting a course of becoming radically local.

Afterword: Vale Stringybark

November 2, 2021

In the midst of this hot dry land, precious water quietly flows where I sit. This stream, scarcely more than a creek here, will eventually flow into the Western River. It is an untamed space. Minutes ago, I walked through a swaying sea of grasses, baked and glowing by a sun amplified in the vast, brittle blue sky. It is almost two years to the day from the first pages of this book, I am here to visit my friend once more.

Only hours ago, I stood five kilometres away in the shade of living stringybarks. I was beside a First Nations fire practitioner and we looked across at the scars of another skeletonised valley and another river. I had just told him about my friend—this beautiful multi-centenarian tree. In a powerful moment he will almost certainly not remember, he turned to me and said 'it's sad this Country has lost so many of its Elders. Who will teach the young trees how to listen to the river, or to the birds? You can see all these young trees are crowding each other not knowing what to do. It will be hard for them without the shelter of their Elders'. Desperate to maintain the appearance of professional calm, I fought back tears, but his words cut through to my soul. It was poetic, and sad, and exactly how I felt, but from my rigid adherence to science and defensible statements had struggled to articulate. Then he said, 'But, Country is one of our oldest and greatest Elders of all, and that is where knowledge comes from'.

I drew his gift in and let it settle in my heart.

Now I am back, under the blackened branches of my dear friend, to thank her, acknowledge her family that will miss her, and to say goodbye.

Oblivious to the long history and understanding of this tree held by the First Nations of this land, her stringybark kin were the first Eucalyptus species discovered and published by European explorers. Collected in 1777 by botanist David Nelson. They were the species used by Charles Louis L'Héritier de Brutelle in 1788 as the type species for the new Eucalyptus genus. He named her kind 'oblique', from the Latin 'obliquus' referring to the base of the leaves that are larger on one side than the other. There is little recognition of her wisdom in that title. I am sure, had L'Héritier passed an afternoon under her branches or with the ancient peoples of this land—had he listened to the opus trees and water perform together—he would have given her kin the name of a sage.

She is part of a community, here on this hill. Not too far away stand her younger family. A few have survived the fire. Now, at the height of summer, the creek appears still, but this is a deception. Running water is naturally rare in this landscape, and rarer still in the last five decades because my species has cleared and dammed much of the terrain, annihilating many creeks and streams. I imagine the remaining creeks trying to hide from view, lest someone comes to destroy their songs, but these creeks are too joyful to ever really hide. They give themselves away by their flute-notes as the water dances around the stringybark trunks and roots. On hot, dry days, everything that can move makes its way towards them to survive the heat, enjoy their cheerful company, and wait for nightfall.

This place we call Bates Creek begins on our farm, rainfall collecting in the large fields to the west, pooling in rivulets, and sinking deep into the soil and underground streams that eventually make their way to this point. Below ground, it is as deep as the trees are tall and as dark as storm clouds. Above ground, it is shallow and tea-coloured glass.

Where the shade from the stringybarks meet the field, the wattle leaves bob in the breeze, keeping time with a rhythm my ears cannot hear. Their young roots cling to the edge of the damp soil, their branches thrust out into the brightness of the sun. Purple thistle blossoms sit tightly knotted, waiting to erupt with splashes of purple and blue.

Pushing their way to the fore, bracken cloaks the ground in a pillowed blanket of miniature Christmas trees along slender stems. Small clumps of fish-bone water ferns hug the water's edge, separated by the more abundant but no less beautiful coral ferns, their leaves lines of small green swords standing in formation along russet shoots. Pale rushes, adorned with straw-coloured flower heads, find space here and there. Other grasses twine between the trunks, ferns and rocks, some with early purple flower heads ripening to shining cream, others morphing between pale green and silver-white.

I contemplate the journey of this creek and stringybark family. From here, it flows into the South Branch of the Western River. As the water meanders its way across the landscape, it moves from our farm through a charred plantation of Tasmanian blue gums; massive stands of trees that were to be harvested to make paper. Then it flows briefly through another farm before it weaves north into bushland untouched by time, but devastated by un-natural fire. As it trickles along, many other creeks feed its fantasia, the hills become steeper and the valleys deeper. Close to the coastline, it meets what is called the Western and Eastern Branches and falls into the final valley, where the river becomes wide and slow, the crescendo embracing the sea.

The river, at this coastal end, has created a place of breathtaking beauty, as it flows into a wetland nestled at the base of two perilously steep hills. Standing in this wetland feels as if the world around shuttled vertical and forgot to take the wetland with it. On either side, the hills rise abruptly, too steep to climb for anyone but billy-goats. Although sheep have been grazing these hills for decades, persistent woody plants still grip the soil, creating a patchwork of living texture.

The river mixes with the salt of the ocean in an estuary flanked on one side by a pearl white beach and on the other by weathered ironstone rocks, etched and carved into honeycomb. As the hills themselves round to meet the deep blue water, their faces become sheer cliffs anchored beneath the waves. Sentinels standing either side of the small bay. At that end, there are only two ways to commune with this river; by a single dirt road that rolls its way into the valley, or by boat arriving into the small bay as naturalists did centuries ago.

A distant 'scwreee-ahhh, scwreee-ahhh, scwreee-ahhh' of black cockatoos echoes across the hill tops. Perhaps in reply, crimson rosellas land in the empty canopy above me, their chorus a staccato cacophony, amplified by raucous flashes of green, red, and blue. Small living rainbows, twisting and twirling, and then they are gone.

This is all her family and her symphony. She stood for centuries as a matriarch at the start of this river. Her wisdom and song flowed through her roots, into the stream, and all the way to the river's mouth. Her spirit is gone, but I know now Country holds her knowledge.

Vale Stringybark.

Thank you.

Acknowledgements

It is frequently said that writing is a solo art; an introspective process that an author does alone. For me, that has never rung true. Writing, in all it forms springs from the interaction between an author's inner microcosm and the world around them, the people who fill their days, the memories of times past, and the visions of the future. I have felt that interaction keenly writing this book. I started in one place with a clear picture of the story ahead and, through the interactions with my community and people around the world, arrived at a finishing line in an entirely different universe. I am as surprised as grateful.

My deepest thanks to Nicolas Entrup, you are my eternal friend. There is never a day when I don't cherish you in my life. Donna Mulvenna, without you, in so many ways, the pages would not have filled. Jenny Fraser, Amii Larsen, James Doube, Johannes Steyn, and Suzie Keynes you kept me standing, and walking, and breathing. That was never a guarantee. Sigrid Lüber and Fabienne McLellan your generosity and grace knows no bounds. Sue Arlidge, your intervention and navigation saved us many times over. The opportunity to reflect on the world with a mind like yours shone the light of insight into dark moments. Jayne, Ashleigh, and Shane Bates, Graham and Kathy Barrett, Colin Hopkins, Sophie Thomson, the CFS Foundation, and Mark Tazewell, your rescues are a debt will never be able to repay.

Erich Hoyt, Heidrun Frisch-Nwakanma, Melanie Virtue, Marissa Slaven, Cara Miller, Júlia Both, Maximin Djondo, David McLellan, Vera Buergi, and June Cullen, without your generosity and trust the book would not have been started. Colman O Criodain, Alexia Wellbelove, Nicolas Hodgins, Mary Woodbury, Ralf Kober, Susan Lieberman, Leeza Irwin, Giuseppe Notarbartolo di Sciara, Gerold Rudle, Oliver Schall, Lisa Wallner Declan Andrews, Maria T. Stadtmüller, Georg Hauptfeld, Judith Bauer, Joseph Martino, Marybeth Holleman, Robyn Campbell, Donna Gavin, Sue Fisher, Paulina Wörnhör, Barb Baker, Susan Farquhar, Jim Farquhar, Pat Fairhead, Barbara Entrup, Tan Ian Sheng, Sandra Farquhar, Lori Myers, Magdolene Dykstra, Nancy Wells, Evan Quartermain, Ana, Felix MacNeill, Jennifer Nicklyn, Matthew Collis, Sarah Fowler, Martina Närr-Fuchs, Sheryl Richard, Louise Duff, Caitlin Barthold, Arioch Morningstar, Cheyne Morris, José Truda Palazzo, Jr., Darry Fraser, Florian Keil, Tony and Phyll Bartram, Anthony Burke, and Werner Fuhry, without you I wouldn't have finished.

Rodney Laid, Peter Fuller, Tim Leewenberg, Kevin Riggs, Katrina Wills, Wendy Wallace, Ben and Sabrina Davis, Susan Hayes, Becky

Westbrook, Leeza and Dave Irwin, Naomi Murton, Bruce and Alison Buck, Peter Nash, Wendy Booker, Peter and Julie Ingram, Daniel Plewright, Jayne and Ashleigh Bates, Fred and Fleur Peters, Colin and Sue Florance, Michael Pengilly, Anne McLean, Graham and Kathy Barrett, Jason Barrett, Caroline Patterson, Heidi Grieg and Kimball Cuddihy, Robert Benny, Alice Teasdale, Lara Tillbrook, Melanie Moffatt, Shauna Black, Rick Morris, Dan Florance, Tina Wang, Meaghan May, Maree Perkins, Anne Morrison, Brogan-Li Berry, Katie Welz, Peter and Bett Clements, Steph Wurst, John Matheson and Reiko Hosokawa, Kayne Davis, Maree Baldwin, Leon Bignell, Linda Irwin, Peter Denholm, Pat Goodwin and Les Montanjees, Daniel Clarke, and the hundred or so other Kangaroo Islanders who remain anonymous for this project, thank you for generously sharing your reflections with me either in writing, during interviews or through casual chats in the main street of town. You've shaped the thoughts that built this book. Any errors in interpretation or the conclusion drawn rests solely with me.

Gratitude to the crews at Cactus, Ingram, BiRite, Beaumont, Turbill, and Nepean as well as Andy Boardman, Nigel Richardson, Brad, Michelle, and Melanie Pink for getting us on our feet. Deepest thanks to Denis and Maree Perkins and Bernie and Meaghan May for your tireless work on the precious community garden. Sabrina Davis, huge appreciation for your early proofread. Be assured, all remaining errors are my own.

Peter Garrett, I am immensely appreciative of your beautiful words, especially knowing they were written during such an important tour. And, Michael Bollen, Wakefield Press, thank you for inheriting this book and running with it. It came to you through an unconventional route and I am immensely proud it wears Wakefield's name.

Finally, Geoff, you are my heart's champion and my soul's deepest friend. Each word on these pages vibrates with your journey, too. Thank you for walking this fraught and tangled life beside me. There has never been, nor ever will be another I have loved so deeply.

About the Author

Margi Prideaux has written about wildlife, international politics and law almost every day for the past 33 years. As an international negotiator and independent academic, with a Ph.D. in wildlife policy and law, her words have been tuned to inform policy audiences in more than 20 different international conservation processes.

She is the author of two other nonfiction books, *Birdsong After the Storm; Averting the Tragedy of Global Wildlife Loss* and *Global*

Environmental Governance, Civil Society and Wildlife, and co-author of *Tales from the River: An Anthology of River Literature* as well as *All Things Breathe Alike: A Wildlife Anthology*.

Along the way, her shorter musings have been published in *Dark Mountain, openDemocracy, Global Policy, Live Encounters, AlterNet, Wildlife Articles,* and *Ecologist*.

After living and losing through the Black Summer wildfires, Margi has shifted her writing to direction to advocacy for human and non-human communities impacted by unfolding climate chaos. With this radical new focus, she has joined the *Planet Politics Institute* as the academic home for her writing in the period to come.

Connect with Margi through her author website
www.wildpolitics.co

References

1. Kangaroo Island Local Recovery Committee., Kangaroo Island Community Recovery Plan: 2020-2022. 2020, Government of South Australia: Adelaide.
2. National Recovery and Resilience Agency. 2019-20 Black Summer bushfires. 2021; Available from: https://recovery.gov.au/impact/Black-Summer-bushfires.
3. Nolan, R., et al., What Do the Australian Black Summer Fires signify for the global fire crisis? Fire, 2021. 4(4): p. 97.
4. Stocker, T., et al., Climate Change 2013: The Physical Science Basis. Contribution of Working Group I to the Fifth Assessment Report of the Intergovernmental Panel on Climate Change. 2013, Cambridge

University Press: Cambridge, United Kingdom and New York. p. 1535.

5. Shukla, P., et al., Special Report on climate change, desertification, land degradation, sustainable land management, food security, and greenhouse gas fluxes in terrestrial ecosystems. 2019, Cambridge University Press: Cambridge, United Kingdom and New York.
6. Arias, P., et al., Working Group I: The Physical Science Basis. 2021, Intergovernmental Panel on Climate Change.
7. Pörtner, H., et al., Working Group II: Impacts, Adaptation and Vulnerability. 2021, Intergovernmental Panel on Climate Change.
8. Pathak, M., et al., Working Group III: Mitigation of Climate Change. 2022, Intergovernmental Panel on Climate Change.
9. Martin, S., Australia already 'carrying its load' on emissions and must adapt to warmer climate, PM says, in The Guardian. 2020.
10. Field, C., et al., Summary for policymakers. In: Climate Change 2014: Impacts, Adaptation, and Vulnerability. Part A: Global and Sectoral Aspects. Contribution of Working Group II to the Fifth Assessment Report of the Intergovernmental Panel on Climate Change. 2014, Cambridge University Press: Cambridge, United Kingdom and New York. p. 32.
11. Field, C., et al., Climate Change 2014: Impacts, Adaptation, and Vulnerability. Part A: Global and Sectoral Aspects. Contribution of Working Group II to the Fifth Assessment Report of the Intergovernmental Panel on Climate Change. 2014, Cambridge University Press: Cambridge, United Kingdom and New York. p. 1132.
12. Bouckaert, B., et al., Net Zero by 2050: A Roadmap for the Global Energy Sector. 2021, International Energy Agency: Paris.
13. Al Jazeera, COP26: What's in the Glasgow Climate Pact?, in Al Jazeera. 2021, Al Jazeera online.
14. United Nations Framework Convention on Climate Change., Transformational Action Needed for Paris Agreement Targets–United in Science Report. 2020, United Nations Framework Convention on Climate Change.
15. Luterbacher, J., et al., eds. United in Science 2020: A multi-organization high-level compilation of the latest climate science information. 2020, World Meteorological Organization: Geneva.
16. Australian Academy of Science, The risks to Australia of a 3°C warmer world,. 2021, Australian Academy of Science: Canberra.
17. Readfearn, G. and A. Morton, Every choice matters': can we cling to hope of avoiding 1.5C heating? The Guardian online, 2021.
18. United Nations Office for Disaster Risk Reduction, Sendai Framework for Disaster Risk Reduction 2015-2030. 2015, United Nations Office for Disaster Risk Reduction: Sendai.
19. ClimateNexus. Right Here, Right Now: How Climate Change Impacts Us Today. 2020; Available from: https://theyearsproject.com/learn/news/right-here-right-now/.
20. Union of Concerned Scientists. Climate Impacts: The consequences of climate change are already here. 2020; Available from: https://www.ucsusa.org/climate/impacts.

21. McDonnell, T., Climate change creates a new migration crisis for Bangladesh. 2019, National Geographic.
22. Merino, D., The First Undeniable Climate Change Deaths. 2019, Slate.
23. Mashal, M., India Heat Wave, Soaring Up to 123 Degrees, Has Killed at Least 36. 2019, The New York Times.
24. Silberner, J., Heat wave causes hundreds of deaths and hospitalisations in Pacific north west. British Medical Journal, 2021. 374.
25. Rice, M., et al., A Supercharged Climate: Rain Bombs, Flash Flooding and Destruction. 2022, Climate Council of Australia: Sydney.
26. Freund, M., et al., Recent Australian droughts may be the worst in 800 years. 2018, The Conversation.
27. Giffiths, T., Savage Summer. 2020, Inside Story: Carlton.
28. Flannery, T., The Climate Cure: Solving the Climate Emergency in the Era of COVID-19. 2020, Melbourne: Text Publishing.
29. Cal Fire. 2021 Incident Archive. California Department of Forestry and Fire Protection 2021 December 12, 2021; Available from: https://www.fire.ca.gov/incidents/2021/.
30. Taylor, C., Deforestation in Brazil's Amazon rainforest hits 15-year high, data shows, in CNBC Online. 2021.
31. Wikipedia, 2021 Greece wildfires. Wikipedia, 2021.
32. Roth, A., Russia forest fire damage worst since records began, says Greenpeace, in The Guardian. 2021.
33. Batsakis, A., N. Hasham, and W. Mountain, Summer bushfires: how are the plant and animal survivors 6 months on? We mapped their recovery, in The Conversation. 2020.
34. Griffiths, T., Season of reckoning. 2020, Australian Book Review: Melbourne.
35. Weber, D., et al., #ArsonEmergency and Australia's" Black Summer": Polarisation and misinformation on social media. 2020, Cornell University: arXiv.
36. Read, P. and R. Denniss, With costs approaching $100 billion, the fires are Australia's costliest natural disaster, in The Conversation. 2020.
37. Williams, R., et al., Interactions between climate change, fire regimes and biodiversity in Australia: a preliminary assessment. 2009, Department of Climate Change and Department of the Environment, Water, Heritage and the Arts: Canberra, Australia.
38. Harris, S. and C. Lucas, Understanding the variability of Australian fire weather between 1973 and 2017. PLoS ONE, 2019. 14(9).
39. Cai, W., T. Cowan, and M. Raupach, Positive Indian Ocean dipole events precondition southeast Australia bushfires. Geophysical Research Letters, 2009. 36(19).
40. Dowdy, A., Climatological Variability of Fire Weather in Australia. Journal of Applied Meteorology and Climatology, 2018. 57(2): p. 221-234.
41. Dowdy, A., Seasonal forecasting of lightning and thunderstorm

activity in tropical and temperate regions of the world. Scientific Reports, 2016. 6(1): p. 20874.

42. Hewitson, B., et al., eds. Regional context. In: Climate Change 2014: Impacts, Adaptation, and Vulnerability. Part B: Regional Aspects. Contribution of Working Group II to the Fifth Assessment Report of the Intergovernmental Panel on Climate Change. ed. V. Barros, et al. 2014, Cambridge University Press: Cambridge and New York. 688.
43. Clarke, H., P. Smith, and A. Pitman, Regional signatures of future fire weather over eastern Australia from global climate models. International Journal of Wildland Fire, 2011. 20(4): p. 550-562.
44. Hasson, A., et al., Assessing the impact of climate change on extreme fire weather events over southeastern Australia. Climate Research, 2009. 39(2): p. 159-172.
45. Colvin, R., et al., Implications of Climate Change for Future Disasters, in Natural Hazards and Disaster Justice. 2020, Springer. p. 25-48.
46. Filkov, A., et al., Impact of Australia's catastrophic 2019/20 bushfire season on communities and environment. Retrospective analysis and current trends. Journal of Safety Science and Resilience, 2020. 1(1): p. 44-56.
47. Attiwill, P. and M. Adams, Mega-fires, inquiries and politics in the eucalypt forests of Victoria, south-eastern Australia. Forest Ecology and Management, 2013. 294: p. 45-53.
48. Adams, M. and P. Attiwill, Burning issues: sustainability and management of Australia's southern forests. 2011: CSIRO publishing.
49. Williams, J., Exploring the onset of high-impact mega-fires through a forest land management prism. Forest Ecology and Management, 2013. 294: p. 4-10.
50. Adams, M., Mega-fires, tipping points and ecosystem services: Managing forests and woodlands in an uncertain future. Forest Ecology and Management, 2013. 294: p. 250-261.
51. Moreira, F., et al., Wildfire management in Mediterranean-type regions: paradigm change needed. Environmental Research Letters, 2020. 15(1).
52. Nolan, R., et al., Causes and consequences of eastern Australia's 2019–20 season of mega-fires. Global change biology, 2020. 26(3): p. 1039-1041.
53. Brookhouse, M., G. Farquhar, and M. Roderick, The impact of bushfires on water yield from south-east Australia's ash forests. Water Resources Research, 2013. 49(7): p. 4493-4505.
54. Gharun, M., T. Turnbull, and M. Adams, Stand water use status in relation to fire in a mixed species eucalypt forest. Forest Ecology and Management, 2013. 304: p. 162-170.
55. Abram, N., et al., Connections of climate change and variability to large and extreme forest fires in southeast Australia. Communications Earth & Environment, 2021. 2(1): p. 1-17.
56. Spencer, S., Setting the Record Straight on Climate Change and Arson in Australia's Bushfires. 2020, Annenberg Public Policy Center: FactCheck.org.

57. Dowdy, A. Large-scale modelling of environments favourable for dry lightning occurrence. in Proc. 21st Int. Congress on Modelling and Simulation. 2015. Broadbeach: Modelling and Simulation Society of Australia and New Zealand.
58. Dowdy, A., Climatology of thunderstorms, convective rainfall and dry lightning environments in Australia. Climate Dynamics, 2020. 54(5): p. 3041-3052.
59. Dowdy, A. and G. Mills, Characteristics of lightning-attributed wildland fires in south-east Australia. International Journal of Wildland Fire, 2012. 21(5): p. 521-524.
60. Sullivan, A., Bushfire in Australia: understanding 'hell on Earth'. 2015, CSIRO: ECOS.
61. Finneran, M., Fire-Breathing Storm Systems. 2014, NASA: NASA Langley Research Center.
62. Badlan, R., et al. The role of deep flaming in violent pyroconvection. in 22nd International Congress on Modelling and Simulation, Hobart, Tasmania, Australia. 2017.
63. Tory, K. and W. Thurston, Pyrocumulonimbus: A literature review. 2015, Bushfire and Natural Hazards CRC:: East Melbourne.
64. Dowdy, A., et al., Future changes in extreme weather and pyroconvection risk factors for Australian wildfires. Scientific Reports, 2019. 9(1): p. 1-11.
65. Tory, K. and J. Kepert, Pyrocumulonimbus Firepower Threshold: Assessing the atmospheric potential for pyroCb. Weather and Forecasting, 2021. 36(2): p. 439-456.
66. Fromm, M., et al., Violent pyro-convective storm devastates Australia's capital and pollutes the stratosphere. Geophysical Research Letters, 2006. 33(5).
67. Canadell, J., et al., Multi-decadal increase of forest burned area in Australia is linked to climate change. Nature Communications, 2021. 12(1): p. 1-11.
68. Ndalila, M., et al., Evolution of a pyrocumulonimbus event associated with an extreme wildfire in Tasmania, Australia. Natural Hazards and Earth System Sciences, 2020. 20(5): p. 1497-1511.
69. Peace, M., et al., Meteorological drivers of extreme fire behaviour during the Waroona bushfire, Western Australia, January 2016. Journal of Southern Hemisphere Earth Systems Science, 2017. 67(2): p. 79-106.
70. Di Virgilio, G., et al., Climate Change Increases the Potential for Extreme Wildfires. Geophysical Research Letters, 2019. 46(14): p. 8517-8526.
71. McRae, R. and J. Sharples, A conceptual framework for assessing the risk posed by extreme bushfires. Australian Journal of Emergency Management, 2011. 26(2): p. 47.
72. Mills, G., Abrupt surface drying and fire weather Part 1: overview and case study of the South Australian fires of 11 January 2005. Australian Meteorological Magazine, 2008. 57(4): p. 299-309.

73. Pyne, S. The Pyrocene comes to Australia: A commentary. in Journal and Proceedings of the Royal Society of New South Wales. 2020. Royal Society of New South Wales.

74. Jager, H. and C. Coutant, Knitting while Australia burns. Nature Climate Change, 2020. 10(3): p. 170-170.

75. Burgess, T., et al., Black Summer: Australian newspaper reporting on the nation's worst bushfire season. Monash Climate Change Communication Research Hub, Monash University, 2020.

76. Chapman, A., Australian firefighter's message to PM Scott Morrison. 2020, 7 News.

77. Moustafa, A., Australian bushfire latest: Scott Morrison's embarrassing gaffe on Kangaroo Island. 2020, 7 News.

78. Chester, L., The 2019–2020 Australian bushfires: a potent mix of climate change, problematisation, indigenous disregard, a fractured federation, volunteerism, social media, and more. Review of Evolutionary Political Economy, 2020. 1(2): p. 245-264.

79. Cull, M., Value beyond money: Australia's special dependence on volunteer firefighters. The Conversation, 2020.

80. Keelty, M., et al., Independent Review into South Australia's 2019-20 Bushfire Season. 2020, Government of South Australia.

81. Australian Institute for Disaster Resilience. Australian Disaster Resilience Handbook Collection. 2020; Available from: https://knowledge.aidr.org.au/collections/handbook-collection/.

82. Australian Institute for Disaster Resilience, Community Recovery, in Australian Disaster Resilience Handbook Collection. 2018, Australian Institute for Disaster Resilience/Australian Government Department of Home Affairs: Canberra.

83. Commonwealth of Australia, Community Engagement for Disaster Resilience, in Australian Disaster Resilience Handbook Collection. 2020, Australian Institute for Disaster Resilience/Australian Government Department of Home Affairs: Canberra.

84. Government of South Australia, Ministerial Building Standard MBS 008: Designated bushfire prone areas - additional requirements, D.P.T.a. Infrastructure, Editor. 2020, Government of South Australia.

85. Government of South Australia, Minister's code: Undertaking developmnet in Bushfire Protection Areas, M.f. Planning, Editor. 2009 (amended 2012), Government of South Australia.

86. Government of South Australia, Minister's Specification: Additional requirements in designated bushfire prone areas, D.o.P.a.L. Government, Editor. 2011, Government of South Australia.

87. Penney, G. and S. Richardson, Modelling of the radiant heat flux and rate of spread of wildfire within the urban environment. Fire, 2019. 2(1): p. 4.

88. My Building Certifier, Construction Standards to Comply with Australian Standard 3959 – 2009 & Appendix 3 of Planning for Bushfire Protection Bushfire Attack Level (BAL) - 12.5 (Low). 2014, My Building Certifier.

89. Preston, B., et al., Igniting change in local government: lessons learned from a bushfire vulnerability assessment. Mitigation and Adaptation Strategies for Global Change, 2009. 14(3): p. 251-283.

90. My Building Certifier, Construction Standards to Comply with Australian Standard 3959 – 2009 & Appendix 3 of Planning for Bushfire Protection Bushfire Attack Level (BAL) - 40 (Very High). 2014, My Building Certifier.

91. Telegraph, T.D., What you need to know about building in a bushfire prone area. 2018, The Daily Telegraph.

92. Penman, S., et al., The role of defensible space on the likelihood of house impact from wildfires in forested landscapes of south eastern Australia. International Journal of Wildland Fire, 2018. 28(1): p. 4-14.

93. Sullivan, A., P. Ellis, and I. Knight, A review of radiant heat flux models used in bushfire applications. International Journal of Wildland Fire, 2003. 12(1): p. 101-110.

94. Pattee, E., The Difference Between Worry, Stress and Anxiety. The New York Times. The New York Times, 2020.

95. Vaishnav, P., et al., Stress Induced Diabetes. Asian Journal of Research in Pharmaceutical Science, 2021. 11(2).

96. Dai, S., et al., Chronic stress promotes Cancer development. Frontiers in Oncology, 2020. 10: p. 1492.

97. Ricchiardi, S., After the adrenaline: Once the excitement of chasing the big story subsides, journalists struggle to cope with the horror of the tragic events they've witnessed. American Journalism Review, 2001. 23(9): p. 35-40.

98. Brown, N., Building disaster resilience: Why community gardens improve community resilience. 2015: California State University, Long Beach.

99. McIlvaine-Newsad, H., R. Porter, and G. Delany-Barmann, Change the Game, Not the Rules: The Role of Community Gardens in Disaster Resilience. Journal of Park and Recreation Administration, 2020. 38(3).

100. Okvat, H. and A. Zautra, Sowing seeds of resilience: community gardening in a post-disaster context, in Greening in the red zone. 2014, Springer. p. 73-90.

101. Shimpo, N., A. Wesener, and W. McWilliam, How community gardens may contribute to community resilience following an earthquake. Urban Forestry & Urban Greening, 2019. 38: p. 124-132.

102. Clatworthy, J., J. Hinds, and P. Camic, Gardening as a mental health intervention: a review. Mental Health Review Journal, 2013.

103. Schmutz, U., et al., The benefits of gardening and food growing for health and well-being. Garden Organic and Sustain, 2014.

104. Tidball, K., Urgent biophilia: Human-nature interactions in red zone recovery and resilience, in Greening in the Red Zone. 2014, Springer. p. 53-71.

105. Montgomery, R., A. Wesener, and F. Davies, Bottom-up governance after a natural disaster: a temporary post-earthquake community

garden in Central Christchurch, New Zealand. NA, 2017. 28(3).

106. Stefanidou, M., S. Athanaselis, and C. Spiliopoulou, Health impacts of fire smoke inhalation. Inhalation toxicology, 2008. 20(8): p. 761-766.

107. De Vos, A., et al., Respiratory irritants in Australian bushfire smoke: air toxics sampling in a smoke chamber and during prescribed burns. Archives of environmental contamination and toxicology, 2009. 56(3): p. 380-388.

108. Vardoulakis, S., et al., Bushfire smoke: urgent need for a national health protection strategy. Medical Journal of Australia, 2020. 212(8): p. 349-353. e1.

109. Milton, L. and A. White, The Potential Impact of Bushfire Smoke on Brain Health. Neurochemistry International, 2020: p. 104796.

110. National Center for PTSD. PCL-5 Assessment Resources. Available from: http://www.ptsd.va.gov/professional/assessment/adult-sr/ptsd-checklist.asp.

111. Silveira, S., et al., Chronic mental health sequelae of climate change extremes: a case study of the deadliest Californian wildfire. International Journal of Environmental Research and Public Health, 2021. 18(4): p. 1487.

112. Van der Kolk, B., The body keeps the score: Brain, mind, and body in the healing of trauma. 2015: Penguin Books.

113. Shapiro, F., EMDR 12 years after its introduction: Past and future research. Journal of Clinical Psychology, 2002. 58(1): p. 1-22.

114. Bae, H., et al., Add-on eye movement desensitization and reprocessing (EMDR) therapy for adults with post-traumatic stress disorder who failed to respond to initial antidepressant pharmacotherapy. Journal of Korean medical science, 2018. 33(48).

115. de Jongh, A., et al., The status of EMDR therapy in the treatment of posttraumatic stress disorder 30 years after its introduction. Journal of EMDR Practice and Research, 2019. 13(4): p. 261-269.

116. Cunsolo, A. and N. Ellis, Ecological grief as a mental health response to climate change-related loss. Nature Climate Change, 2018. 8(4): p. 275-281.

117. To, P., E. Eboreime, and V.I. Agyapong, The impact of wildfires on mental health: a scoping review. Behavioral Sciences, 2021. 11(9): p. 126.

118. Cianconi, P., S. Betrò, and L. Janiri, The impact of climate change on mental health: a systematic descriptive review. Frontiers in Psychiatry, 2020. 11: p. 74.

119. Tschakert, P., et al., One thousand ways to experience loss: A systematic analysis of climate-related intangible harm from around the world. Global Environmental Change, 2019. 55: p. 58-72.

120. Comtesse, H., et al., Ecological grief as a response to environmental change: a mental health risk or functional response? International Journal of Environmental Research and Public Health, 2021. 18(2): p. 734.

121. Nightingale, A., N. Gonda, and S. Eriksen, Affective adaptation=

effective transformation? Shifting the politics of climate change adaptation and transformation from the status quo. Wiley Interdisciplinary Reviews: Climate Change, 2021: p. e740.

122. Kieft, J., The responsibility of communicating difficult truths about climate influenced societal disruption and collapse. Journal of Psychotherapy Aotearoa New Zealand, 2021. 25(1): p. 65-97.

123. Kieft, J. and J. Bendell, The responsibility of communicating difficult truths about climate influenced societal disruption and collapse: an introduction to psychological research. 2021, Institute for Leadership and Sustainability (IFLAS) Occasional Papers: University of Cumbria.

124. Girons Lopez, M., G. Di Baldassarre, and J. Seibert, Impact of social preparedness on flood early warning systems. Water Resources Research, 2017. 53(1): p. 522-534.

125. Garcia, D. and B. Rimé, Collective emotions and social resilience in the digital traces after a terrorist attack. Psychological Science, 2019. 30(4): p. 617-628.

126. Sifaki-Pistolla, D., et al., Who is going to rescue the rescuers? Post-traumatic stress disorder among rescue workers operating in Greece during the European refugee crisis. Social Psychiatry and Psychiatric Epidemiology, 2017. 52(1): p. 45-54.

127. McFarlane, A. and R. Williams, Mental health services required after disasters: Learning from the lasting effects of disasters. Depression research and treatment. 2012.

128. Holgersen, K., et al., Disaster survivors in their third decade: Trajectories of initial stress responses and long-term course of mental health. Journal of traumatic stress, 2011. 24(3): p. 334-341.

129. Walter, C., et al., Health impacts of bushfire smoke exposure in Australia. Respirology, 2020. 25(5): p. 495-501.

130. MacIntyre, R., et al., Adverse Health Effects in People with and without Preexisting Respiratory Conditions during Bushfire Smoke Exposure in the 2019/2020 Australian Summer. American Journal of Respiratory and Critical Care Medicine, 2021. 204(3): p. 368-371.

131. Vardoulakis, S., G. Marks, and M. Abramson, Lessons learned from the Australian bushfires: climate change, air pollution, and public health. JAMA Internal Medicine, 2020. 180(5): p. 635-636.

132. Vardoulakis, S., et al., Bushfire smoke: urgent need for a national health protection strategy. The Medical Journal of Australia, 2020. 212(8): p. 349.

133. Milton, L. and A. White, The potential impact of bushfire smoke on brain health. Neurochemistry International, 2020. 139: p. 104796.

134. Jarosz, N., Humans see just 4.7km into the distance. So how can we truly understand what the bushfires destroyed?, in The Conversation. 2020.

135. Senate Environment and Communications References Committee, Australia's Faunal Extinction Crisis, Tuesday, 29 September 2020. 2020, Commonwealth of Australia.

136. Morton, A., Bushfire devastation leaves almost 50 Australian native species at risk of becoming threatened, in The Guardian. 2020.

137. Dickman, C., Australia's 2019-2020 Bushfires: The Wildlife Toll. WWF Australia, 2020.

138. Wintle, B., S. Legge, and J. Woinarski, After the Mega-fires: What Next for Australian Wildlife? Trends in Ecology & Evolution, 2020. 35(9): p. 753-757.

139. Urban Dictionary. Hopium. 2022 January 2022]; Available from: https://www.urbandictionary.com/define.php?term=Hopium.

140. Jenkinson, S., Die Wise: A Menifesto for Sanity and Soul. 2015, Berkley: North Atlantic Books.

141. Bazzano, M., The tyranny of hope and the transformative tendency. Person-Centered & Experiential Psychotherapies, 2019. 18(2): p. 151-165.

142. Gergis, J., The great unravelling: 'I never thought I'd live to see the horror of planetary collapse'. 2020, The Guardian.

143. Clode, D., A Future in Flames. 2018, Melbourne: Melbourne University Press.

144. Baker, A., C. Catterall, and M. Wiseman, Rainforest persistence and recruitment after Australia's 2019–2020 fires in subtropical, temperate, dry and littoral rainforests. Australian Journal of Botany, 2022.

145. Lawes, M., et al., Appraising widespread resprouting but variable levels of postfire seeding in Australian ecosystems: the effect of phylogeny, fire regime and productivity. Australian Journal of Botany, 2022. 70(2): p. 114-130.

146. Zimmer, H., et al., Post-fire recruitment and resprouting of a threatened montane eucalypt. Australian Journal of Botany, 2021. 69(1): p. 21-29.

147. Lamont, B., Groundbreaking discovery in plant adaptations to fire. 2011, Department of Environment and Agriculture, Curtin University: Bentley.

148. Williamson, G., et al., Yes, the Australian bush is recovering from bushfires – but it may never be the same, in The Conversation. 2020.

149. Binskin, M., A. Bennett, and A. Macintosh, Hearings: Royal Commission into National Natural Disaster Arrangements. 2020, Commonwealth of Australia: Canberra.

150. Luterbacher, J., et al., United in Science 2021: A multi-organization high-level compilation of the latest climate science information. 2021, World Meteorological Organization (WMO) ; United Nations Environment Programme ; Intergovernmental Panel on Climate Change ; United Nations Educational, Scientific and Cultural Organization (UNESCO); Intergovernmental Oceanographic Commission (IOC); Global Carbon Project.

151. Mountford, H., et al., COP26: Key Outcomes From the UN Climate Talks in Glasgow. 2021, The World Resources Institute: Washington.

152. Rowling, M., Climate 'loss and damage' earns recognition but little action in COP26 deal, in Reuters. 2021, New York.

153. Shawoo, Z., How the Glasgow Dialogue can deliver on loss and damage finance. 2021, Climate Home News: Kent.

154. United Nations Office for Disaster Risk Reduction. History. 2022; Available from: https://www.undrr.org/about-undrr/history.
155. United Nations Office for Disaster Risk Reduction. What is the Sendai Framework for Disaster Risk Reduction? 2022; Available from: https://www.undrr.org/implementing-sendai-framework/what-sendai-framework.
156. Binskin, M., A. Bennett, and A. Macintosh, Royal Commission into National Natural Disaster Arrangements. 2020, Commonwealth of Australia: Canberra.
157. United Nations General Assembly, Resolution adopted by the General Assembly on 3 June 2015: 69/283. Sendai Framework for Disaster Risk Reduction 2015–2030, in A/RES/69/283. 2015, United Nations General Assembly: New York.
158. National Resilience Taskforce, Deconstructing Disaster: The strategic case for developing an Australian Vulnerability Profile to enhance national preparedness – March 2017. 2018, Department of Home Affairs.
159. Butler, J., Scott Morrison says defence force 'not available on a moment's notice' to respond to floods disaster, in The Guardian. 2022.
160. Knaus, C., Scott Morrison circus fails to impress Lismore, a town that has lost everything, in The Guardian. 2022.
161. Visontay, E., Locals take charge of NSW floods helicopter food and rescue efforts amid frustration with ADF, in The Guardian. 2022.
162. McLeod, C., 'Seriously?': Disaster relief chief fires back amid flood controversy, in News.com.au. 2022.
163. Claughton, D., Black Summer donations from Australians nudged $640 million. Getting it to those in need was a miracle, in ABC Rural. 2021.
164. Ryan, M., Lessons From the Island: An independent review of the fires that burnt across Kangaroo Island during December 2019 - February 2020. 2020, C3 Resilience/SA Country Fire Service/Government of South Australia.
165. Caudle, S. and E. Broussard Jr, With a disaster, pain is inevitable, but suffering is optional. Homeland Security Affairs, 2011. 7(1).
166. de Almeida Kumlien, A. and P. Coughlan, Wicked problems and how to solve them. 1998, The Conversation.
167. Peters, B., What is so wicked about wicked problems? A conceptual analysis and a research program. Policy and Society, 2017. 36(3): p. 385-396.
168. Levin, K., et al., Overcoming the tragedy of super wicked problems: constraining our future selves to ameliorate global climate change. Policy Sciences, 2012. 45(2): p. 123-152.
169. Lazarus, R., Super wicked problems and climate change: Restraining the present to liberate the future. Cornell Law Review, 2008. 94: p. 1153.
170. Drury, J., et al., Facilitating collective psychosocial resilience in the public in emergencies: Twelve recommendations based on the social

identity approach. Frontiers in Public Health, 2019. 7: p. 141.

171. Kaniasty, K., Social support, interpersonal, and community dynamics following disasters caused by natural hazards. Current Opinion in Psychology, 2020. 32: p. 105-109.

172. Ntontis, E., et al., Endurance or decline of emergent groups following a flood disaster: Implications for community resilience. International Journal of Disaster Risk Reduction, 2020. 45(101493): p. 10.1016.

173. Barnett, J., et al., A science of loss. Nature Climate Change, 2016. 6(11): p. 976-978.

174. McFarlane, A. and R. Williams, Mental health services required after disasters: Learning from the lasting effects of disasters. Depression Research and Treatment, 2012. 2012.

175. Goldmann, E. and S. Galea, Mental health consequences of disasters. Annual Review of Public Health, 2014. 35: p. 169-183.

176. Agyapong, V., et al., Long-Term Mental Health Effects of a Devastating Wildfire Are Amplified by Socio-Demographic and Clinical Antecedents in Elementary and High School Staff. Frontiers in Psychiatry, 2020. 11: p. 448.

177. Fairman, T., C. Nitschke, and L. Bennett, Too much, too soon? A review of the effects of increasing wildfire frequency on tree mortality and regeneration in temperate eucalypt forests. International Journal of Wildland Fire, 2015. 25(8): p. 831-848.

178. Godfree, R., et al., Implications of the 2019–2020 mega-fires for the biogeography and conservation of Australian vegetation. Nature Communications, 2021. 12(1): p. 1-13.

179. Kelly, L., et al., Fire and biodiversity in the Anthropocene. Science, 2020. 370(6519): p. eabb0355.

180. Pyne, S., Fire: A Brief History (Second/Australian Edition). 2020, Sydney: NewSouth Publishing.

181. Abram, N., et al., Connections of climate change and variability to large and extreme forest fires in southeast Australia. Communications Earth & Environment, 2021. 2(1): p. 1-17.

182. Kangaroo Island Local Recovery Committee, Kangaroo Island Community Recovery Plan: 2020-2022. 2020, Government of South Australia.

183. Kangaroo Island Council, Kangaroo Island Council Strategic Plan 2020-2024. 2020, Kangaroo Island Council.

184. Kruse, S., et al., Conceptualizing community resilience to natural hazards–the emBRACE framework. Natural Hazards and Earth System Sciences, 2017. 17(12): p. 2321-2333.

185. Lake, F. and A. Christianson, Indigenous fire stewardship, in Encyclopedia of Wildfires and Wildland-Urban Interface (WUI) Fires, S. Manzello, Editor. 2019, Spinger Nature: Switzerland.

186. Langton, M., The fire at the centre of each family: Aboriginal traditional fire regimes and the challenges for reproducing ancient fire management in the protected areas of northern Australia, in FIRE! The Australian Experience, N.A. Forum, Editor. 1999, Australian Academy of Technological Sciences and Engineering: Canberra.

187. Gillies, M., Introduction, in FIRE! The Australian Experience, N.A. Forum, Editor. 1999, Australian Academy of Technological Sciences and Engineering: Canberra.

188. Cavanagh, V., J. Weir, and B. Williamson, Strength from perpetual grief: how Aboriginal people experience the bushfire crisis. 2020, University of Woolongong: Woolongong.

189. Firesticks Alliance Indigenous Corporation, What is cultural burning? 2020, Firesticks Alliance Indigenous Corporation.

190. Betigeri, A., How Australia's Indigenous Experts Could Help Deal With Devastating Wildfires. 2020, Time: Washington.

191. Mistry, J., et al., Indigenous fire management in the cerrado of Brazil: the case of the Krahô of Tocantíns. Human Ecology, 2005. 33(3): p. 365-386.

192. Rodríguez, I., Pemon perspectives of fire management in Canaima National Park, southeastern Venezuela. Human Ecology, 2007. 35(3): p. 331-343.

193. Laris, P., Burning the seasonal mosaic: preventative burning strategies in the wooded savannah of southern Mali. Human Ecology, 2002. 30(2): p. 155-186.

194. United Nations, United Nations Declaration on the Rights of Indigenous Peoples. 2007, United Nations: New York.

195. Neale, T., What are whitefellas talking about when we talk about "cultural burning"? 2020, Inside Story.

196. Milton, V., Indigenous fire management set to scale up in Bega Valley after devastating Black Summer bushfires. 2020, ABC South East NSW.

197. Griffiths, T., Born in the ice age, humankind now faces the age of fire – and Australia is on the frontline. 2020, The Guardian.

198. Allam, L., For First Nations people the bushfires bring a particular grief, burning what makes us who we are, in The Guardian. 2020.

199. Smith, E., California's bushfires rival Australia's. They're turning to Indigenous knowledge, too. 2020, Dateline.

200. United Nations, Guterres: The IPCC Report is a code red for humanity. 2022, United Nations.

201. World Meteorological Organization, IPCC: 'Now or Never' on 1.5°C warming limit. 2022, World Meteorological Organization.

202. Earth Science Communications Team, Is it too late to prevent climate change? 2022, NASA Jet Propulsion Laboratory

203. ScienceDaily Editor, Climate change impacts already locked in, but the worst can still be avoided. ScienceDaily, 2017. 16.

204. Chefurka, P., Climbing The Ladder of Awareness. 2012, Paul Chefurka: Approaching the Limits of Growth.

205. Patel, S., et al., What do we mean by 'community resilience'?: A systematic literature review of how it is defined in the literature. PLoS Currents, 2017. 9.

206. Guo, C., T. Sim, and H. Ho, Impact of information seeking, disaster preparedness and typhoon emergency response on perceived

community resilience in Hong Kong. International Journal of Disaster Risk Reduction, 2020. 50: p. 101744.

207. Morelli, A., et al., The disaster resilience assessment of coastal areas: A method for improving the stakeholders' participation. Ocean & Coastal Management, 2021. 214: p. 105867.

208. Oyedotun, T. and H. Burningham, The need for data integration to address the challenges of climate change on the Guyana coast. Geography and Sustainability, 2021. 2(4): p. 288-297.

209. Twigger-Ross, C., et al., Community resilience to climate change: an evidence review. 2015.

210. Smith, T., et al., A method for building community resilience to climate change in emerging coastal cities. Futures, 2011. 43(7): p. 673-679.

211. Pomeroy, A. and J. Newell, Rural community resilience and climate change. A report to the Ministry of Agriculture and Forestry, New Zealand. University of Otago, 2011.

212. Satizábal, P., et al., The power of connection: Navigating the constraints of community engagement for disaster risk reduction. International Journal of Disaster Risk Reduction, 2022. 68: p. 102699.

213. Carrington, D., Critical climate indicators broke records in 2021, says UN, in The Guardian. 2022.

214. Weston, P., Wildfires likely to increase by a third by 2050, warns UN, in The Guardian. 2022.

215. United Nations Environment Programme, Spreading like Wildfire: The Rising Threat of Extraordinary Landscape Fires, in A UNEP Rapid Response Assessment. 2022, UNEP and GRID-Arendal: Nairobi.

216. May, N., 'Disaster's in the recovery': bushfire survivors still waiting for homes, in The Guardian. 2022.

217. Blainey, G., 'How Fire Shaped A Continent: Australian Experiences of Fire Since 1788', in FIRE! The Australian Experience, N.A. Forum, Editor. 1999, Australian Academy of Technological Sciences and Engineering: Canberra.

218. Berkes F and C. Folke, 'Linking social and ecological systems for resilience and sustainability.' in Linking social and ecological systems: management practices and social mechanisms for building resilience. 1998. 1(4):4.

219. Ross H. and F. Berkes, 'Research approaches for understanding, enhancing, and monitoring community resilience.' in Society & Natural Resources. 2014. 27(8):787-804.

220. Cote M. and AJ. Nightingale, 'Resilience thinking meets social theory: situating social change in socio-ecological systems (SES) research'. Progress in human geography. 2012. 36(4):475-89.

221. Sadri AM, Ukkusuri SV, Lee S, Clawson R, Aldrich D, Nelson MS, Seipel J. and D. Kelly, 'The role of social capital, personal networks, and emergency responders in post-disaster recovery and resilience: a study of rural communities in Indiana' in Natural hazards. 2018 90(3):1377-406.

Power

Letter to Editor, The Islander

(Kangaroo Island's local newspaper)

January 9, 2020

The past two weeks have been an exhausting and confusing roller coaster—dizzying elation followed by deep devastation. For many in our community the ordeal is not over. We are not through this threatening weather, and we are nowhere near through summer.

Power seems to be the theme that ripples below the surface of our collective experience.

There is the venal power of pride as our federal politics careens from one blunder to the next, oblivious to a country in desperate need.

There is the expansive power of the Earth, who shudders and shrugs at our insanity, for it is us alone that are destroying its thin, life-sustaining embrace. We wonder, 'is this the new normal?' Regardless, when we are gone, Earth will still glide through the heavens as it did long before we evolved.

There is the destructive power of the fire-storm that ripped through our landscape, leaving a charred time capsule of what we were doing the days before the fury was unleashed. The impact has imprinted on many of us, in a multitude of ways.

And for those of us who have lost homes, farms, and livelihoods, there is the embracing power of community, as we've stood shoulder to shoulder with each other facing the hell-hole, and then again to reconstruct life in the vacuum of the fire's aftermath. Our home-grown emergency services led the charge, but hundreds of farmers and others just as bravely defy the flames, day after day. Treasured efforts vitally refuelled by community support.

We loved this place, deeply, before these fires. Now the bond is sealed as we stand in the cinders of our previous life, because of the power of community.

Geoff and Margi Prideaux
from the ashes of Berrymans Road, Gosse

Only Together

Letter to Editor, The Islander

(Kangaroo Island's local newspaper)

January 13, 2022

It has been two years and some days since the Black Summer wildfires changed the landscape of our community. Only weeks ago, we were reminded what this means.

Lightning and fire have been ever present on this island, but reports tell us the threat of big fire will be more frequent. Call it climate change or a natural cycle, it doesn't matter. The labels are a distraction. Something has shifted and the risk of record-breaking fires will not go away.

In the aftermath of the Black Summer wildfire, despite our collective hardships and bone weariness, or the aching loss many bore, despite the influx of disaster tourists that fed off our misfortune, we wrapped each other in a collective embrace. That embrace—that togetherness—saved lives.

As time rolls on, faces have brightened. New things are built. Some businesses flourish. Others fail. The embrace is fading.

It is easy to slide into denial that everything will be fine without our intervention. It is comforting to imagine the government has learned from experience and will protect us next time. There is solace, when jaded by charred trees and bad news, to blindly seek what is bright and hopeful on the horizon.

We are exhausted, but now is not the time to sleep.

Learning to live safely in an unsafe space requires discussion and dramatic changes. We need to trust our neighbours. We need to better understand our entire community, not just our tribes. We need to collectively control decisions about our island.

Only together can we survive the future.

Geoff and Margi Prideaux
from the burn scar of Berrymans Road, Gosse

Statement to the Senate Inquiry into Australia's Faunal Extinction Crisis

Dr Margi Prideaux
September 29, 2020

They say pain makes people change. I can attest it is true. The pain and loss of this year has tested my personal resilience and reshaped my beliefs. Last year, had I sat before you, I would have constructed a different statement. I would have urged Australia to commit to the important international targets of Paris and CBD.

I am a landholder—we have a farm and a vineyard. I am also a card-carrying member of the conservation movement. For thirty years my raison d'etre has been as a voice for nature in human affairs. I am an author and have written a PhD about the international relations of wildlife conservation. I am a member of the IUCN WCPA Transboundary Conservation Specialist Group, the Joint IUCN SSC/ WCPA Marine Mammal Taskforce, and the Planet Politics Institute. I am the Chair of the UNEP Convention on Migratory Species Aquatic Wild Meat Working Group. Conservation is, literally, my life. But the pain of this year has stripped away a veil.

Knowing I commit my words to Hansard, I sit here today prepared to say in public it is too late. Too late to continue as we are. Too late to continue with our old plans.

And, I am done.

Division is Dangerous

The revelation that we have left it too late to implement outdated plans has woken a new insight in me.

Steve Biko, a brave anti-apartheid activist, once said 'A community is easily divided when their perception of the same thing is different'. I'm finding the wisdom in this statement now. Division surrounds humankind right. The uber-rich elite—in a quest for resource and power—benefit from us being separated into camps fuelling our divisions. The conservation sector further fuels that division by casting us into tribes—those for and those against nature.

Division ripples through governments, propping up the very systems that are driving the dual climate and extinction crises. Nowhere is this more apparent than amongst the fossil fuel industry that invests millions of dollars convincing both the public and politicians to make the same catastrophic mistakes we have been making for decades.

In the shadow of the CBD COP and the global pledge, last week my husband gave evidence to the Senate Inquiry into the impact of seismic testing on fisheries and the marine environment.[1] Despite the depth of science, the miles of journal papers, and the wisdom of the fishing industry – despite the Back Summer travesty—some Senators on the panel persisted with the myth that we could not substantiate the science of harm. That my husband was the lead author of CMS Family Guidelines on Environmental Impact Assessment for Marine Noise-generating Activities,[2] endorsed in 2017 by nearly 130 countries, carried no weight. This inquiry was not about whales, or seals, or beautiful reefs. This was an inquiry into the impact of a devastating industry on fisheries and the environment on which those fisheries depend—it was about the fossil fuel industry. A juggernaut of power and privilege that is directly complicit in the changing climatic conditions that created the fire-storm that devastated this island in January 2020. The inquiry should be a gift for change. It is being served on a plate. Yet both sides of politics protect the fossil fuel industry, even in the face of the laws and international commitments that say it must end.

Meanwhile, the conservation industry persists with the myth that we must lock away tracts of land for nature, because only that will save nature from climate change. Big conservation argues the people closest to the land are too ignorant. The powerful voice of the conservation industry fuels a distrust for anyone using the land and sea to grow or harvest food or fibre—dismissing the connections many in modern agriculture, horticulture, viticulture, and fisheries have to a healthy landscape—while blithely continuing in their roles as consumers who demand cheap food and fibre from the very production systems they vilify. They demonise those who depend on wild resources for their food, while speaking from the privileged access to city supermarkets with ladened shelves of packaged goods. The conservation sector's mantra of 'parks and distrust' tolls like a drumbeat at a wake.

This year I saw first-hand when the chips are down, many in the conservation industry prioritize fundraising—foolishly forgetting that people are part of nature—collecting millions of dollars to support wildlife rescue and feeding stations, while farmers on Kangaroo Island bent their backs to destroying their suffering farm animals without a whiff of support. These were the men and women who had faced weeks of unrelenting firefighting.

Never have I felt so disconnected from my peers. Never has it been so clear how disconnected the conservation industry can be to people.

Division is dangerous.

We Were Warned

Never have I felt that politics served another master as deeply as I do now. They warned us this disaster was coming. Scientists have been telling us a changing global climate is affecting Australia's fire weather by modifying the underlying climate drivers.[3] During the Royal Commission into National Natural Disaster Arrangements, I watched the live-stream of Karl Braganza from the Australian Bureau of Meteorology present with exquisite detail those climate drivers and predictions for the 2019/20 fire seasons. At the end of the presentation the Commission Chair, Mark Binskin, asked 'About mid 2019 when you were starting to provide advice to those committees that look at what's coming up in the fire season, how did it play out in real time?' Braganza replied 'Things really played out the way our forecast models, both in climate and weather, suggested they would'.[4]

We know state fire services were aware of the dangers and prepared as much as they could, but they have been systematically starved of funds and resources for years. Governments ignored direct appeals from people they should trust to address the situation early,[5] and did almost nothing to get ready. Since, although the vast scale, intensity and destructiveness of Black Summer fires represents a major national security crisis for Australia in the sheer impact to biodiversity,[6] the political response has been to fiddle at the margins.

Thirteen days after Geoff and I lost our home, farm, and wildlife sanctuary, academic Anthony Burke wrote that Australia's failure to prepare for the Black Summer's fires was a product of three things:

1) the narrow way we think about national security;

2) anthropocentric thinking that fails to value how humans are enmeshed in natural ecosystems; and

3) four decades in which our system of government has been vandalised for the benefit of the powerful at the expense of the rest.[6]

Unspoken Truths

As a landholder stripped bare by the Black Summer fires, I have moved—psychologically and physically—into the camp of people who are now living inside the grip of climate change. Climate change is not a theoretical or distant horizon. It is real. It is now. And it bites hard. I know, and my community knows, it threatens the future of the entire country, and the vast tapestry of biodiversity on which we depend. There is no question this threatens national security.

In this climate-changed bardo there are unspoken truths we must confront. We've just witnessed the might of fire to destroy decades of conservation in a single night, despite the razor wire in our minds we believed would protect it. Chris Dickman and Lily Van Eeden coordinated a study for WWF that found almost 3 billion wild animals—143 million mammals, 2.46 billion reptiles, 180 million birds, 51 million frogs—were killed or displaced in the Black Summer fires.[7] Alongside these were 125,000 sheep and cattle.[8] Nowhere was the livestock tragedy deeper than on Kangaroo Island. The full impacts on Kangaroo Island's biodiversity will not be fully understood for years to come, as extinction debts are slowly, painfully realised. Sure, trees will regrow. 'Nature will rebound' people are fond of saying, but we know these fires burned hotter, deeper, and were far more extreme than this landscape is adapted to.

Some coarse surrogates are being developed now. Brendan Wintle, Sarah Legge, and John Woinarski have projected that, across Australia, 327 (272 plants, and 55 animals, including five invertebrates) of the ~1800 listed threatened species in Australia had a significant portion (>10 percent) of their known distribution within the Black

Summer fire footprint. 31 of these were already critically endangered. Among the significantly impacted species, 114 have lost at least half of their habitat and 49 have lost over 80 percent.[9]

Parks didn't protect them. Arguably, the misuse of environmental laws sealed their doom. And, who was it that stood in the face of the firestorms? Farmers and landholders fought harder than anyone to save nature along with their farms. These are the same individuals that have been hampered for decades by a scientific bureaucracy administering land clearing laws that 'count' rather than 'feel', 'prescribe' rather than 'support', and have designed themselves into an impenetrable mess arguably designed to exclude landholders from managing the risk of fire to biodiversity on their own land—trees, and animals, and insects they cherish. Our balled-up, metric-driven interpretation of laws, suppressed cool, controlled fires that might have saved a significant portion of those species and habitats. Landholders were dis-empowered by bureaucracies because we don't trust.

Adapting to Survive

The manifesto of the multi-disciplinary Planet Politics Institute [12] calls for the 'political imagination that can rise from the ashes of our canonical texts. It is about meditating on our failures and finding the will needed for our continued survival'. ... 'we must ask questions that are intimately connected to capitalism, modernity, and oppression. We must ensure that our diplomacy, our politics, and our institutions are open to those who will bear the brunt of ecological change'.[12]

It is too late for another round of argument and obfuscation. My small community, and the nature we love, must adapt on our own to survive. We feel our connection to this landscape; we understand we are a part of its ecosystems. We must banish the division and come together—all of us—conservation, farming, fishing, and forestry to work out how to carry on. We need to learn to hear and understand each other because we want the same thing. We want this landscape—one we all love deeply—to endure.

To prevail, our community and our wild landscapes need a tenure-blind plan for managing our collective future in the presence of climate change—a plan that empowers us all, together. A plan we develop to suit us, not to a formula designed in Canberra, or New York, or Brussels. A community-based landscape plan that decides the proper application of land-use fires (weed control, wildfire prevention, and preparedness and suppression of wildfires) because we are the first to bear the losses from uncontrolled fires in our locality.

A few short years ago, I wrote that the empowerment of communities, who depend on healthy ecosystems for their lives and livelihoods, makes them effective stewards.[11] My words then were tuned to the ecological justice of communities in developing regions of the world, but those words now ring true for my community as well. This ethic is more than hiring local people as park rangers or eco-tour guides or systematically enabling individuals to monitor and blow the whistle on illegal activities. It means truly acknowledging a community connection to a place and the wildlife they live with—recognising these forests, grassy plains, or wetlands as their home—can build powerful local conservation bonds. Our biodiversity is the most important element in our lives. It is the life force that sustains us, the food that feeds us, and the context that enlivens our souls. We cannot survive without it.

Ironically, community-level land management is a mantra Australia finds easy to suggest for other places—developing countries where our aid and support is offered. In these other places we recognise that colonial fire suppression policies have caused conflicts, wildfire, and livelihood impacts. For these other places we suggest that fire policies should address adaptive, inclusive and integrative within land management.[10] So why not here? Because we are divided.

Conservation goals should be set by governments, but the conservation form should be born of the community—our homes, our solutions, our management. Communities should have the power to speak for the wildlife that surrounds us in national and international environmental governance. We should be free to adapt, change, and evolve. We should have the liberty to choose if we want to pursue voluntary area closures, or to consider if new activities should start. The solutions we form should be born of our context.[11]

This proposal requires a leap of faith and commitment from the conservation industry and government actors, to genuinely devolve decision making to the community level and to adapt the national and international political system to embrace a multitude of conservation expressions—a tapestry of conservation diversity.

To make it work, there will need to be a high degree of monitoring and transparency, supported capacity to take part in community-based landscape plan committees, and deep and sustained conservation science programmes.[11] I appreciate the governance I propose is a complex and diffuse logistical programme, but it mirrors life.

Becoming Radically Local

I believed it before, but I know it now. We have run out of time. Climate change is already upon us. Our community can no longer afford the opinions of people in a city far away dividing us—no community can. We cannot survive the scientific bureaucracy of Adelaide or Canberra, or Brussels, or New York that listens to a disconnected, distrustful conservation elite instead of us. We cannot persist if we are beholden to the budget cuts and sleight of hand as the priority of governments shifts with the wind. We must control our own destiny and the destiny of the millions of souls we share this landscape with—the carpenter bees, the pygmy possums, the kangaroos, and the stringybarks. These are our neighbours and our kin.

If this Inquiry is serious, I urge it to consider radical change in how Australia operates; an adaptation to the climate-changed world we have created. The big-picture, command-and-control system inherent in this Inquiry's own terms of reference—administration by distant government departments, the metrics of percentages—has not worked. Australia's laws are good when you compare them to other biodiverse regions of the world, yet both sides of politics have abused those laws and permitted the powerful to destroy nature, anyway. Nauseating as that track record is, a single fire season eclipsed its damage. This year, a vast network of the natural heritage estate became ash in the wind.

We killed three billion animals.

We are on the brink of losing everything. We have no choice left but to do what was obvious all along—to empower radically local conservation, immediately—not incrementally, aiming for ten- or twenty-years' time. We need local round tables of planning and decision, populated by those who carry the knowledge of our land, and of fire, flood, and drought—First Nations, farmers, fishers, and conservation landholders—with science there to educate and empower. We should seek agreement and understand compromise. We should banish division.

Kangaroo Island's plans won't be the same as Kangaroo Valley's. We are different communities and different regions. We have different priorities. Devolving the power to communities to plan and manage means we must accept this mosaic of difference. We won't be able to easily 'measure and count' anymore, and politics won't like that. But we have no time left to pander to niceties. The time for slow action is past.

Remembering that our diplomacy, our politics, and our institutions must be open to those who will bear the brunt of ecological change, the Kangaroo Island community stands in that space, right now—we are living ecological change.

Recommendations

Embracing radically local conservation means:

1) National environment and land management laws should provide the guiding principles and baselines for the development of a mosaic of community landscape plans that are based on identifiable ecoregions.
2) Community-based landscape plans should be adaptive and embraced by the whole community, guiding how that community lives and uses their land, when they burn that land, what and where they grow and how they farm. Everyone should have a seat at the table and be accountable to each other.
3) Science should be nested, permanently into each community, providing deep support, rather than being abused as a regulatory tool.
4) When a plan is made, federal and state government roles should support the plan's implementation and to manage outlier behaviour.

This year I've stood on the very cliff edge of my beliefs, tempted to jump for the shame. Three billion souls perished on our watch. I am done. Done with the plans on paper. Done with the talk into the wind. I have become radically local.

References

1. Environment and Communications References Committee. 2020. Senate Inquiry into the impact of seismic testing on fisheries and the marine environment, Public Hearings.

2. CMS. 2017. CMS Family Guidelines on Environmental Impact Assessment for Marine Noise-generating Activities, Resolution 12.14: Adverse Impacts of Anthropogenic Noise on Cetaceans and Other Migratory Species, CMS COP12, Manilla.

3. Harris, S., & Lucas, C., 2019. Understanding the variability of Australian fire weather between 1973 and 2017, PLoS ONE 14(9); Dowdy, A., H. Ye, et al. (2019). Future changes in extreme weather and pyroconvection risk factors for Australian wildfires, Scientific Reports 9(1)

4. Royal Commission into National Natural Disaster Arrangements, 2020. Hearing Block 1.

5 Cox, L., 2019. Former fire chiefs warn Australia unprepared for escalating climate threat, The Guardian Online; Daniel, Z and Donaldson, A. 2019, As fire seasons overlap in Australia and California, sharing firefighting resources will only get harder, ABC News Online; Taylor, J., 2019. Home affairs warned the Australian government of growing climate disaster risk after May election, The Guardian Online.

6. Burke, A., 2020. We Spent $17b On One Fleet, We Won't Spend $500m On The Other. Which Do You Think Is More Urgent?, New Matilda.

7. Dickman, C., 2020. Australia's 2019-2020 Bushfires: The Wildlife Toll. WWF Australia.

8. Wahlquist, C., 2020. Up to 100,000 sheep killed in Kangaroo Island fires, as farmers tally livestock losses. The Guardian online.

9. Wintle, B.A., Legge, S. and Woinarski, J.C., 2020. After the Mega-fires: What Next for Australian Wildlife?. Trends in Ecology & Evolution, 35(9), pp.753-757.

10. Moura, L.C., Scariot, A.O., Schmidt, I.B., Beatty, R. and Russell-Smith, J., 2019. The legacy of colonial fire management policies on traditional livelihoods and ecological sustainability in savannas: Impacts, consequences, new directions. Journal of Environmental Management, 232, pp.600-606.

11. Prideaux, M., 2017. Global Environmental Governance, Civil Society and Wildlife: Birdsong After the Storm. Taylor & Francis.

12. Burke, A., Fishel, S., Mitchell, A., Dalby, S. and Levine, D.J., 2016. Planet Politics: A manifesto from the end of IR. Millennium, 44(3), pp.499-523.

Index

Printed by BoD™ in Norderstedt, Germany

9 781925 856552